# RWANDA SINCE 1994

## Stories of Change

FRANCOPHONE POSTCOLONIAL STUDIES

The annual publication of the Society for Francophone Postcolonial Studies
New Series, Vol. 10

# Francophone Postcolonial Studies

The annual publication of the Society for Francophone Postcolonial Studies

The Society for Francophone Postcolonial Studies (SFPS) is an international association which exists in order to promote, facilitate and otherwise support the work of all scholars and researchers working on colonial/postcolonial studies in the French-speaking world. SFPS was created in 2002 with the aim of continuing and developing the pioneering work of its predecessor organization, the Association for the Study of Caribbean and African Literature in French (ASCALF). SFPS does not seek to impose a monolithic understanding of the 'postcolonial' and it consciously aims to appeal to as diverse a range of members as possible, in order to engage in wide-ranging debate on the nature and legacy of colonialism in and beyond the French-speaking world. SFPS encourages work of a transcultural, transhistorical, comparative and interdisciplinary nature. It implicitly seeks to decolonize the term Francophone, emphasizing that it should refer to all cultures where French is spoken (including, of course, France itself), and it encourages a critical reflection on the nature of the cognate disciplines of French Studies, on the one hand, and Anglophone Postcolonial Studies, on the other.

Our vision for this publication with Liverpool University Press is that each volume will constitute a sort of *état présent* on a significant topic embracing various expressions of Francophone Postcolonial Cultures (e.g. literature, film, music, history), in relation to pertinent geographical areas (e.g. France/Belgium, the Caribbean, Africa, the Indian Ocean, Asia, Polynesia) and different periods (slavery, colonialism, the post-colonial era, etc.): above all, we are looking to publish research that will help to set new research agendas across our field. The editorial board of *Francophone Postcolonial Studies* invites proposals for edited volumes touching on any of the areas listed above: proposals should be sent to Kate Marsh (clmarsh@ liverpool.ac.uk). For further details, visit: http://sfps.org.uk/.

**General Editor:** Kate Marsh (University of Liverpool, UK)

**Editorial Board**
Charlotte Baker (Lancaster University)
Leslie Barnes (The Australian National University)
Lia Brozgal (UCLA)
Patrick Crowley (University College Cork)
Nicki Hitchcott (University of St Andrews)
Kate Hodgson (University College Cork)
Maeve McCusker (Queen's University Belfast)
H Adlai Murdoch (Tufts University)
Srilata Ravi (University of Alberta)
Ieme van der Poel (University of Amsterdam)
John Walsh (University of Pittsburgh)

# RWANDA SINCE 1994

## Stories of Change

Edited by
Hannah Grayson and Nicki Hitchcott

Liverpool University Press

First published 2019 by
Liverpool University Press
4 Cambridge Street
Liverpool
L69 7ZU

British Library Cataloguing-in-Publication data
A British Library CIP record is available

ISBN 978-1-78694-199-2 cased

Typeset by Carnegie Book Production, Lancaster
Printed and bound by TJ International Ltd, Padstow, Cornwall, PL28 8RW

# Contents

# Introduction: Rwanda since 1994

*Hannah Grayson and Nicki Hitchcott*

In July 1994, after 100 days of the most brutal massacres imaginable, in which it is estimated that over a million people died, the Rwandan Patriotic Front (RPF) army captured the Rwandan capital of Kigali and brought the Genocide against the Tutsi to an end. The city, as Jean-Paul Kimonyo notes, was almost totally destroyed:

> Au lendemain de la prise de Kigali le 4 juillet 1994 et au terme de trois mois de massacres intenses et de combats acharnés, Kigali est une ville fantôme. Il y règne le silence, le vide et l'odeur de la mort. Quelques rares véhicules des militaires du FPR, de petites patrouilles, circulent dans les rues vides encombrées de carcasses de voitures. Des survivants, véritables spectres ambulants, émergent de leur cachette [...] Des chiens repus de cadavres errent en meutes agressives et, de loin en loin, les tirs qui les abattent percent le silence.[1] (2017: 129)

---

[1] 'The day after the capture of Kigali on 4 July 1994 and at the end of three months of intense killings and relentless fighting, Kigali is a ghost town. The city is shrouded in silence, emptiness and the smell of death. A few RPF military vehicles, in small patrols, move around the empty streets littered with the shells of cars. Survivors – truly the walking dead – come out from their hiding places [...] Dogs, full up on corpses, wander in fierce packs and, every now and then, the silence is broken by shots that kill the dogs'. Translations are our own unless otherwise stated.

1

Kigali today looks nothing like this. The city centre's high-rise buildings and immaculate roadsides are a far cry from the violence, chaos and confusion of 1994 when Rwandans did not know which of their family members were alive or dead. Although films such as Terry George's *Hotel Rwanda* have contributed to the overdetermination of Rwanda by the events of 1994, Malaika Uwamahoro's opening poem in this volume challenges this image and points to a new version of the country as 'The world's example and definition of hope, resilience and ambition'. Over the past 25 years, Rwanda has been transforming itself from the devastation of 1994 into what is seen by government donors and the international community as a remarkable success story: 'an example for the East African region and perhaps even for the whole continent' (Marijnen and van de Lijn, 2012: 13).

This book is about the changing nature of Rwanda: how individual people and the nation as a whole have changed in manifold ways since suffering the horror of the Genocide against the Tutsi in 1994. Our aim with this volume is to explore from a range of disciplinary perspectives how Rwanda has undergone transformations. The Rwandan government narrative of progress represents a particular developmental trajectory that is tied to a nation-building project at home and the dissemination of a particular image beyond Rwanda's borders. But change in Rwanda is multifaceted, and the heterogeneous areas and experiences of change described in this volume demonstrate that range. Crucially, this book explores the multiple narratives about Rwanda that have emerged at individual, regional, national and international levels. These interact with each other and, as well as reporting change, also contribute to further change. All these stories contribute to the conscious and subconscious reimaginings of Rwanda taking place across the board, including through literature, politics and the media.

The book is divided into two parts. Part One, 'A Changing Nation', explores some of the ways in which the Rwandan government has responded to the multiple challenges created by the near-total destruction of the nation in 1994. The question of how to commemorate the Genocide against the Tutsi in ways that are appropriate and inclusive while still moving the country forwards is discussed in the opening chapter by Eloïse Brezault through the examples of cultural memory work by South African artist Bruce Clarke and Senegalese playwright Felwine Sarr. How, Brezault asks, can commemorative artworks 'open a safe space to talk about the genocide inside and outside Rwanda'? The role of the arts in commemoration then returns in Part Two of the book, 'Changing People', which focuses on individual Rwandans' stories of change. Here, Catherine Gilbert's discussion of written testimonies by two Rwandan women survivors sets up a dialogue with Madelaine Hron's more specific focus on Christian testimonials of forgiveness. In the final chapter,

Laura Apol's presentation of her experience of running writing workshops with Rwandan survivors speaks back to Brezault's opening question. Apol shows that creative writing can be a safe space for narrating the trauma of the genocide and can help individual people move forward with their lives. These authors' analyses of the therapeutic benefits of artistic expression for genocide survivors offer an interesting contrast to the therapeutic practices sometimes used by psychotherapists in Rwanda. Caroline Williamson Sinalo's chapter draws attention to the limitations of Western therapy traditions in the Rwandan context and emphasizes the importance of acknowledging historical, cultural and linguistic factors in the clinical treatment of trauma.

Through its critical perspective on Western narratives, Williamson Sinalo's essay offers points of connection with Benjamin Thorne and Julia Viebach's analysis of human rights reports on Rwanda in Part One. Thorne and Viebach's contribution is one of two chapters in the volume to focus on *gacaca*, the transitional justice system based on traditional community courts (see below). The other chapter is by Ananda Breed and Astrid Jamar. Both chapters use a narrative-based approach to *gacaca*, but draw on different stories and generate quite different conclusions: for Thorne and Viebach, external narratives on *gacaca* by human rights organizations such as Amnesty International and Human Rights Watch 'tell a story that leaves little room for different interpretations or meaning attached to *gacaca*', whereas Breed and Jamar focus on what they describe as the 'competing narratives and variances within the *gacaca* system'.

The interdisciplinary approach of *Rwanda Since 1994: Stories of Change* aims to avoid interpretations of Rwanda that are determined by polarized views of the genocide or the RPF government. In her chapter on post-genocide governance, Louise Umutoni-Bower focuses on the key transitional decade following 1994 and shows how the post-genocide period was an opportunity for renegotiating old systems and customs, including gender norms. Indeed, as Georgina Holmes and Ilaria Buscaglia demonstrate, the government of Rwanda has been rebuilding and transforming the country in a myriad of ways. Focusing on Rwanda's role as an international peacekeeper, Holmes and Buscaglia evaluate the ways in which the government has attempted to create a new brand identity, becoming what Rwandan daily *The New Times* describes as 'a strong advocate for reforming peacekeeping across the world' (in Holmes and Buscaglia, this volume).

In *Rwanda Since 1994: Stories of Change*, we have also chosen to include a focus on groups of people sometimes overshadowed by particular debates. As such, we want to move beyond binary identity dichotomies (Hutu and Tutsi), which tend to dominate Rwanda scholarship, and which have had such fatal consequences in Rwanda's history. The chapter by Meghan Laws,

Richard Ntakirutimana and Bennett Collins gives voice to the often unheard stories of the Rwandan Twa, known as a 'historically marginalized people'. Richard Benda's chapter shifts the discussion of Rwandan identity in another direction by analysing stories from children of perpetrators in relation to the national narrative of Rwandan identity (see below). We have placed chapters on social, economic, political and judicial change alongside one another to indicate how these areas of change are interconnected, and indeed driven by a range of motivations. We also aim to highlight how change occurs in different stages and periods of time. As Benda explains, a comprehensive account of post-genocide change must account for this multilevel and multistage dimension if we are to avoid scholarship that is characterized by misleading dualistic assessments of Rwanda (Benda, this volume). The drive for change inevitably comes from multiple sources and directions, whilst also having influences that are less tangible, for instance on intergenerational relations, or on expectations around memory and healing. These are some of the areas this volume seeks to explore.

## The Weight of History

Reflecting on forward-moving change must come alongside historical awareness, not least because in Rwanda the past weighs so heavily on the present, and in many ways determines the direction of the country's transformations.[2] The changes we describe evidently come in the wake of the genocide, but also continue changes which were taking place politically, socially and economically in the run-up to that nation-changing period of mass violence in 1994. In his recent study, *Rwanda demain! Une longue marche vers la transformation*, Rwandan scholar and presidential advisor Jean-Paul Kimonyo (2017) describes the instability which ultimately resulted in the genocide, including fluctuations in economic growth, and numerous waves of refugee migration around the Great Lakes region in the preceding decades.

The research questions in the present volume are raised within an interdisciplinary and postcolonial frame. The context for the genocide was also of course deeply marked by Belgian colonial influence, and illustrates just some of the complex legacy of colonialism in Rwanda. The genocide grew out of constructed narratives about the Other, which had been deliberately instilled over many years before 1994. As part of his revolutionary propaganda,

---

[2] For a range of historical accounts of the Genocide against the Tutsi, see Braeckman (1994), Des Forges (1999), Prunier (1995), Mamdani (2001), Semujanga (2003), Guichaoua (2015), Jessee (2017).

the first Rwandan President Grégoire Kayibanda entrenched interethnic enmity by formalizing distinctions between Hutu and Tutsi, who had priorly existed as fluid socio-economic groups, and had been concretized in part by the introduction of identity cards under Belgian rule in the 1930s. During and since the genocide, it has remained clear that Rwanda exists in the afterlife of European colonial projects – not least in France's implication in the genocide, the failure of the international community to intervene and the fraught relationships which continue over access to French archives.[3] Ongoing violence in the surrounding region, as well as genocide trials happening abroad, mean that Rwanda remains impacted by other countries, particularly in Europe. International actors (governmental, third sector, academic) continue to engage with Rwanda – some of the entangled influences on state formation and cultural development that come from abroad are analysed in the chapters that follow.

The road to Rwandan independence was marked by discrimination, persecution and bloodshed. Calls for independence from Belgium were accompanied by growing Hutu nationalism, with Kayibanda's MDR-Parmehutu party leading what is euphemistically known as the 'Social Revolution' of 1959–61. Following independence, Kayibanda's MDR government ruled with increasing violence and extremism, encouraging attacks on Tutsi populations and facing counter-attacks from the exiled RPF. When Juvénal Habyarimana took over from Kayibanda in the 1973 coup d'état, MDR-Parmehutu was outlawed, but seasons of unrest and instability continued, and Rwanda was a single-party state until 1991. It was within Habyarimana's party, the MRND (Mouvement révolutionnaire pour le développement) that the youth wing, the Interahamwe, and the extremist faction, the CDR (Coalition pour la défense de la république) were formed. Both would play a key role in the orchestration of the Genocide against the Tutsi in 1994.

In October 1990, the RPF's army invaded from Uganda and the Civil War began, a war that continued until a ceasefire agreement was negotiated in August 1993 along with plans for a power-sharing government. Identity politics were at the heart of this conflict and also central to the attempts at establishing peace. When Habyarimana's plane was shot down in April 1994, identity politics remained at the crux of hate-fuelled violence for the following 100 days. The horror of the genocide came not only in its scale and isolation, but also in its intimacy. Where other contemporary acts of mass

---

[3] The most recent book on France's involvement in the Genocide against the Tutsi is the testimony of former French army officer Guillaume Ancel (2018). Other key studies on France's role in Rwanda are Kroslak (2008) and Wallis (2014).

violence had recourse to concentration camps or means of transportation and imprisonment, the means of physical control and extermination in Rwanda was the mobilization of the population itself. The massacres happened in an unnervingly intimate way. Neighbours, friends, family members, as well as priests, teachers and students, were all complicit with the genocidal militia, the Interahamwe. The official number of people killed between April and July 1994 is now over a million and mass graves are still being discovered.

## Memory Landscape

Remembering those who were killed, and accounting for their deaths, has understandably dominated much of the last 25 years in Rwanda. A complex memory landscape has been built as Rwandans move forwards while inevitably having to look backwards. At a national level, annual programmes of commemoration come under the name *Kwibuka* and begin with an official week of mourning from 7–13 April (*Icyunamo*). During this time, work is put on hold and events are held locally, nationally and amongst the Rwandan diaspora around the world, where survivors share their testimonies. In Kigali there is a 'Walk to Remember', and a night vigil at the Amahoro national stadium, where many people sought refuge during the genocide. Organized gatherings over the three months that follow seek to provide space for healing and reconciliation, as well as build understanding, in order to prevent future violence. Within this context, 'ethnic' heritage determines who can openly mourn their dead at genocide commemorations and whether one is categorized as victim, survivor or perpetrator (Eramian, 2018: 60). This can risk reproducing oppositional groupings of Tutsi-victim and Hutu-perpetrator, and must be negotiated with care (Blackie and Hitchcott, 2018). The memorial landscape is one that must be navigated gently, not least because of the intense pain and loss that thousands of Rwandans still live with. The role of memorials and museums has been central to this process, as Eloïse Brezault explains in her chapter here, and remains a contested one, for instance regarding the display of victims' remains at public memorials such as Murambi. The museum infrastructure continues to evolve, with the recent opening of the Campaign Against Genocide museum inside the Rwandan parliament building. This new museum is a further indication of the importance placed on the production of historical knowledge in Rwanda and undeniably a retrospective response to the charged history of knowledge production preceding the genocide. As Brezault explores, the production of memory in Rwanda is shaped in part by the material and immaterial traces of cultural production, but also in dynamic relation to state and individual agency.

These official programmes and structures provide a backdrop of remembrance against which each family and individual deals with grief and loss every day of their lives. Managing the absence of relations whilst also reconstructing life is an ongoing challenge for thousands of Rwandans, faced with the breakdown of family and community structures which existed prior to the genocide and having to recreate senses of belonging and purpose in its aftermath. Informal remembering is thus a part of everyday life too: loved ones are talked about, and photographs used to prompt recollections, as Piotr Cieplak explores in his 2017 documentary, *The Faces We Lost*. Revisiting and re-narrating the pre-genocide past is also important for individuals, as Laura Apol describes in her chapter in this volume. The need to provide for this kind of personal memory work has led to the gradual development of a therapeutic infrastructure in the country.

## Therapy

When the tragedy of the Genocide against the Tutsi occurred in 1994, Rwanda's provision for psychiatric care was practically non-existent, as Caroline Williamson Sinalo outlines (this volume). Building an infrastructure for healing and therapy is one of many examples of Rwanda's pursuit of post-genocide change with a mixture of home-grown and imported approaches. Thanks to a number of individuals and institutions (Naasson Munyandamutsa, University of Rwanda, Community Based Sociotherapy, Prison Fellowship Rwanda, among others), the provision for psychological interventions in Rwanda is now wide-ranging and well established, although not available to all. Since the Rwandan government committed to training clinical psychologists in 1998, the country is now better served to support those suffering from PTSD and the multiple other effects of trauma. Williamson Sinalo writes of the shortcomings of importing Western medical approaches, which do not leave room for traditional beliefs, nor for the necessary overlaps of past and present. As this volume demonstrates, the advantages of such recourse to pre-genocide Rwandan tradition are not limited to therapy but can also be seen in areas of justice, governance and cultural development. Alongside responding to trauma, individuals must negotiate their personhood in a country whose social fabric was completely destroyed in 1994. Laura Eramian (2017) explores this at length in a sociocultural study of personhood, and we have elsewhere presented multiple testimonies of individuals who have negotiated their own psychosocial recovery (Grayson et al., 2019). In more established literary forms, narrating personal journeys in writing is a process people come back to multiple times (Gilbert, this volume), and these kinds of engagement with writing have been shown not only to relate change effectively, but also to promote further positive change (Apol, this volume).

## Justice and Reconciliation

A huge part of moving forward in Rwanda has been the pursuit of prosecutorial justice and the related emergence of reconciliation narratives. The government established the National Unity and Reconciliation Commission (NURC) in March 1999 to facilitate awareness-raising, truth-telling and reconciliation processes. Subsequently, the government introduced a system of transitional justice known as *gacaca*. Based on a traditional means of conflict resolution, the system aimed to reconcile Rwandans while also issuing punishments. At the heart of the trials was the participation of the whole community: as truth-tellers, witnesses and judges. Retaining the traditional structure, the *gacaca* trials were readopted in 2002 to prosecute the thousands of perpetrators charged with killing and other crimes committed during the genocide. Over a period of ten years, 1,958,634 genocide related cases were tried through *gacaca*.[4] *Gacaca* acted as a mechanism of both retributive and restorative justice: punishments were given but the trials were also designed for confession, reintegration and reconciliation. *Gacaca* is one element of the highly entangled repair processes of post-genocide Rwanda, and the complexities and shortcomings of this system of justice have been explored extensively (Clark and Kaufman, 2009; Clark, 2010; Gahima, 2013; Ingelaere, 2016). In this volume, Thorne and Viebach compare the RPF government's justification for using *gacaca* with other reports that depict it as a failure. Discussing the same shifting terrain of legal mechanisms, Breed and Jamar examine the staging of particular narratives around *gacaca* and the ways policy and practice interact to build a particular image of post-genocide Rwanda whilst failing to address the system's fundamental weaknesses. The major restorative element of *gacaca* was the bringing together of so many people, and this continues in other community-based initiatives such as Unity and Reconciliation associations. These are local groups which draw together survivors and perpetrators and allow for the public acknowledgement of crimes. This in turn has led to shifting relationships at a local level, particularly following the release from prison of huge numbers of former perpetrators thanks to a presidential pardon.

For understandable reasons, unity and peace building are of the utmost importance in Rwanda. In 2007 the RPF government (often referred to as the

---

[4]  'Governance and Home-Grown Solutions', http://gov.rw/about-the-government/governance-home-grown-solutions/ (consulted on 25 May 2018).

Government of National Unity and Reconciliation) established the National Commission for the Fight Against Genocide (CNLG) to combat genocide ideology, conduct research on genocide and raise awareness. Because of the intimate nature and vast scale of violence during the genocide, and also because one of its consequences was the dispersal of the population, unity is at the forefront of state-led initiatives. Stories of organized and spontaneous forgiveness abound, and in her chapter, Madelaine Hron untangles differences between religious and secular understandings of forgiveness, accounting for its limitations (in terms of justice) as well as its benefits (both social and spiritual). The religious landscape in Rwanda has changed considerably in the wake of the genocide, not least because of the Catholic Church's complicity in so many deaths (Longman, 2010). Although Pentecostal churches are on the rise, the relationships between churches and the state, and possibilities for ecumenism, remain precarious (Kubai, 2007; Grant, 2018). More broadly too, unity remains contentious and complicated. Focusing on what has become known as a 'historically marginalized people', Laws et al. (this volume) discuss national unity in terms of ethnicity, and ask who fits the official narrative of inclusive, pan-Rwandan identity, and who does not quite belong. Benda (this volume) looks further at the *Ndi Umunyarwanda* [I am Rwandan] programme and its influence on different generations. He shows how particular initiatives can shift the parameters of public narratives and which groups get included in them, in order to move beyond restrictive 'single stories'. In these ways, reconciliation and unity, and the narratives developed around them, form a vital part of Rwanda's nation-building project.

## Narrative of Progress

The project of building a post-genocide Rwanda is narrated by the RPF government in a rhetoric of progress and development. In defining modern nationhood for Rwanda, two themes that feature highly are self-sufficiency and ambition. Although foreign investment and NGO activity are currently ongoing, President Kagame recently spoke of setting a deadline to stop foreign aid dependency, saying, 'Our dignity is not about wealth but self-belief that we can do it.'[5] Partly in response to the failures of the international community during the genocide, there is a prevailing sense of Rwandans needing to build Rwanda for themselves. The *gacaca* trials, described above, are just one of many 'home-grown solutions' the government has implemented. These are distinctly Rwandan initiatives

[5] 'Kagame Orders Govt to Set Deadline on Aid Dependence', http://en.igihe. com/spip.php?page=mv2_article&id_article=31146 (consulted on 25 May 2018).

introduced to contribute 'to Rwanda's journey of transformation'.[6] The following home-grown solutions have come within a broader programme of decentralization and post-conflict rebuilding, which has concentrated on restructuring administration and government, and promoting social welfare. *Abunzi* is a conflict-resolution system that was institutionalized in 2004 to decentralize justice and make it more accessible and affordable for citizens without them needing to attend court. *Imihigo* gives an indication of the forward-moving drive pushed by the RPF government. It describes a precolonial practice of setting targets and completing them, and is used as a means of accountability so that the national government can evaluate the achievements of local governments, ministries and public services. *Umwiherero*, the National Leadership Retreat, works in much the same vein. Again based on traditional practice, once a year the president chairs a retreat for ministers to present on development challenges. These are then discussed and solutions proposed. Decentralization has also aimed to widen the sense of responsibility and ownership so that every citizen can be involved in rebuilding the nation. This is partly enacted in *Umuganda*, a mandatory day of community work which happens on the last Saturday of each month. Rwandans between the ages of 18 and 65 are obliged to participate, and tasks include building roads, fixing buildings and community meetings to discuss local and national issues.

Economic recovery has been a crucial part of post-conflict rebuilding, and all this whilst dealing with the physical and psychological effects of genocidal violence. This area of growth is, like many others, shaped by looking back to the past, since it was a context of extreme poverty in the late 1980s and early 1990s that prepared the ground for the genocide. At the end of the 1980s Rwanda was among the five worst-off countries in the world in terms of the percentage of population with access to health services, the number of calories consumed daily per person and the percentage of children at secondary school (Kimonyo, 2017: 86). In 1990, life expectancy in Rwanda was recorded as 33.4 years (Kimonyo, 2017: 88) compared to 66.6 years in 2017 (NISR, n.d.). Today Rwanda's economy is growing at an average rate of 7 per cent each year,[7] and where huge disparity exists between urban and rural space, programmes are in place to improve agricultural production and rural livelihoods. *Girinka* is one example of this, where a dairy cow is provided to poor households to generate income and improve nutrition.

---

[6] 'Governance and Home-Grown Solutions', http://gov.rw/about-the-government/governance-home-grown-solutions/ (consulted on 25 May 2018).

[7] 'The World Bank in Rwanda', http://www.worldbank.org/en/country/rwanda/overview (consulted on 25 April 2018).

Hundreds of thousands of people have benefited since *girinka* was introduced in 2006, and economic stability remains a key goal. These initiatives have also seen provinces and regions reorganized and renamed – in many cases to write over negative names associated with the genocide. These are geospatial inscriptions of the changes which have also occurred in the fields of language and education.

## Francophone to Anglophone

In 2008, Rwanda applied to join the Commonwealth. At the same time, English was adopted as the official language of public administration and replaced French as the main language of education in Rwandan schools. Joseph Assan and Lawrence Walker read the switch to English as a symbol of 'the new national development strategy within a forward-looking post-conflict society' (2012: 176). What Assan and Walker do not consider is the impact of the switch on cultural production in Rwanda. Most published fiction to date has been published in French (Hitchcott, 2015) and French remains the language of intellectuals, particularly among the older generation. For university staff, the new policy has been a challenge for some academics who are unhappy to find themselves now obliged to write and teach in English rather than French or their mother-tongue of Kinyarwanda. However, as Assam and Walker rightly note (2012: 185), a number of causal factors informed the switch from French to English: firstly, Rwanda's decision to join the East African Community (EAC) in 2007, which was followed in 2017 by the adoption of Swahili, the universal language of the EAC, as the fourth official language of Rwanda. A second motivation was the role of English as a world language, particularly in science and technology, reflecting Paul Kagame's ambition for Rwanda to become a middle-income country with influence on the world stage. Finally, a not insignificant factor in the move away from French as a major language of communication was undoubtedly the increasingly strained political relationship between Rwanda and France. In 2014, then President of France François Hollande refused to send a delegate to the twentieth anniversary commemorations of the Genocide against the Tutsi following the publication in *Jeune Afrique* of an interview with Rwandan President Kagame in which he spoke of 'le rôle direct de la Belgique et de la France dans la préparation politique du génocide et la participation de cette dernière à son exécution même' (Soudan, 2014: 23).[8]

---

[8] 'the direct role of Belgium and France in the political preparation of the genocide and the latter's participation in its very execution'.

## Stories of Change

Rwanda is certainly not without its critics, most of them focused on the country's president and former RPF military commander, Paul Kagame. Indeed, as Laura Mann and Marie Berry note, 'Rwanda's experience has received polarised interpretations' which, they argue, must be considered together for the transformation of the country to be fully understood (2015: 138). Critics highlight allegations of autocratic rule, lack of freedom of speech, political disappearances, human rights abuses and war crimes in the neighbouring Democratic Republic of the Congo. While we do not wish to undermine the importance of these allegations, which, where relevant, are acknowledged in the chapters that follow, the focus of the present volume is on the stories of change that are emerging from Rwanda: creative writing and testimonies, as well as national and international political narratives. The book's two parts trace the ways in which the Rwandan nation and its people have evolved from the almost total destruction of 1994 to a regional leader in the EAC and a pioneer in a number of areas that are now having an impact on the rest of the world. These include Rwanda's role as international peacekeeper, as discussed by Buscaglia and Holmes (this volume) and Rwanda now having the highest percentage of women holding seats in parliament in the world (see Umutoni-Bower, this volume), as well as a number of green initiatives, including a ban on plastic bags, car-free days and sustainable tourism. Developments in the creative arts such as spoken word, cinema, fashion and photography are also beginning to put Rwanda on the map. The importance of Rwandan youth in rebuilding their nation cannot be overemphasized and is foregrounded from the outset of this volume in Malaika Uwamahoro's poem. Where in 1994, the world refused to acknowledge what was taking place in Rwanda, 25 years later Rwanda is making itself highly visible through stories of individual and societal change.

## Acknowledgement

This publication was made possible through the support of a research grant AH/M004155/2 from the Arts and Humanities Research Council, UK.

## Works Cited

Ancel, Guillaume. 2018. *Rwanda, la fin du silence: témoignage d'un officier français*. Paris: Les Belles Lettres.

Assan, Joseph, and Lawrence Walker. 2012. 'The Political Economy of Contemporary Education and the Challenges of Switching Formal Language to English in Rwanda'. In Maddelena Campioni and Patrick Noack (eds), *Rwanda Fast Forward*. Basingstoke: Palgrave Macmillan: 176–91.

Blackie, Laura, and Nicki Hitchcott. 2018. '"I am Rwandan": Unity and Reconciliation in Post-Genocide Rwanda'. *Genocide Studies and Prevention* 12.1: 24–37.

Braeckman, Colette. 1994. *Rwanda. Histoire d'un génocide*. Paris: Fayard.

Cieplak, Piotr (dir.). 2017. *The Faces We Lost*.

Clark, Phil. 2010. *The Gacaca Courts, Post-Genocide Justice and Reconciliation in Rwanda: Justice without Lawyers*. Cambridge: Cambridge University Press.

Clark, Phil, and Zachary Kaufman. 2009. *After Genocide: Transitional Justice, Post-Conflict Reconstruction and Reconciliation in Rwanda and Beyond*. New York: Columbia University Press.

Des Forges, Alison. 1999. *'Leave None to Tell the Story': Genocide in Rwanda*. New York: Human Rights Watch.

Eramian, Laura. 2018. *Peaceful Selves: Personhood, Nationhood, and the Post-Conflict Moment in Rwanda*. New York: Berghahn Books.

Gahima, Gerald. 2013. *Transitional Justice in Rwanda: Accountability for Atrocity*. Abingdon and New York: Routledge.

George, Terry (dir.). 2004. *Hotel Rwanda*.

'Governance and Home-Grown Solutions'. Available at http://gov.rw/about-the-government/governance-home-grown-solutions/ (consulted on 25 May 2018).

Grant, Andrea Mariko. 2018. 'Ecumenism in Question: Rwanda's Contentious Post-Genocide Religious Landscape'. *Journal of Southern African Studies* 44.2: 221–38.

Grayson, Hannah, Nicki Hitchcott, Laura Blackie and Stephen Joseph (eds). 2019. *After the Genocide in Rwanda: Testimonies of Violence, Change and Reconciliation*. London: I.B. Tauris.

Guichaoua, André. 2015. *From War to Genocide: Criminal Politics in Rwanda, 1990–1994*. Madison, WI: University of Wisconsin Press.

Hitchcott, Nicki. 2015. *Rwanda Genocide Stories: Fiction after 1994*. Liverpool: Liverpool University Press.

Ingelaere, Bert. 2016. *Inside Rwanda's Gacaca Courts: Seeking Justice after Genocide*. Madison, WI: University of Wisconsin Press.

Jessee, Erin. 2017. *Negotiating Genocide in Rwanda: The Politics of History*. London: Palgrave Macmillan.

'Kagame Orders Govt to Set Deadline on Aid Dependence'. 17 December 2016. Available at http://en.igihe.com/spip.php?page=mv2_article&id_article=31146 (consulted on 25 May 2018).

Kimonyo, Jean-Paul. 2017. *Rwanda demain! Une longue marche vers la transformation*. Paris: Karthala.

Kroslak, Daniela. 2007. *The French Betrayal of Rwanda*. Bloomington, IN: Indiana University Press.

Kubai, Anne. 2007. 'Post-Genocide Rwanda: The Changing Religious Landscape'. *Exchange* 36.2: 198–214.

Longman, Timothy. 2010. *Christianity and Genocide in Rwanda*. Cambridge: Cambridge University Press.

Mamdani, Mahmood. 2001. *When Victims Become Killers: Colonialism, Nativism, and the Genocide in Rwanda*. Princeton, NJ: Princeton University Press.

Mann, Laura, and Marie Berry. 2015. 'Understanding the Political Motivations that Shape Rwanda's Emergent Development State'. *New Political Economy* 21.1: 119–44.

Marijnen, Esther, and Jaïr van der Lijn. 2012. 'Rwandan 2025: Scenarios for the Future Political Stability of Rwanda'. In Maddelena Campioni and Patrick Noack (eds), *Rwanda Fast Forward*. Basingstoke: Palgrave Macmillan: 13–28.

NISR (National Institute of Statistics of Rwanda). 'Life Expectancy at Birth'. Available at http://statistics.gov.rw/publication/life-expectancy-birth (consulted on 13 August 2018).

Prunier, Gérard. 1995. *The Rwanda Crisis: History of a Genocide*. New York: Columbia University Press.

Semujanga, Josias. 2003. *Origins of the Rwandan Genocide*. Amherst, NY: Humanity Books.

Soudan, François. 2014. 'Paul Kagamé: du génocide à la rwandité'. *Jeune Afrique* 2778 (6–12 April): 22–28.

Wallis, Andrew. 2014. *Silent Accomplice: The Untold Story of France's Role in the Rwandan Genocide*. 2nd ed. London: I.B. Tauris.

'The World Bank in Rwanda'. 7 March 2017. Available at http://www.worldbank.org/en/country/rwanda/overview (consulted on 25 April 2018).

# Rwanda Is NOT *Hotel Rwanda*!!!

*Malaika Uwamahoro*

Rwanda –
is not hotel Rwanda
No –
Rwanda is the heart beating life of Africa –
The world's example and definition of hope, resilience and ambition
If you haven't yet heard
listen,
Grab a pen and learn –
Rwanda is a lesson.

Rwanda is where the great Kivu lake
Rests in –
Where the birds of the Nyungwe forest
Nest in
and the foreign investors fly all the way to
Invest in
What's happening right now in Rwanda
Is interestin'
And its amazin'
To be a part of and watch …

Watch …

Rwanda

Rwanda is
**Tens** of growing cities
**Hundreds** of opportunities
The land of a **thousand** hills –
The faces of a **million** smiles –
And just
**one people** –
We are united back home –
Where I come from ...

In Rwanda there is freedom
Where we live in peace
And live as we please
*Yemwe simvuga amahanga*
*Nda vuga iwacu murwanda*
*Ahari kubera ibitangaza* –

Rwanda Is
birds and lakes
Lights and city streets,
Volcanoes and silver backs,
Restaurants,
Cinemas and coffee beans,
teas, industries, electricity and honey bees ...
**I come from the earth's last piece of paradise**

**A big-hearted land**
Where my people
Chose forgiveness
From the atrocities they witnessed
**A land**
Where we are not afraid to speak the truth
**A land**
Where there is room for the youth
**A land**
Where one people work hard hand in hand
To demand,
Justice and dignity –

**We come from a land –**
That has risen from the ashes of sorrow
To the rose blossom of tomorrow
**A land**
of Agaciro –
**We come from that land**

So NO –
Rwanda
is not hotel Rwanda –
We will not be defined by the genocide
Rwanda is
A land of pride –
The home to
dreamers, believers and achievers,
Learners and teachers
Humans and creatures
the heart beating life of Africa –
The world's example and definition of hope, resilience and ambition
If you haven't yet heard
Yo, I hope you listened
Rwanda is a lesson!!!

# Part One:
# A Changing Nation

# 'Memory-Traces' in the Work of Felwine Sarr and Bruce Clarke: What Stories of Change Can Commemorate the Genocide against the Tutsi?

*Eloïse Brezault*

In March 2014, Kizito Mihigo, one of the most popular Rwandan singers and well-known peace activist, released a song very critical of the wartime actions of Paul Kagame's political party, the Rwandan Patriotic Front: 'Igisobanuro Cy'urupfu' [The Meaning of Death].[1] After the song went viral (it had more than 30,000 views within two days of posting) and sparked a nationwide dialogue about the genocide, Mihigo was accused of conspiracy to assassinate the president of Rwanda and sentenced to ten years in prison. He confessed, probably after being tortured. In September 2018, he was officially pardoned by President Kagame and released from prison. American journalist Charulata Sihna wrote a piece in *Afropop worldwide*, wondering if 'Mihigo [was] truly guilty of conspiracy or only of speaking (and singing) truth to power'?[2] Indeed, Mihigo, co-writer of the Rwandan National Anthem, is a Tutsi survivor of the 1994 genocide and was invited several times to perform at commemorations of the genocide between 2004 and 2008; before being incarcerated, he was scheduled to perform for the twentieth anniversary in front of world leaders. Mihigo's song advocates peace and reconciliation, talks about the necessity of empathy for others (Tutsi *and* Hutu) and remembering

---

[1] The English translation is from the YouTube clip of Mihigo's song that circulated widely after his imprisonment at https://www.youtube.com/watch?v=S2n8hTQl2lI.

[2] See Sinha (2018).

the lives of all (without directly naming them), specifically those whose lives were 'brutally taken', although 'not qualified as Genocide' victims because they are not part of the government narrative. Mihigo became *persona non grata* because he alludes not only to the Tutsi victims of the genocide, but also the Hutu who were killed by RPF soldiers during the civil war and after the genocide. The song was abruptly banned from public broadcast, along with all of Mihigo's other songs. As scholar Susan Thomson puts it in Sinha's piece, Mihigo's song goes against the simple story of the official commemoration, which is 'Tutsi dies, Hutu kills, RPF saves and they are ultimately the heroes.' It is clear that the role of the government's commemoration is to unify the country behind one single narrative that cannot be contested. In that context, it might be assumed that Hutu lives cannot matter, despite what Mihigo's song advocates. This example is one of many recent challenges to Paul Kagame's vision of the 1994 Genocide against the Tutsi.

Though Rwanda does not lack memorials, their overabundance has become highly problematic since it carefully 'stages' a very specific narrative orchestrated by the Rwandan government, creating what Alexandre Dauge-Roth calls an 'excess of memory' (2012: 15) and a 'powerful legitimizing gesture directed toward the present' (2012: 16). Far from being neutral, these national museums build an 'imaginary community', to paraphrase Benedict Anderson (2006), whose overarching goal is to unify a nation decimated by genocide. Museums therefore have a specific task: to show that the reconstruction of a nation is still possible if our humanity can be rebuilt, which results in the idea of a saviour emerging slowly from the narrative. Museums bear acknowledgements of what happened, which is essential in post-genocide peacebuilding, but 'selecting which civilian memories of violence to include and which to exclude in these sites is a political process that has important implications for "hard" politics – for the success of peacebuilding and future security', as Elisabeth King argues (2010: 293). Kizito Mihigo's song threatens this false equilibrium and must be severed: no heroes in his words, only frail humans to forgive and remember. In a country where there had been a moratorium on teaching the Tutsi genocide for ten years,[3] the museums became the place where such a horrific event was told and explained. In the

---

[3] In her recent essay *From Classrooms to Conflict in Rwanda*, Elisabeth King recalls that Rwanda's government suspended the teaching of history in schools in 1994. 'In 1999, the government suggested that history should be taught in schools for two hours each week but did not offer substantial guidelines, or any textbooks or teaching material, thereby continuing a de facto moratorium' (2014: 121). In 2004, the government introduced a primary-level civics textbook, *A Guide to Civic Education*, with units on 'Genocide and Reconciliation' (King, 2014: 131).

Kigali Genocide Memorial for example, it is said that 'Hutus who did not comply [help kill Tutsi] were threatened with death. A number of Hutus who did not subscribe to the genocidal ideology, as well as those who tried to protect Tutsis were persecuted and killed' (Aegis Trust, 2004: 20). But nothing is said about the violence of RPF soldiers upon civilians (King, 2014: 300). In the national narrative, there is only space for the Tutsi survivor saved by the RPF and the moderate Hutu. The grand narrative of the genocide has been fixed, implying that those who do not fit into those categories become genocide deniers, such as Kizito Mihigo. I would like to explore further the role which art can play in this particular context of memorialization. King writes that 'Many Rwandans' memories are inconsistent with public ones and there is friction between state discourses and personal narratives' (2014: 303) and thus the lack of acknowledgement of memories from the majority Hutu community can jeopardize the peace-building process, creating an 'us' versus 'them' mentality that could divide the country further. Indeed, many Hutu think that the memorialization process creates more collective guilt and excludes them from political power.[4] If Rwandans themselves feel threatened not to speak out in public, who is left in Rwanda to contest the official narrative? If such a prominent and public figure as Mihigo has been arrested, where can change come from? Can art and literature mobilize an external and somewhat more critical memory that could slowly transform the official narrative or speak directly to the younger generations born after the genocide? In this chapter, I would like to investigate, through the lens of Marianne Hirsch's concept of 'postmemory', two recent artistic projects that commemorate the Genocide against the Tutsi of 1994 from an external perspective, 20 years after: the latest play by Senegalese intellectual Felwine Sarr, *Sur la barrière* [*On the Roadblock*] (written in 2015 in Kigali) and the mural project *Upright Men* (2014) by South African photographer Bruce Clarke. According to Hirsch, 'Postmemory describes the relationship that the "generation after" bears to the personal, collective and cultural trauma of those who came before – to experiences they "remember" only

---

And in 2008, the National Curriculum Development Center set a curriculum guideline 'for history teaching for the first three years of secondary school [...] and in 2010 for the second three years, called advanced or upper secondary school level' (King, 2014: 134) with a section on 'The War of 1990–1994 and the genocide of Tutsi'. However, King recalls that critical thinking is carefully controlled by the government narrative and that the teachers she interviewed felt uncomfortable with teaching that part of the curriculum (2014: 132).

⁴ See the work of Lemarchand (2009), Coquio (2004) or Brandstetter (2010) on this question.

by means of stories, images and behaviors among which they grew up
[...] *Postmemory's connection to the past is thus actually mediated not by
recall but by imaginative investment, projection and creation'* (2012: 5; my
emphasis). How much do those projects, by bringing different generations
and different voices together, reconnect Rwandans to their own specific oral
traditions and thus alter the official narrative? Indeed, Asumpta Mugiraneza,
the head of Iriba Center for Multimedia in Kigali, underlined the importance
of art and oral traditions in the transmission of memory in Rwanda at a
symposium at Columbia University on Postmemory and Creation: 'Rwanda's
artistic tradition has [...] a highly sophisticated and elaborate language that
paints pictures worthy of the greatest painters [...] The Rwandan expresses
himself through songs or poetry more than any other art form' (2013: 15). I
will argue that Sarr's and Clarke's projects open a safe space to talk about the
genocide inside and outside Rwanda and underline the importance of orality
in the transmission process.

*Upright Men* is a public mural built collectively with the contribution of
Rwandan artists 'to give a presence to the victims, restoring their individuality, reaffirming their status in the human community' (Clarke, 'Upright
Men'). Reproduced in many sites around the world, this artwork combines
newspapers, torn fragments and posters. The words and images are combined
and resurface on the canvas to create a collage that is never meant to be
an illustration. Then the fragmented pieces are drenched, coated in paint
and repeated elsewhere to create a palimpsest. Clarke organized workshops
in Rwanda to train Rwandan artists in the techniques so that they could
participate fully in the project by making their own collage. Three techniques
were used to give life to the figures. Not only were mural paintings created
on the façades of the buildings of the memorial sites to commemorate the
anniversary of the genocide, but also large-scale printed tarpaulins bearing
representations of Rwandans were also shown in symbolic locations inside
and outside Rwanda to heighten awareness in a wider audience: the Slave
Route in Benin, Neumunster Abbey in Luxembourg, the UN headquarters
in New York, the Place des Nations in Geneva, the Casa Africa in Mexico,
UNESCO in Paris and La Grand-Place in Brussels. Artists also used light
projections and digital reproductions during the nights of commemoration
in Rwanda and elsewhere. This ephemeral art reminds us of the silence of
the international community who did not want to see and acknowledge what
happened. Reproduced on many sites at the same time, the project bears
witness to Rwandan people standing up and remembering the genocide.

When in 2015 the Rwandan actress Carole Karemera invited Felwine Sarr
to a writing residency project, she told him the story of her aunt, who ended
up adopting the murderer of her son. The project became *Sur la barrière*,

which Sarr documented by interviewing people on site. *Sur la barrière* depicts the complex relationships between a mother, Isaro, and her son's murderer, Faustin, a young Hutu farmer who became an interahamwe during the genocide.

These projects show how memorialization in Rwanda can be shaped by international actors and underline a trend that Rachel Ibreck has also observed with the official memorials: 'It reflects a worldwide turn towards "post-national" commemoration [...] and a shift towards the transnational production and dissemination of memories in the context of globalization [...] The national hold on memory, never entirely firm, has been loosened by international norms, narratives and finances' (2013: 150). Ibreck explains how the Kigali Memorial was completely conceptualized, designed and built by a UK NGO, the Aegis Trust, modelled on the Beth Shalom Holocaust Centre in Nottinghamshire. The Aegis Trust even organized and wrote the main exhibit for the official opening in April 2004, flying experts from the UK to Rwanda for the occasion, instead of using people on site (Ibreck, 2013: 158). The Kigali memorial strengthens relationships between Europe and Rwanda. However, the transnational movement seems to operate in only one direction, from North to South, from an old colonial power to a former colony, maintaining the country in a relationship of dependency and showing how the Rwandan government is still influenced by European actors to rebuild its political legitimacy after the genocide.[5] I would argue that the two works of art presented in this chapter break with this paternalistic vision and inject fresh momentum, since they start a dialogue between South and South (Felwine Sarr is Senegalese)[6] but also from South to North and vice versa (the artists present copies of their art in European countries, while the original creation belongs to Rwanda). It is also worth noting that while Bruce Clarke was born and raised in the UK by South African parents, he divides his life between Europe and Africa, and his art is heavily influenced by his

---

[5] We could even say that, because the UK is not a former colonizer of Rwanda like Belgium and Germany, Aegis (which is based in the UK) has more leeway to implement its policies without being criticized for paternalistic gestures. King mentions that 'between 2000 and 2005, about 5% of all British aid to Africa went to Rwanda, totaling approximatively 168 million pounds sterling. The United Kingdom remains the largest bilateral donor to Rwanda, alongside the United States' (2014: 120).

[6] With Bénédicte Savoy, Professor of Art History at the Technische Universität Berlin, Sarr has recently been appointed by French President Emmanuel Macron to a huge task: the restitution of African artefacts stolen by French museums during colonization to their country of origin.

experience on the African continent.[7] Sarr and Clarke create stories of a new type: they question the government's narrative and build an immaterial *lieu de mémoire*[8] that cannot be censored because of its transnational impact.

## Renewing and Changing a Post-National Tradition of Commemoration

As I mentioned earlier, these two projects are by artists whose interests have focused on the African continent: Bruce Clarke is a white photographer, visual artist and activist whose parents emigrated from South Africa to London in the 1960s; Felwine Sarr is a Senegalese economist and thinker who teaches at the Université Gaston-Berger (Saint-Louis, Senegal). With Achille Mbembe he created 'Les Ateliers de la pensée' in Senegal in 2016 in order to reposition the continent back at the centre of ideas and reflections.

In some ways, Sarr's play echoes the Fest'Africa project organized in 1998 by Chadian writer Nocky Djedanoum and Ivorian artist Maïmouna Coulibaly to commemorate the genocide in Rwanda. Djedanoum and Coulibaly brought a group of ten African writers (only two were Rwandan)[9] to bear witness to the genocide by visiting memorial sites and speaking to survivors. 'Rwanda: Writing as a Duty to Remember' aimed to fill a void four years after the events. At the time the writers denounced the framework of ethnic killings (as told by the Western world) and the rhetoric of hatred; they also rebutted the thesis of a double genocide promoted by pro-Hutu people fighting against the RPF soldiers (Dauge-Roth, 2012: 92). After a two-month residency in Rwanda, they produced a body of literature that has been published by African and French publishers and translated into various languages. Nicki Hitchcott justly points

---

[7] As stated on his website: 'For Bruce Clarke his artistic work is inseparable from his political activism, firstly in relation to South Africa where he played a role in the anti-apartheid movement in France and with the ANC (African National Congress). He continues working on cultural projects in this country, particularly with the Afrika Cultural Centre in Johannesburg' (Clarke, 'Biography').

[8] Even if both projects are also material in the sense that Nora described *lieux de mémoire* – Sarr wrote a book and Clarke painted murals – I am more interested here in how their mobility has created discussions and stories that go beyond Rwanda and Rwandans as I will develop further in the chapter, creating a space I would call immaterial because it is not restricted to a sole object.

[9] Participants in the Fest'Africa project: Boubacar Boris Diop (Senegal), Monique Ilboudo (Burkina Faso), Vénuste Kayimahe (Rwanda), Koulsy Lamko (Chad), Tierno Monénembo (Guinea), Meja Mwangi (Kenya), Nocky Djedanoum (Chad), Jean-Marie Vianney Rurangwa (Rwanda), Véronique Tadjo (Ivory Coast) and Abdourahman Waberi (Djibouti).

out that 'the Fest'Africa project [...] attempted to drag Rwanda out of the "heart of Darkness" into the global imagination': by writing back to the old colonial centres, the authors were able to 'situate the Rwanda genocide within a transnational, transhistorical and transcultural framework' (2009: 158–59).

Almost 20 years later, Felwine Sarr was invited to Rwanda to write a play about redemption and humanity. His focus is slightly different because the issues of memorialization have evolved since then: what matters today is less the rhetoric of hatred or the criticism of Françafrique and its neocolonialism than the possibility of reconciliation after everything has been lost. Isaro, the main character, is distraught after her husband died fighting for the RPF and her son was murdered by Faustin and his gang of Interahamwe on the 'barrière'. There are very few direct allusions to ethnicity in the text. Faustin hunted Tutsi with his group of friends: his use of the words 'hunting' and 'working' alludes to the general propaganda produced by the government at the time and shows that he has completely internalized it. Could it also be a way to distance himself from what he did by reducing the people he killed to animals? He objectifies Tutsi and compares them to *inyenzi* (cockroaches) but, interestingly enough, as soon as he uses the word in front of Isaro, he corrects himself and adopts the word 'Tutsi' instead (Sarr, 2017: 7). However, he is not able to see anything wrong with using words such as 'hunt' or 'work' (real euphemisms used for killing people during the genocide). His recollection of the event seems limited, as if he cannot escape (even today) the politics of objectification that have targeted the Tutsi for years, before and during the genocide. Is there a limit to the process of forgiveness and redemption? Sarr does not alleviate problems in post-genocide Rwanda: issues remain and the memorialization is imperfect, but it is all we have.

Both Isaro and Faustin come from families of farmers: she has a plantation of bananas; he cultivated his own *rugo*[10] with his stepfather when he was a child. Sarr goes against the classifications that defined colonial Rwanda (that Hutu were farmers and Tutsi owned cattle). In a phone interview, he said that he did a lot of research when he was in Rwanda and discovered that those social categories used to be more fluid in precolonial Rwanda (a Hutu could become a Tutsi by buying his own cattle). He wanted the reader to think critically about those categories as social constructions. Faustin makes only one allusion to Albert's height – 'sa grande taille' (Sarr, 2017: 15) – which could imply that Albert is a Tutsi. However, nothing can explain why Faustin killed him, except the fact that he was told to do it. Faustin does not resent Albert because he is a Tutsi, he does not kill Albert because he hates him, he kills him to follow orders. Sarr makes a clear statement that the rhetoric of

---

[10] Sarr uses the Kinyarwanda word for 'family compound'.

hatred was less efficient for Faustin than the fear of being killed by his own people if he did not comply with orders. After talking to a lot of Rwandans, Sarr was struck by the fact that perpetrators had different motives for their actions. Faustin is not an evil character per se: he did not plan the killings; he is able to articulate without guilt or shame that he is only human and acted for his own survival. However, just because he is asking for forgiveness does not mean he should be forgiven. Sarr adds layers of complexity to the narrative of a post-genocide society. His play offers a journey into a killer's mind without being dramatic or judgemental; it gives a voice to a majority of people who have been silenced for years. The audience is then able to better understand what motivated Faustin:

> Faustin: Je l'ai poursuivi et attrapé. Je lui ai tenu fermement le cou. J'ai senti son sang bouillir. C'était plus mou qu'un plant de maïs. Il ne disait rien. Ça m'a un peu refroidi, puis je me suis repris. Juvénal et Kamanzi me regardaient avec fierté. J'ai pris le gourdin et je l'ai frappé. [...]
> Isaro: Et il est mort?
> Faustin: Non, pas tout de suite. J'ai dû frapper à nouveau sur la nuque. Encore et encore: il était robuste. Et le cou a craqué. (Sarr, 2017: 15)[11]

Faustin expresses himself in short sentences that are stripped of emotion. He describes Albert's murder in a bland style that recalls Barthes's (1972) idea of *écriture blanche*, symbolic of post-war attempts to strip language down to a *degré zéro*, to a supposed absence of style, as if Sarr refused to commit to either side of the conflict in order to let the audience decide what they think of Faustin. *Écriture blanche*, Barthes believed, forces the reader to make sense of a novel by questioning the character's inner motives. Indeed, the writer is not there to take sides, claims Sarr, but to stay close to the reality he witnessed. It is all the more powerful that Faustin can talk about his crime with Isaro, who is able to listen in return. The dialogue has been restored and they can move on, signalling that change can happen.

Similarly, Clarke's project, *Upright Men*, describes our lost humanity without any judgement:

---

[11] 'Faustin: I followed him and caught him. I grabbed his neck firmly. I felt his blood boiling. It was softer than a young corn plant. He said nothing, which stopped me, but I got a grip on myself. Juvénal and Kamanzi looked at me proudly. I took the club and I hit him [...].
Isaro: And he was dead?
Faustin: No, not right away. I had to hit him on the back of the neck. Again and again. He was strong. And his neck snapped'. All translations are mine unless otherwise stated.

The figures are larger than life, often 6–8 m high, silhouettes sketched with a strong affirmed presence. They are symbols of the dignity of human beings who lived and died in this barbarous genocide [...] The intention is to give presence to the victims, restoring their individuality and reaffirming their status in the human community. (2018: 159)

The project is composed of tall murals of Rwandans that were exhibited not only in Rwanda but also outside the country to raise awareness of the genocide among young people. Clarke does not put any emphasis on ethnicity either; the figures are all Rwandans who belong to the same country. They are all human beings whose dignity is there to give a presence to those who were killed. Clarke says that the figures carry with them a message of hope: they testify about what happened while asserting to the rest of the world that Rwandans will never be crushed by genocide; they will always stand up (Brinker et al., 2017: 442).

By creating a dialogue with the Rwandan population and its young generation, the artistic process in Clarke's and Sarr's works was also a learning experience and it opened a safe space to talk about the genocide from a personal viewpoint. Instead of being only a *lieu de mémoire*, these projects illustrate and discuss Rothberg's idea of 'memory knots': 'Noeuds de mémoire as we conceive them here are not static conglomerations of heterogeneous elements [...] sites of memory do not remember by themselves – they require the active agency of individuals and publics. Such agency entails recognizing and revealing the production of memory as an ongoing process involving inscription and reinscription, coding and recoding' (2010: 8).

As Clarke recalls, Rwandans told him that a foreigner had to do this work to help them move forward and make peace with their past,[12] and Sarr heard the same.[13] The artists' foreignness was essential to convincing Rwandans to tell their own stories. In both cases, Rwandans affirmed their need for an external person to initiate a public discussion about the commemoration. I think the format chosen by the artists helped to expand the conversation. The choice of the mural (along with the workshops in which Rwandan artists were trained and shared their own perspective on Rwandan people) and the medium of theatre allowed Clarke and Sarr to further involve the audience in a more dynamic way. They 'question the spectator, not to give ready-made

---

[12] 'Plusieurs fois on m'a dit: Il fallait qu'un étranger fasse ce travail avec nous pour nous aider à aller de l'avant; nous, nous sommes trop prêt de la chose, trop meurtris' [Several times, I was told: a foreigner must do this work to help us move forward; we are too close to the event, too wounded] (Brinker et al., 2017: 444).

[13] We had this conversation during our phone interview (17 December 2017).

answers. Art possesses this ability to provoke curiosity'.[14] Indeed, the space
of performance becomes a cathartic space of dialogue: Rwandan artists are
asked to express and share their own vision of what it means to be Rwandan,
and spectators placed directly on the stage can exchange their own stories
and discuss freely Isaro's and Faustin's fates.[15] As Sarr recalls, the Rwandans
reacted positively to the play, and the empathy created by the project allowed
them to connect and share their own experience after watching the play; they
were moved by Isaro's humanity and wanted to continue the conversation
because the text captured an important moment of their lives.[16]

## Living Museums and Metaphors of Ghostly Figures: The Necessary Traces of Absence

Both projects belong to what Vergès and Marimoutou (2007) call a 'living
museum' because they let the audience contribute to the memorialization process with their own questions and comments. Marimoutou and
Vergès coined the term with the Maison des Civilisations et de la Culture
Réunionnaise (MCUR), whose goal was to restore the culture and the history
of a society without any precolonial past and to bear witness to the absence
of those traces. The concept of a 'living museum' aimed to build a new
narrative opened to all memories, a 'récit partagé qui fasse place à toutes les
mémoires' [a shared story that would accommodate all memories] (Vergès
and Marimoutou, 2005: 16). Even if the MCUR was eventually abandoned
for political reasons, it raises an interesting question about commemoration
in a formerly colonized country: how to stage the absence of a given culture
(a precolonial Creole culture for Vergès and Marimoutou), the erasure of
a culture with the Tutsi genocide? How is it even possible to have a public
debate about a culture that is no longer tangible and visible? As Marimoutou
and Vergès argue, it is essential to reinscribe those questions into a broader

---

[14] See the official site of the project: https://www.uprightmen.org/home.

[15] Indeed, Karemera outlines her vision of theatre in an article for the French
newspaper *Le Monde*: theatre connects people together, restoring social links
(Kodjo-Grandvaux, 2017).

[16] Sarr told me that, after the main rehearsal in Kigali, he and the actors had
a two-hour discussion with the audience. Rwandans said that the play was true
to what they had experienced: the emotions the story conveyed were faithful
to what they had gone through (phone call interview). When the play was
performed in Dakar (Senegal) during the Ateliers de la Pensée in November 2017,
a journalist recalled the conversations that followed the play with the audience
(Marin La Meslée, 2017).

and more fruitful debate about postcolonial cultures. The grand narratives of colonial history have absorbed and assimilated colonized cultures, such as in Réunion: 'Nous étions un peuple "parlé" par d'autres, notre espace était occupé par des représentations dans lesquelles nous ne nous reconnaissions pas' [We were a people 'spoken' by others, our space was occupied by representations in which we did not recognize ourselves] (Vergès and Marimoutou, 2005: 34). The absence of traces and their eradication led to a mute society incapable of making sense of its own present. In that context, a 'living museum' can underline a useful and productive foreign intervention in the form of artistic commemorative projects that allow voices from inside Rwanda to cohabit with external voices.[17] It can offer a way to examine and confront different voices in order to question and understand the past and the present.

Though the political and historical context is different in postcolonial Rwanda, the memorialization of the absence which the genocide carries with it (the loss of 800,000 to one million Rwandans killed and hidden in mass graves) has been defined in a very specific way, as I discussed earlier in relation to the role national museums play in the commemoration and the education of younger generations born after the genocide. Reacting to this official vision, Clarke's and Sarr's artistic projects liberate the words of Rwandans and bring together different voices, perpetuating and expanding on the Garden of Memory which Clarke started in 2000.[18]

With the Garden of Memory, Clarke wanted to keep a trace and debunk the revisionist thesis that dismissed the existence of a genocide in Rwanda. By taking the shape of a blank space that is slowly covered with personalized stones and reclaimed by Rwandans who make their voice heard, the Garden could also materialize the muteness of the international community during the massacres and question the dangers of oblivion. Even if the project gave agency to Rwandans by letting them grieve, it was soon abandoned for lack

---

[17] Indeed, neither Sarr nor Clarke tries to speak *for* the Rwandans, they speak *with* them. They want to open a safe space where Rwandans and non-Rwandans from different generations feel free to share their own experience and learn from each other through the emotional connection created by a work of art.

[18] At the outset of the project, Clarke wanted one million stones – each bearing the name or a distinctive sign of a victim – to be placed on a specific site in Kigali, by victims' families. This collective act of memorialization would be cathartic because it required the participation of Rwandans: 'For this reason, it is being built as a collective monument in partnership with the principal civil society associations: IBUKA, Pro-Femmes, AVEGA amongst others [...] The construction of the memorial will in itself be a process of remembrance and of contemplation' (Clarke, 'The Garden of Memory').

of funding and political interest because it did not combine 'the display of remains and the spaces of mourning' that many other memorial sites did (Dauge-Roth, 2012: 94). Dauge-Roth also mentions that the Garden of Memory did not fit into the very didactic promotion of official history which had then become a distinctive evolution of the museographic narratives in Rwanda. I would add that the participatory act of commemoration by Rwandans might open up competing voices within the official narrative that were difficult to muzzle.

Clarke's *Upright Men* and Sarr's *Sur la barrière* bring the catharsis further because not only do they let the audience participate, they also let them openly question the core of the official narrative of the genocide. The mourning mutated into interrogation. Their work does not give one explanation but materializes the pain of absence for the living. Clarke does this by using the medium of photography. His artistic work recalls what Marianne Hirsch writes in her book on postmemory: 'Photography's relation to loss and death is not to mediate the process of individual and collective memory but to bring the past back in the form of a ghostly revenant, emphasizing, at the same time, its immutable and irreversible pastness and irretrievability' (1997: 20).

Even if Hirsch does not mention Clarke, her essay is nonetheless pertinent for analysing Clarke's and Sarr's projects. Clarke's work seems to bring to the forefront the ghostly remnants of the genocide. If Clarke's figures belong to the living, they carry with them all those traces from the past. Anchored on a wall, the silhouettes are never clearly delineated; their bodies can be blurred by layers and layers of hidden history, or words. These pictures, by connecting past and present, function as what Nora calls 'lieux de mémoire' and 'block the work of forgetting' (Hirsch, 1997: 19). Clarke's *Upright Men* 'suggest[s] both the desire and the necessity, and at the same time, the difficulty, the impossibility, of mourning' (Hirsch, 2017: 20). When one looks at Clarke's murals, one can feel the presence of the dead in the body of the living, the silhouettes look towards the future while being inhabited by the past.

Similarly, Sarr's play resurrects the dead who materialize on stage in front of the audience. The story stages the souls (*muzimu*) of Albert and his father talking about their own death. Similar to Clarke's project, the play gives a voice to the dead who have been silenced; it gives them a strong presence through the void that their absence represents for Isaro: they still belong to the world of the living, despite years of colonization and Christianity. They thus embody a trace that cannot be erased. The post-genocide generation is constructed collectively in relation to those ghosts and is shaped by the trauma. By illustrating the impossibility of silencing the dead, those ghostly figures develop a space of rebellion in which to rewrite the non-official history, mixing past and present together in the same space: the pain is openly discussed; the trace of the trauma is acknowledged on both sides, recalling the necessity of hearing different voices during the commemorations.

Sarr's and Clarke's projects also promote another vision of the world that no longer separates the living from the dead; rather, they reconnect with the old Rwandan cosmology – the world of Imana is fluid and belongs to the living – that had been eradicated by Christianity. These projects do not fix memory but encourage 'memory work' (Rothberg) inside and outside Rwanda. In that sense, they contribute to what Marianne Hirsch has called 'postmemory' and offer another type of memorialization to which everybody can connect, creating new transnational conversations in the context of globalization.

## Memory Work and Counter-Monuments

If Sarr and Clarke mobilize a memory that is not theirs, it is nonetheless powerful. The artists do not try to influence the memorialization process by telling their audience how to remember; they give a voice to those who have been silenced, they raise legitimate questions about reconstruction, forgiveness and amnesty. Sarr's play is based on a true story and the writer enriched it with testimonies from people he met in Rwanda. Clarke's mural is also inspired by the artist's encounters and interaction with Rwandans. The artists can identify from a distance with those who have been persecuted. Following Hirsch, the Self connects to the Other with a 'familial or group relation through an understanding of what it means to be' Rwandan (2012: 86). Postmemory is highly heteropathic in the sense that the Self identifies with the Other because of the emotion transmitted through a work of art. The emotional connection diminishes spatial, temporal and cultural distances, puts into contact historical events that would not otherwise be connected and helps to soothe the trauma.

Sarr told me that the play originated also in a personal family story. He comes from a military family and in 1993, his father was working for UNAMIR to observe the Arusha agreements.[19] Sarr's father was still in Rwanda when the bloodbath started. He was writing letters to his son, who was then a student in Orléans in France. Sarr's interest in Rwanda thus

---

[19] The United Nations Assistance Mission for Rwanda (UNAMIR) was intended to assist in the implementation of the Arusha Accords (4 August 1993), which were meant to end the Rwandan Civil War between the Government of the Republic of Rwanda and the Rwandan Patriotic Front. According to the UN website, 'The principal functions of UNAMIR would be to assist in ensuring the security of the capital city of Kigali; monitor the ceasefire agreement, including establishment of an expanded demilitarized zone (DMZ) and demobilization

emanates from a familial connection; it is an indirect one but is rooted in his father's personal past and his own, given his concern for his father being in a conflict zone. Clarke's interest in Rwanda stems from his militant past as an activist against the apartheid regime in South Africa. Clarke is a committed artist whose work is very political. As he said in an interview,

> They [journalists] used clichés to explain the situation, clichés that were false historically [...] In my work, words help us to misunderstand the world. And that is what I wanted to underline with this, it was a *mise en garde*, a way to say to people: be vigilant about what you think you are seeing [...] Rwanda is healing alone but it is good that people from the outside and the inside help it to heal a bit more [...] and we can't ignore it. It is us. (Clarke, 'Thinking Africa 1: Interview')

Both artistic projects acknowledge civilians' memories of suffering and violence: by restoring words to the living but also to the dead, they raise questions about whose stories to tell. These 'Memory-Traces', to quote Chamoiseau and Hammadi,[20] by non-Rwandan artists build a counter-monument that constantly questions official memory and encourages public agency. They also capture in their form the importance of absence and forgetting, especially in the ephemeral palimpsests imagined by Clarke and other Rwandan artists, or, in Sarr's play, that perpetually starts anew with each performance. At that precise moment of repetition/reproduction, memorialization becomes narrative. The artist creates counter-monuments that represent and discuss the absence of the trace. It is in a sense what Erica Johnson called a 'migration of memorial art from physical to literary form'[21] – and, by extension, also to other

---

procedures; monitor the security situation during the final period of the transitional Government's mandate leading up to elections' ('Historical Background', https://peacekeeping.un.org/mission/past/unamirFT.htm).

[20] Their project transforms monuments into a temporal and spatial knot of memory-traces, or 'sedimented memories' (Chamoiseau and Hammadi, 1994: 25). The traces characterize the authors' journey into the occulted space of colonial memories, and they uncover all the marginalized voices that have resisted assimilation into dominant structures. Chamoiseau writes: 'Qu'est-ce qu'une Trace-mémoires? C'est un espace oublié par l'Histoire et par la Mémoire-une, car elle témoigne des histoires dominées, des mémoires écrasées, et tend à les préserver' [What is a Memory-trace? It's the space forgotten by History and by monolithic Memory, since it witnesses dominated histories, erased memories and tends to preserve them] (Chamoiseau and Hammadi, 1994: 16). For more information on this topic, see Johnson and Brezault (2017).

[21] Erica Johnson talked about this idea in her paper 'Countermonuments to the Middle Passage' at the MLA conference in January 2018.

forms – that is made possible by the affective impact the counter-monument conveys on the viewer, activating 'a highly self-reflexive relationship to the past': 'the remembrance of things not witnessed' (Cronshaw, 2010: 186) or discussed in public places. Sarr's play and Clarke's project reconnect with an ancestral tradition that combines memorialization and oral stories. Indeed, the anthropologist Anna-Maria Brandstetter reminds us that official memorial sites in Rwanda are considered burial places for the victims of the genocide. They have become symbolic sites that borrow heavily from Christian and colonial religious practices. In precolonial Rwanda, there were no cemeteries: people were buried in marshes, forests or sometimes in the house they had inhabited:

> and even today cemeteries are not particularly well kept. In most cases only simple wooden crosses adorn the graves, and visits to the cemetery are not usual. Remembering the dead in Rwandan culture was, and still is, not based on a 'cult of the corpse', rather the dead are remembered in ancestral worship, in family stories and historical narratives. (Brandstetter, 2010: 11)[22]

Worshipping the dead happened through stories and public speeches, which is what Sarr's and Clarke's projects of memorialization reconnect with. Their art creates connections and allows people's words to be heard in safe public spaces. It allows the emergence of a non-official memory that resonates not only within Rwanda but also outside the country. Both projects were performed/exhibited outside Rwanda and successfully targeted a non-African audience born after the 1994 genocide. In Paris, for example, the project *Upright Men* was accompanied by a concert organized by the young songwriter and author of *Petit Pays*, Gaël Faye. Faye, who is Franco-Rwandan, invited French and francophone artists to sing during the twentieth anniversary of the genocide. The concert, like the murals, was another ephemeral attempt to mobilize and connect the current generation with what happened by creating an emotional connection through music that reduced cultural distances.[23] It brought awareness and created meaning:

> Artistic representations, in all eras or conditions of production, contribute to the construction of memory in such a way that in time, years later, they can become the only records of the event. It is Guernica [by Picasso]

---

[22] For more information on how Rwandan rituals of burial and mourning have changed, see Gerard van't Spijker's doctoral dissertation *Les Usages funéraires et la mission de l'Église. Une étude anthropologique et théologique des rites funéraires au Rwanda* (1990: 51–128). See also Hertefelt, Trouwborst and Scherer (1962).

[23] See the short documentary on YouTube, 'Concert: Les Hommes Debout, #Kwibuka20': https://www.youtube.com/watch?v=6cbtwbaH4qY&t=17s.

an artwork [*sic*], which reminds us today, over [seventy] years after it happened, of the tragedy of the small Basque village, not the newspapers of the time or scholarly history textbooks. (Clarke, 2018: 161)

Since its creation in 2015, Sarr's play has been performed in the DRC, Tunisia and France. It is staged in a very specific way to better involve the audience in the story: the setting is intimate (no more than 100 people) and the public is divided into two rows and sat directly on the stage facing each other to follow the *huis-clos* from the inside. In the middle of the stage, between the two rows, the director creates a small empty space where the two actors face each other and talk about the murder of Albert. At that moment, they share their own feelings, pain and misunderstandings about Albert's death. The audience is completely immersed in the dialogue and participates directly in the redemption process, trying to make sense of the differences that separated the mother and the young man. Indeed, Isaro is essential to Faustin's redemption, the characters cannot move forward without understanding and acknowledging each other's point of view. Isaro shares her pain and listens to Faustin's motivations while Faustin says he wants to help her take care of her banana plantation. By the end of the play, Isaro accepts his offer and is ready to forgive him:

De toute manière que puis-je faire? Te haïr? Je ne ferais que propager les ombres que nous portons tous en nous [...] Nous devons franchir la barrière de la perte, de l'humiliation et de l'offense, pour reconstruire la communauté. Il n'y a que nous – que vous appelez 'victimes' – qui puissions commencer à rebâtir la communauté. Avant la prochaine tempête, pour que, peut-être, elle résiste. (Sarr, 2017: 24)[24]

Despite what Isaro is saying (she underlines the importance of the role of victims in the peace-building decision process), it is worth noting that there can be no peace and redemption without Faustin's will. Indeed, he is the one who will work on the plantation, carefully taking care of the trees year after year, cropping, planting, protecting them. He has the technical knowledge to take care of the plantation, while she owns the land; without him, her land will die. Metaphorically, Sarr emphasizes the symbiotic relationships that now exist between victim and perpetrator in time of peace and reconstruction.

---

[24] 'Anyway, what can I do? Should I hate you? I would only spread the shadows we are carrying in us [...] We should cross the roadblock of loss, of humiliation and of offence in order to rebuild the community. There is only us – you call us "victims" – who could rebuild the community. Before the next storm so that, maybe, it could resist'.

They cannot function without each other; they have to work together to move on and rebuild the nation, now that all the traces of Albert's story have been dug up and discussed openly. Faustin confesses what he did, but he is not really able to explain why he struck Albert with a club. However, that does not diminish his responsibility and he knows it: 'Tantie, il n'y a que l'impardonnable qui puisse être pardonné' [Auntie, only the unforgiveable can be forgiven] (Sarr, 2017: 22). To resume his life, he needs Isaro's blessing. By acknowledging that he did unforgiveable things, he affirms that he is ready to be forgiven by the person he hurt. The absence of explanation goes against a didactic project of commemoration. Sarr underlines the complexities of all human beings and does not try to confine Faustin to his past or his guilt.

In acknowledging civilians' memory of suffering and violence, both artistic projects create counter-monuments. They downplay the tragic story to focus on the present of the survivors (Hutu and Tutsi together), fostering human dignity and triggering conversations with young people who were born after the genocide in Rwanda, but also all around the world. Their work exemplifies Rothberg's concept of 'memory knots':

> It suggests that [...] acts of memory are rhizomatic networks of temporality and cultural reference that exceed attempts at territorialization (whether at the local or national level) and identitarian reduction. Performances of memory may well have territorializing or identity-forming effects, but those effects will always be contingent and open to resignification. (2010: 7)

These immaterial and artistic memorials require the public's participation and resignification based on their culture, history and background, which makes censorship more difficult to implement given the rhizomatic nature of this new form of memorialization. They are enriched by a transnational audience that is now able to read the events of the genocide in a more critical way. To a certain extent, they expand what had been started in 2000 with the Fest'Africa initiative or even with Bruce Clarke's Garden of Memory. However, the Garden of Memory is anchored in Kigali and it seems difficult to envision it elsewhere without distorting its essence. The Fest'Africa texts published around 2000 were a first attempt to touch a wider audience inside and outside Rwanda, but the result was mitigated because the books are costly for Rwandans and they have not been translated into Kinyarwanda.[25] Clarke's and Sarr's new artistic projects operate differently in the sense that

---

[25] During a presentation of these texts at the University of Butare in 2000, Catherine Coquio noticed that they were studied on photocopies (2009: 7). Mostly, these texts are aimed at a very specific Western audience, underlining the limits of Djedanoum's pan-African dream within the Fest'Africa project.

they speak directly to their viewer's consciousness without the medium of a book. The murals in the streets of Rwanda and elsewhere connect to people's emotions; they don't need translation to operate fully. Even though *Sur la barrière* was written in French, it reconnects with oral traditions through the performance of the actors. Their words breathe empathy and emotions into the audience, they speak to our humanity. These projects externalize further and embrace the concept of a transnational tradition by giving more agency to the reader/spectator to remember the Tutsi genocide. Through the work of postmemory, they connect with the new generation and alter the governmental narrative, opening the way to other possibilities of commemorating the tragedy, with different affects and emotions.

## Works Cited

Aegis Trust. 2004. *Jenocide: Kigali Memorial Center*. Kigali: Kigali Genocide Memorial.

Anderson, Benedict. 2006. *Imagined Communities: Reflections on the Origin and Spread of Nationalism*. London: Verso.

Barthes, Roland. 1972. *Le Degré zéro de l'écriture*. Paris: Éditions du Seuil.

Brandstetter, Anna-Maria. 2010. 'Contested Past: Politics of Remembrance in Post-genocide Rwanda'. *Netherlands Institute for Advanced Studies in the Humanities and Social Sciences: Ortelius Lecture* 1: 1–21.

Brinker, Virginie, Catherine Coquio, Alexandre Dauge-Roth, Eric Hoppenot, Nathan Réra and François Robinet. 2017. *Rwanda, 1994–2014: Histoire, Mémoires et récits*. Paris: Les Presses du Réel.

Chamoiseau, Patrick, and Rodolphe Hammadi. 1994. *Guyane: traces-mémoires du Bagne*. Paris: Caisse nationale des monuments historiques et des sites.

Clarke, Bruce. 'Biography'. Available at https://www.bruce-clarke.com/index.php?p=pages&title=Biographie&locale=en_US (consulted on 20 February 2018).

—. 'The Garden of Memory'. Available at https://www.bruce-clarke.com/index.php?p=pages&title=Le-Jardin-de-la-M-moire&locale=en_US (consulted on 20 February 2018).

—. 'Upright Men: Collective Project of Public Mural Art on the Places of Memory of the Tutsi Genocide in Rwanda'. Available at https://www.bruce-clarke.com/index.php?album=hommes-debout (consulted on 20 February 2018).

—. 2014. 'Thinking Africa 1: Interview'. Available at https://www.youtube.com/watch?v=J8c3pAmFiSc (consulted on 20 February 2018).

—. 2018. 'Genocide, Memory and the Arts: Memorial Projects in Rwanda of "Upright Men" and "The Garden Memory"'. In Martin Leiner and Christine Schliesser (eds), *Alternative Approaches in Conflict Resolution*. Cham: Palgrave Macmillan: 153–63.

Coquio, Catherine. 2004. *Rwanda: le récit et les réels*. Paris: Belin.

—. 2009. 'Le Malentendu culturel: Quelle "traversée des mémoires" pour le génocide du Rwanda?' Available at https://francegenocidetutsi.org/CoquioMalentendu. pdf (consulted on 4 January 2018).

Cronshaw, Richard. 2010. *The Afterlife of Holocaust Memory in Contemporary Literature and Culture*. New York: Palgrave Macmillan.

Dauge-Roth, Alexandre. 2012. *Writing and Filming the Genocide of the Tutsis in Rwanda: Dismembering and Remembering Traumatic History*. Lanham, MD: Lexington Books.

Hertefelt, Marcel, Albert A. Trouwborst and J.H. Scherer. 1962. *Les Anciens Royaumes de la zone interlacustre méridionale: Rwanda, Burundi, Buha*. London: International African Institute.

Hirsch, Marianne. 1997. *Family Frames*. Cambridge: Harvard University Press.

—. 2012. *The Generation of Postmemory: Writing and Visual Culture after the Holocaust*. New York: Columbia University Press.

'Historical Background'. United Nations Peacekeeping. Available at https:// peacekeeping.un.org/mission/past/unamirFT.htm (consulted on 20 February 2018).

Hitchcott, Nicki. 2009. 'A Global African Commemoration – Rwanda: écrire par devoir de mémoire'. *Forum for Modern Language Studies* 45.2: 151–61.

Ibreck, Rachel. 2013. 'International Constructions of National Memories: The Aims and Effects of Foreign Donors' Support for Genocide Remembrance in Rwanda'. *Journal of Intervention and Statebuilding* 7.2: 149–69.

Johnson, Erica L., and Éloïse Brezault (eds). 2017. *Memory as Colonial Capital: Cross Cultural Encounter in French and in English*. Cham: Palgrave Macmillan.

King, Elisabeth. 2010. 'Memory Controversies in Post-Genocide Rwanda: Implications for Peacebuilding'. *Genocide Studies and Prevention* 5.3: 293–309.

—. 2014. *From Classrooms to Conflict in Rwanda*. New York: Cambridge University Press.

Kodjo-Grandvaux, Séverine. 2017. 'Théâtre: le génocide mis en pièce'. *Le Monde Afrique*. 28 April. Available at https://www.lemonde.fr/afrique/article/2017/ 04/28/theatre-le-genocide-rwandais-mis-en-pieces_5119704_3212.html (consulted on 15 August 2018).

Lemarchand, René. 2009. *The Dynamics of Violence in Central Africa*. Philadelphia: University of Pennsylvania Press.

Marin La Meslée, Valérie. 2017. 'Elsa Dorlin: ce qui se passe à Dakar relève d'un geste révolutionnaire'. *Le Point Afrique*. 6 November. Available at http://afrique. lepoint.fr/culture/elsa-dorlin-ce-qui-se-passe-a-dakar-releve-d-un-geste-revolu- tionnaire-06-11-2017-2170246_2256.php (consulted on 14 August 2018).

Mugiraneza, Asumpta. 'Postmemory in Rwanda'. 2013. Conference on *Creation and Postmemory* at Columbia University 10 April–4 May 2013.

Available at http://docplayer.fr/24477545-Creation-et-postmemoire-creation-and-postmemory-10-avril-4-mai-2013-april-10-2013-may-4-2013-universite-columbia-colloque-et-exposition.html (consulted on 15 April 2018).

Rothberg, Michael. 2010. 'Introduction: Between Memory and Memory. From *Lieux de mémoire* to *Nœuds de mémoire*'. *Yale French Studies* 118–19: 3–12.

Sarr, Felwine. 2017. *Ishindenshin: de mon âme à ton âme*. Montreal: Mémoire d'encrier.

Sinha, Charulata. 2018. 'Kizito Mihigo and the Politics of Music in Post-genocide Rwanda'. Available at https://soundcloud.com/afropop-worldwide/kizito-mihigo-and-the-politics-of-music-in-post-genocide-rwanda-closeup (consulted on 4 January 2018).

van't Spijker, Gerard. 1990. *Les Usages funéraires et la mission de l'Église. Une étude anthropologique et théologique des rites funéraires au Rwanda*. Kampen: Kok.

Vergès, Françoise, and Jean-Claude Carpanin Marimoutou. 2005. *Amarres, créolisations india-océanes*. Paris: L'Harmattan.

—. 2007. 'Pour un musée du temps présent'. Available at http://africultures.com/pour-un-musee-du-temps-present-6725/ (consulted on 20 February 2018).

# Human Rights Reporting
# on Rwanda's *Gacaca* Courts:
# A Story of Stagnation and Failure

*Benjamin Thorne and Julia Viebach*

The human rights report has become a new genre in the proliferation and application of human rights, centred on the idea of professionalized, objective reporting in a depoliticized, dispassionate tone that speaks from the vantage point of universal human rights rather than from a leftist view or from that of an opposition party. The human rights report has become a key locus in knowledge production about human rights violations globally. These reports fundamentally and profoundly inform our understanding of conflict, violence and accountability measures in the aftermath of conflict. We understand the human rights report not only as a genre, but as a site of knowledge production in and of itself. Therefore, we want to ask how such knowledge is constructed and with what purpose, what story is told, what is concealed, silenced or sidelined in human rights reports. Specifically, this chapter aims to deconstruct the human rights knowledge production around Rwanda's *gacaca* courts by using the analytical tools provided in French philosopher Paul Ricoeur's seminal work on narrative and memory. His insights into the construction of the past in the present support our aim to demonstrate the ways in which human rights reports establish a fixed and static conception of *gacaca*.

Like Doughty (2015), we understand societal change in the aftermath of atrocities to be a complex, multifaceted and fluid process. Through negotiating and attaching meaning to the numerous formal and informal processes of justice and reconciliation, Rwandans have been able to begin rebuilding lives and restructuring social relationships. After the 1994 Genocide against the Tutsi, the Rwandan Patriotic Front (RPF) government decided to fight impunity by modernizing *gacaca*, a traditional conflict-resolution mechanism that had been used to resolve minor disputes at community level. The courts operated between 2002 and 2012 and tried around two million genocide-related cases (http://gov.rw/about-the-government/justice-reconciliation/) *Gacaca* aimed not only to fight impunity but, importantly, to give the population ownership of the justice process, by keeping community participation as one of its core objectives. Rooted in Rwandan culture, *gacaca* should therefore demonstrate the country's ability to deal with its own conflicts (Clark, 2014: 134). The consensual decision-making process in *gacaca* should lead to unity and reconciliation. The government perceives *gacaca* as a success based on its efficient working and its ability to resolve conflicts in local communities on Rwanda's hills.

This perception of the RPF government stands in stark contrast to some commentators' views (e.g. Thomson, 2013; Waldorf, 2011; Ingelaere, 2014) and in particular to the analysis of human rights reports by Amnesty International and Human Rights Watch. These reports claim that *gacaca* was 'mob justice', that it failed to apply core and minimal human rights standards such as the right to a fair trial and the impartiality of the justice system. These human rights reports depict the Rwandan government as a 'bad agent' who willingly sacrificed human rights to speed up trials and interfered in *gacaca* hearings for the purpose of silencing political opponents and human rights activists.

This chapter focuses on understanding *how* human rights reports on *gacaca* construct a story of stagnation and failure, and the implications therein. At the core of the human rights project is the understanding that human rights define the highest realm of shared moral values for all humanity, which are upheld by the monitoring and advocacy work of human rights organizations (Sokhi-Bulley, 2016).[1] We follow Dudai's call to ask 'meta questions' about the actual product of such human rights advocacy (2006: 783). We do this by unpacking the way a dominant narrative of the *failure* of Rwanda's *gacaca* court was constructed by human rights reports that today fundamentally shape our understanding and interpretation of

---

[1] The universality of human rights as an international norm is rooted in the so-called International Bills of Human Rights, comprised of the Universal Declaration of Human Rights (1948), the International Covenant on Economic, Social, and Cultural Rights and the International Covenant on Civil and Political Rights (1966). For more on the origins and development of human rights see Donnelly (2007).

the workings of *gacaca*. Our discussion begins by briefly outlining how the *gacaca* courts worked before we introduce Ricoeur's work on narrative and memory. We draw particularly on three of his conceptual ideas: the 'object of understanding', the 'representative phase' and 'emplotment'. We use the 'object of understanding' as an analytical tool to deconstruct the universal application of human rights as the foundation upon which human rights reports delegitimize *gacaca* as a localized justice process. This delegitimization is centred on *gacaca*'s failure to adhere to the minimum of the international human rights corpus: the fair trial. We then use Ricoeur's concept of the representative phase to unpack how historical knowledge is produced and what role 'narrative' and 'emplotment' play therein. We analyse Human Rights Watch's report 'Justice Compromised' to demonstrate how the legal plot develops around bad agents, negative events, victims and the Western-style judiciary as a saviour. In the next step, we connect two core themes emerging from the reports – that there is no restorative *gacaca* and the sacrifice of justice – to the legal plot's actors and events. In conclusion, we show how human rights reports remake history into a single imagery by eradicating context and subjectivity. What remains is a story of stagnation and radical exclusion.

## A Brief Introduction to Rwanda's *Gacaca* Courts

In the direct aftermath of the genocide, the RPF began a systematic round-up of thousands of individuals who were suspected of participating in the killings (Eltringham, 2004). By the turn of the millennium, the Rwandan authorities had arrested in excess of 100,000 individuals, who were awaiting trial in prison (Jones, 2009).[2] In light of this crippling caseload of genocide suspects, overcrowded prisons and a completely shattered judiciary,[3] the Rwandan government started thinking about alternatives to the national jurisdiction: the *gacaca* courts.

*Gacaca* is Kinyarwanda for 'sitting in the tall grass'. *Gacaca* was used before and during colonialism as a community-based conflict-resolution mechanism. For instance, if someone harmed a neighbour's chicken, the families concerned would come together with the elders in their community to discuss the case and the possible compensations to be made. This

---

[2] In response to the genocide, the international community – the United Nations – had established the International Criminal Tribunal for Rwanda (ICTR) – located in Arusha, Tanzania – as an ad hoc court to try the genocide's 'most responsible' (Schabas, 2006).

[3] Most intellectuals, including legal staff, had been killed during the genocide.

restorative justice mechanism was adapted and modernized in order to try crimes against humanity and genocide. The government introduced a very complex organic law on *gacaca* in 2002 – when the courts started operating in a pilot phase – and amended the law for *gacaca*'s nationwide cover in 2005. One major component was the introduction of different crime categories starting with murder, rape and torture, to dehumanizing acts on dead bodies, to property crimes. Category One crimes such as rape were tried before the national jurisdiction until the law was changed in 2008, from which time rape could be tried before *gacaca* in private hearings without the involvement of the community. *Gacaca* courts were structured according to Rwanda's decentralized political system.[4] Courts operated at cell and sector level. The cell is the smallest entity and can be best compared with a village, whereas a sector can comprise several villages. The courts had different responsibilities aligned to the categories of crimes. The cell-level court had two responsibilities: first, they carried out the evidence collection phase of *gacaca*, which included compiling lists of victims or property stolen and putting together the dossiers of defendants. This information would then be passed on to the sector-level courts. Second, after the foundational evidence collection phase, the cell level would try property crimes (Category Three) such as theft and looting. The sector level was entrusted with trying Category Two crimes such as murder and killings, then later Category One cases as well, based on the initial evidence collected at the cell level. Appeal cases were also tried at sector level by additional courts of appeal.

One major change compared to traditional *gacaca* was the inclusion of punitive measures, so that the presiding lay judges, who were elected by the community,[5] could sentence defendants to 25 years or even life imprisonment.[6] Prison sentences could be served in part through community work as well. However, in this hybrid punitive and restorative court, defendants could reduce their sentence by a confession and by asking for forgiveness, which had to include full disclosure of the crimes committed. At the core of *gacaca* was the participation of the whole community, which was its essential restorative element (Clark, 2010). Slogans such as 'the truth heals' were key to the official discourse surrounding *gacaca*.

---

[4] Rwanda's political system operates at national, district, sector and cell levels.

[5] The community elected the judges but on the precondition that the judges were 'persons of integrity' (*inyangamugayo*), meaning they could not have been involved in the genocide. As a consequence, many judges were survivors or war returnees from neighbouring countries.

[6] The judges received a two-week training course and had sentencing guidelines and rules of procedures to rely on.

## Analysing Human Rights Reporting on *Gacaca* through a Narrative Lens

Reports produced by human rights and legal advocacy groups have criticized the *gacaca* courts for 'basic violation of the right to a fair trial, flawed decision-making (often caused by judges' ties to the parties in a case, or preconceived views of what happened during the genocide) and lack of witness protection, to name but a few (Human Rights Watch, 2011; Penal Reform International, 2009). Human Rights Watch states that these shortcomings are directly attributable to *gacaca* curtailing the 'fair trial rights' of the accused. According to Human Rights Watch, 'the *gacaca* laws failed to put in place adequate safeguards to ensure that all accused persons appearing before the *gacaca* courts would receive a fair trial' (2011: 4). Former Penal Reform International Coordinator of *gacaca* research Klaas de Jonge took a similarly critical stance, stating that 'if we relate the outcome to its explicit objectives [...] the *gacaca* process was a failure' (2010: 2). Much of the academic literature on *gacaca* (such as Ingelaere, 2014; Thomson, 2013; Waldorf, 2011), expresses a similar critique, but merge a legal critical stance with concerns about political repression and tight political control of the *gacaca* trials. Human Rights Watch uses much of this literature to legitimatize their legal analysis and their conclusion that *gacaca* was a failure. In turn, a predominant view has developed that perceives the legacy of *gacaca* as having failed the broader aims of bringing justice and reconciliation to Rwandan society. There is also a body of literature (such as Clark, 2010; Palmer, 2014; Doughty, 2015) that paints a more complex and nuanced picture of *gacaca*, which we will include in our analysis to emphasize the narrow legalistic way of thinking about *gacaca* in human rights reports. We first introduce the work of Paul Ricoeur to deconstruct *how* leading human rights organizations came to the conclusion that *gacaca* was a failure.

## The 'Object of Understanding'; or in the Beginning there Were Human Rights

The 'object of understanding' can be understood as the specific position from which a past event is framed and perceived in the present (Ricoeur, 2004: 186). According to Ricoeur, an 'object of understanding' is an object which is 'of immediate reference for all the discourses that relate to it' (2004: 188). This immediate reference is what Ricoeur calls a 'pertinent object': an object which comes to be promoted and perceived as embodying some 'special' significance in a given society (2004: 188). For our purposes, we can consider human rights norms as the 'pertinent object', which (re) distributes or sets 'values of importance' that affect the 'scale of importance' of social and political phenomena (Ricoeur, 2004: 188). Therefore, we can understand human rights norms as a set of Western legal and moral values that espouse the existence of a standardized framework which functions as a universal paradigm for the international community (Turner, 2013). In other words, 'pertinent objects' (here, human rights norms) are recognized by society or the international community as embodying moral and symbolic values, which are perceived as socially and politically vital to a way of life. Thus, the moral and symbolic worth – the 'pertinent object' – establishes a hierarchical order for a society, in which certain phenomena that encapsulate moral and symbolic worth take primacy over other phenomena deemed to have 'less' moral worth. In other words, the 'object of understanding' establishes a hierarchy of legitimacy. In our case, human rights take primacy over local understandings of justice or non-legal perceptions of justice (such as restorative measures) that sometimes run counter to the idea of core concepts of the human rights framework, as we will show later in this chapter.

According to Ricoeur, the fixation and manifestation of what is regarded as legitimate through the 'object of understanding' is accomplished through the workings of social institutions and (international) organizations. In the construction of dominant knowledge, both norms and organizations entail scales of coerciveness and effectiveness, and thus can be considered together (Ricoeur, 2004: 220). Ricoeur writes that 'an organization in the broad sense [ties] together values, norms, models of relations and behaviors, roles – [that] lead to the idea of regularity' (2004: 220). This position allows organizations to represent past phenomena in specific ways and in turn to constrain how knowledge is framed. In the context of this chapter, human rights organizations construct knowledge of local realities, such as *gacaca*, upon a 'regulated' understanding of what these organizations regard as legitimate values and behaviours. Ricoeur argues that a dominant norm (frame of knowledge) serves as a 'major epistemological crux' for the construction of past events. This epistemological frame acts as a powerful representation that classifies and constrains. In this, the 'object of understanding' through its normative legitimacy, sets parameters or limits upon what is accepted by society as morally appropriate social action and practice (Ricoeur, 2004: 220). From this 'legitimate' norm a paradigm is established, which acts as a marker determining the legitimacy or non-legitimacy of past social actions and practices (Ricoeur, 2004: 218–22). In other words, the concept of the 'object of understanding' allows us to consider that the construction of the past and, importantly, dominant memory production by international organizations and actors such as Amnesty International, always have a normative frame. Following Ricoeur's idea of the 'object of understanding', human rights norms can be seen as a frame of knowledge used by human rights groups in the construction of the past. The international community (or a society) relies on the moral value of human rights norms to advocate for the universal deployment of a human rights framework. Human rights groups who produce advocacy reports, such as Amnesty International or Human Rights Watch, are perceived as 'norm entrepreneurs' (Sikkink, 2011) lobbying for the upholding of human rights globally. These groups are able to determine the correct way to do rights, telling us 'what human rights are and where and when they are deemed protectable' (Sokhi-Bulley, 2011: 66). As norm entrepreneurs, they sell the idea that such norms encapsulate certain values and behaviours that are purported to be fundamental to all of humanity (Sokhi-Bulley, 2016: 5). It is within this paradigm of morally significant values and behaviours that Amnesty International as a rights organization frames reports on local realities. Amnesty International states in the introduction to its major report on Rwanda that '*gacaca* will be examined on legal grounds':

> Amnesty International believes, however, that *gacaca* trials need to conform to international standards of fairness so that the government's efforts to end impunity, and the trials themselves, are effective [...] This report['s ...] focus is on the *Gacaca* Jurisdictions: the legislation establishing them, their organisation and the various phases of their implementation. *Gacaca* will be examined on legal grounds – minimum fair trial standards – and in relationship to the Rwandese human rights environment in which it will operate. (2002: 2–3)

A dominant presence throughout Amnesty International's report is 'fair trial standards', which are a central component of the international human rights framework. Specifically, fair trial standards form part of the binary categorization of legitimacy and non-legitimacy. According to Amnesty International's 'Fair Trial Manual',

> The right to a fair trial has been reaffirmed and elaborated since 1948 in legally binding treaties such as the International Covenant on Civil and Political Rights (ICCPR), adopted by the UN General Assembly in 1966 [...] These international fair trial standards constitute a collective agreement by the international community on the criteria for assessing how governments treat people suspected, accused and convicted of crimes – from the most egregious to minor crimes. (2014: xvi)

Through the adoption of 'fair trial standards' by treaties and in charters, minimum 'fair trial standards' acts as a threshold for legitimacy for the working of any legal institution. The importance for Amnesty International of 'fair trial standards' as a threshold of legitimacy is evident when they remind the Rwandan government that it has ratified the relevant treaties. The report states:

> The International Covenant on Civil and Political Rights and the African Charter on Human and Peoples' Rights both of which Rwanda has ratified contain specific and considerably detailed international legal obligations to guarantee minimum standards of fair trial. Amnesty International believes that any criminal justice system no matter its form would lose credibility without adherence to these minimum thresholds. The fairness of an individual case therefore depends on the fulfilment of international minimum fair trial standards. (Amnesty International, 2002: 30)

Here, the legitimacy of *gacaca* is constructed as a good-bad binary defined by the threshold of minimum trial standards to which every 'criminal justice system no matter its form' must adhere. Legal institutions are perceived as 'good' as long as they encapsulate this minimum 'fair trial standard'. 'Bad' is defined as any form of criminal proceedings which does not fit the fair trial paradigm. More specifically, what Amnesty International means by 'no matter its form' is the dichotomy of customary legal practice and international legal standards. It seems that rights groups such as Amnesty International cannot move beyond this dichotomy in their understanding of local (semi-) legal processes. For instance, the Amnesty International report claims that 'from the beginning, the Rwandese government's decision to transform Rwanda's customary form of conflict resolution, *gacaca*, into a network of community-based popular tribunals raised human rights concerns regarding their fairness' (2002: 42).

The difficulty for human rights groups to move beyond the binary of 'good' or legitimate legal processes that conform to minimum trial standards versus 'bad' or non-legitimate legal processes which do not, is a cause of tension that has been acknowledged by Mutua. As Mutua (2002) and Turner (2013: 233) note, human rights and transitional justice create binaries of good and evil, just and unjust, peace versus justice, etc., and create an 'other' that does not adhere to the proliferated liberal and legal corpus of human rights. Importantly, this leads in turn to silences and gaps in the production of knowledge on human rights violations and how principles are adapted in the present to deal with those violations in the past. It is no surprise then that key players such as Amnesty International and other organizations perceive locally rooted justice initiatives as problematic when they do not adhere to those principled ideas of the universality and necessarily the standardization of human rights, as is evident in the following excerpt:

> International human rights standards dictate that tribunals, exercising judicial functions, must be legally established and determine matters within their competence on the basis of rules of law and in accordance with proceedings being conducted in a prescribed manner. These standards dramatically affect, however, the customary workings of *gacaca* sessions. The significant differences existing between customary and contemporary forms of *gacaca* force the question of whether these differences negate the anticipated results: justice, the uncovering of truth and national reconciliation. If reconciliation is an essentially personal interaction between victim and perpetrator, one can see how *gacaca*, as previously practiced, would promote it. It is less clear that the state-mandated *Gacaca* Jurisdictions whose focus remains on retributive justice will achieve the same end. (Amnesty International, 2002: 21)

This tension pervades legal discourse since it is rooted in a positivistic understanding of law and truth, and essentializes social categories and identities (Cowan, Dembour and Wilson, 2001: 6). At the same time, though, this tension in the positioning of legal practice and discourse must be seen as under constant flux and a necessary binary without which the continuous transformation of local and global norms is not possible (Cowan, Dembour and Wilson, 2001: 7). As Marie-Bénédicte Dembour reminds us in the context of the universalism of human rights norms, they are never a mere presence, existing in their own right, but always only exist in relation to their opposite (here the relativism of human rights) (Dembour, 2001: 73). Dembour's analysis emphasizes the need for a conversation between local and global worlds of meaning in the sphere of human rights.

## Representative Phase and Emplotment or the Legal Plot

So far, we have looked at how Amnesty International uses the universal human rights framework as an 'object of understanding' to establish the illegitimacy of *gacaca* by claiming that the Rwandan government failed to adhere to the 'minimum' of the human rights corpus: guarantee of a fair trial. In the following section, we demonstrate how, in Human Rights Watch's final report on *gacaca*, 'Justice Compromised', the 'object of understanding' is constructed as rigid and fixed historical knowledge. We argue that the temporal linearity of narrative acts as a process of inclusion and exclusion of meaning based upon the narrow framework of human rights norms.

For Ricoeur, the 'representative phase' is 'the putting into literary or written form of discourse' a temporal rendering of 'how the past was', which in turn constitutes a rigid memory (2004: 136–37). It is in the author's action of writing down events that the intention to represent the past 'as it happened' emerges. The author's written representation of the past consists of what Ricoeur terms the 'contract between an author and a reader' (Ricoeur, 2004: 275).[7] These are written works of 'history' where the 'real' (events, organizational or institutional structures and individuals) is constituted. For Ricoeur, the author-reader contract in a historical text 'agrees that it will deal with situations, events, connections, and characters who [do] or once [did] really exist' (2004: 275). Ricoeur states that it is in the 'reconstruction of the course of past events' that expectation is attached to the production of historical knowledge (2004: 274–75). In short, we have 'nothing better than memory to signify that something has taken place' (Ricoeur, 2004: 137), that an event has happened. In other words, the construction of memory via narrative attaches rigid and fixed temporal meaning to the past (Ricoeur, 2004: 26). It is in the 'representative phase' that the intention of memory to 'represent the truth of past' phenomena 'openly declares itself' (Ricoeur, 2004: 26).

## Emplotment's Agents and Events; or the Savage, the Victim and the Saviour

Narrative constitutes meaning in the production of memory: it is a 'clear sequential order that connects events in a meaningful way [...] and thus offers insights about the world and/or people's experience of it' (Buckley-Zistel, 2012: 73). For Ricoeur, 'narrative' is particularly dependent on time: in order for a narrative to unfold, there must not only be events, but events following one after the other (1984: 3). More specifically, the temporality of the narrative mode is where the 'narrative attains its full meaning when it becomes a condition of temporal existence' (Ricoeur, 1984: 30). Particularly important is the process Ricoeur terms 'emplotment, through which the various components of a narrative are organized into 'an intelligible whole' (1984: 65).

The 'emplotment' in the Human Rights Watch report is centred on a binary of good and evil, as is typical of the language used and stories told in human rights reports more generally (e.g. see Dudai, 2006; Cohen, 1996; Gready, 2010). For instance, Wilson (1997) writes that the realist and legalistic language of human rights reports aims to decontextualize and depoliticize

---

[7] Ricoeur distinguishes between the author-reader contract in works of fiction and that of author-reader in works of 'history'.

events. In this context, Mutua argues that there exists a three-dimensional metaphor in human rights discourse, which he defines as the 'savage-victim-savior-construction' (2002: 10–13). The savage is the actor who violates human rights and does not adhere to its universal principles, in this case the Rwandan government and also the *gacaca* judges, as will be shown in the following paragraphs. This image evokes barbarism and is depicted as a negation of humanity itself. For instance, on the subject of the intimidation of witnesses, the Human Rights Watch authors write that,

> one genocide survivor broke down in tears in September 2007 as he told a Human Rights Watch researcher how ashamed he was at having refused to testify as a defence witness at the *gacaca* hearing of a man accused of genocide who had saved his life and those of more than a dozen members of his family. (2011: 90)

The primary victims in the Human Rights Watch report are not only Rwandans who have been denied justice, including genocide survivors, but first and foremost the defendants who have been stripped of their rights to a fair trial, presumption of innocence and legal counsel, and those who suffered injustice at the hands of the RPF in 1994. The latter were denied their 'right to equal trial'. In Mutua's analysis, the human beings whose 'dignity and worth' are violated are the victims. These are depicted as helpless, powerless and innocent rights-bearing subjects (Mutua 2002: 11). Indeed, the Human Rights Watch report repeatedly makes reference to the plight of defendants being stripped of their rights:

> Human Rights Watch observed cases in which the accused was physically present at trial but was not allowed to follow his or her own trial in any detail. For example, in the south of the country, two different *gacaca* courts made the accused move away from the proceedings so that they were unable to hear or see what was happening in their own trials. A similar case occurred in Kigali in October 2008, when a court told five co-accused to sit apart and well away from trial proceedings, until it was their turn to testify. It was not immediately clear why courts ordered segregation of the accused in these types of cases. It is possible that the judges, who did not have adequate legal training, confused the practice of keeping witnesses outside of earshot of trial proceedings and applied it to accused persons. (2011: 45)

According to the report, the victim of rights abuses is at the mercy of the 'savage' (Mutua, 2002), which includes *gacaca* judges. The language used in the report depicts the judges as greedy individuals whose intention and goal was to transform *gacaca* into a lucrative business. The posting of lay judges unsurprisingly ran counter to 'fair trial standards', and is at the heart of the impartiality critique raised by the report. The human rights language privileges a liberal, universal, legal agenda over personal and local politics (Gready, 2010: 37). In turn, the Human Rights Watch report edits the human experience out of the legal plot.

When we consider the story's endpoint – here the Human Rights Watch legal story of the failure of *gacaca* – we can see the way the report has already embedded this failure as a linear whole from the very beginning of the story. The report brings together the events, agents and goals in the form of an 'emplotment' that is directed towards this failure. This in turn creates a 'synoptic vision' that reduces the substance and complexity of *gacaca*. The Rwandan government is portrayed as the central bad agent, the 'savage', in this narrative. On the first pages, the report remarks that the overcrowded prisons and the slow national prosecution of genocide convicts 'might have been accelerated, had foreign judges and lawyers been brought in to help, but the Rwandan government rejected such proposals. Instead, the government decided to set up community-based courts to try genocide-related crimes' (Human Rights Watch, 2011: 3). It goes on to accuse the government not only of ignoring the legitimate help of the international community but also of neglecting concerns raised by local government authorities that 'turned out to be well-founded' (2011: 3). Furthermore, already in the early description of the genocide's aftermath, the report clearly states that '22 persons convicted of genocide were executed [...] Most had been convicted in unfair and summary trials' (2011: 14). The narrative here begins with what will consequently lead into a story of failure in which a fair trial, the minimum of human rights standards, was not guaranteed. The government had set its priorities in terms of what form of justice it wanted by executing defendants in show trials. This sets the tone for the following accusations that the government had purposefully amended the law and sacrificed justice for its own political ends, a storyline that guides the reader through the whole report.

The storyline in the Human Rights Watch report positions both the Rwandan government and *gacaca* judges as the bad agent of the legal plot. The *gacaca* judges themselves are critiqued for being inadequately trained, for being biased, corrupt and ultimately a prolonged arm of the state. The report describes how in '*gacaca*, the largest number of corruption-related cases documented by Human Rights Watch involved judges taking bribes from accused persons':

As one accused said: 'you have to give money. *Gacaca* judges were not paid so they sometimes made arrangements to receive money from those who were accused.' [...] In a number of cases, judges used intermediaries – persons known to both the judge and the accused – to contact the accused or his or her family to request money in exchange for an acquittal. The accused or the family paid in cash, wrote checks, or deposited money into the intermediary's bank account. (2012: 106–07)

The bad agent narrative becomes particularly evident in the events described as part of the report's 'emplotment'. For instance, pages 29–30 outline the case of human rights activist François-Xavier Byuma, who was falsely accused of crimes because he investigated the sexual assault of a 17-year-old girl by an *inyangamugayo*, a *gacaca* judge. This judge presided over that case even though Byuma requested to have him removed because of the conflict of interest. The bench sentenced him to 19 years in prison, a judgement that was upheld in the appeal court despite the irregularities of due process. The choice of the report's authors to describe an event involving an activist who is sentenced to prison only because he fought for human rights makes the misconduct of the court, the misbehaviour of the judges and the apparently long-reaching arm of the government appear even stronger. All specific events described in the report paint a negative picture of *gacaca* as being utterly unfair, deeply corrupt and a top-down mechanism that suffered from the interference by the government and local authorities.[8] In short, it is presented as having failed Rwandans and the pursuit of justice more generally.

Here, importantly, these renderings of a linear story through 'emplotment' trade individuality for collective experience. As such, the temporal rendering of the narrative presents a causal explanation in which the behaviour and actions of a given group or nation – Rwandan citizens, for instance – are perceived to encapsulate the behaviour and actions of individual members of that group (Simms, 2003). In short, a named phenomenon functions as a temporal collective representation in which a 'whole series of attributes develops in terms of events, structures, agents, and institutions' (Ricoeur, 2004: 277). However, these collectivized attributes provide a 'synoptic vision' of the past. This 'synoptic vision' serves to reduce substance and complexity in favour of breath and scale, which has the effect of 'distancing and at the limit to exile' complexity (Ricoeur, 2004: 277). In short, accounts of the past based on large-scale representations carry with them a sense of closure, 'that of those grand narratives that tend to link up with sagas and foundational legends' (Ricoeur, 2004: 277).

---

[8] In fact, there is not a single passage in the report that describes a positive situation where the lay judges did 'good' work, justice was done and those involved were positive about the outcomes of trials.

The judges are encapsulated within the singular category of impartiality, to which they fail to adhere in the eyes of Human Rights Watch. The report's authors note that:

> *Gacaca* judges try cases relating to events that happened in their own area. Having lived through the genocide, many have their own strong views about what happened and know some or all the parties in any given case, whether they are relatives, friends, neighbors or business partners. Rwandan and international observers believe these factors have given rise to potential conflicts of interest or inherent partiality, and that with even the best will in the world, most *gacaca* judges inevitably struggle to evaluate evidence impartially. (2011: 107)

This view negates the context and, in Ricoeur's sense, collectivizes individuality (2004: 277). In turn, the report narrates the failure of *gacaca*, which is embedded in the miscarriage of justice effected by judges and political interference from the Rwandan state. The report leaves no space to acknowledge that the judges faced many different challenges in their work. In nationwide interviews with former *gacaca* judges conducted by Julia Viebach in 2017 and 2018, judges repeatedly mentioned difficulties in handling different expectations and that they often felt overwhelmed by the work. One female survivor judge echoed many others when she explained that:

> during the trials, it was very difficult and I was close to giving up, but I had a responsibility. It was difficult because you had to stand between two people, the one who wants justice, for example, when someone says her or his property was stolen, but actually did not possess anything really or if someone denies it. Both sides were lying to us but you had to listen to everyone. It was difficult to know the truth. Someone could not be satisfied and you created enemies and didn't feel safe any more.[9]

In these interviews, *gacaca* judges also reported very positive effects of *gacaca*, such as the empowerment of female judges, social progression (many work now as *abunzi*) and a steep learning curve combined with personal development.[10]

---

[9] Personal interview, 27 January 2018.

[10] The *abunzi* (literally 'those who reconcile') are mediators in Rwanda who are mandated by the state (Organic Law No 31/2006) to resolve minor criminal cases and civil cases where the property value is below three million Rwandan Francs. Mediation is obligatory for minor conflicts within the community. Similar to *gacaca*, *abunzi* judges are lay judges elected because of their integrity. Moreover, like *gacaca*, *abunzi* is a hybrid form of mediation combining punitive and restorative measures. It is part of the government's attempt to decentralize

This glimpse into these interviews with former judges demonstrates that the 'Justice Compromised' report excludes the individuality of *gacaca* judges and de-subjectifies them as well as decontextualizing the social embeddedness of *gacaca*.[11] Despite this, the Human Rights Watch report records the past as it happened, suggesting, following Ricoeur's author-reader contract, that the historical knowledge created here concerns real people and real events and is therefore the truth of what happened. In this 'representative phase' the reader only gets a 'synoptic vision' of the working of *gacaca*. At the same time, the linear 'emplotment', starting with the depiction of the Rwandan state as a bad agent, reinforces what Mutua has termed the mutually reinforcing anti-catastrophic and reconstructive strategies, which are inherent to 'the entire human rights structure' (Mutua, 2002: 11): 'the classic human rights document – human rights report – embodies these two mutually reinforcing strategies [...] As a rule, each report carries the diagnostic epilogue and recommended therapies and remedies' (2002: 11). In that sense, the saviour is the human rights corpus itself, which creates better societies based on certain (liberal) values.

The remedies for the failure of *gacaca*, partially due to the actions, intentions and goals of bad agents, is not only the human rights corpus itself but, even more so, recourse to a Western style, 'normal' punitive judiciary, instead of a modernized state-driven local conflict resolution-mechanism that was – as the report suggests – incapable of adhering to the human rights corpus and therefore unable to bring justice and reconciliation to Rwanda. As Amnesty International reminds us, 'the laudable objectives of ending impunity and restoring the social fabric cannot be achieved without respecting human rights' (2002: 1–2).

## Two Core Themes of the Legal Plot: There Is No Restorative *Gacaca* and Sacrificing Justice

At the core of the legal critique which these reports level at *gacaca* is its transformation from a customary model into 'a more formal, state-run judicial apparatus' (Human Rights Watch, 2011: 17). This perspective on *gacaca* enables the authors to question juridical procedures on the basis that *gacaca* was a punitive institution rather than a restorative and traditional one. *Gacaca* therefore needs fully to adhere to the 'object of understanding',

---

and make the justice system more accessible and efficient. For more on *abunzi* see Doughty (2011) and Mutisi (2011).

[11] In total, 80 interviews were conducted in all of Rwanda's provinces and in various districts, at cell and sector level (including appeal courts), and with judges who presided over rape cases.

the universality of human rights. Even though the Human Rights Watch report acknowledges that there is little information on traditional *gacaca*, it concludes that 'the Rwandan government portrayed its decision to use *gacaca* for genocide-related cases as "revert[ing] to our traditional methods of conflict resolution". However, other than in name and certain general characteristics, the version of *gacaca* used to try genocide-related cases bears little resemblance to the customary form' (2011: 17). Based on contestations around the implementation of *gacaca* to try genocide-related cases, the report suggests that it might have been better used 'as an investigative tool to gather evidence at the local level which could assist conventional courts' (2011: 16).

However, studies such as those of Clark (2010) or Palmer (2014) clearly prove the hybrid nature of *gacaca*, emphasizing the crucial importance of the restorative elements of the courts, such as local ownership, community participation, no lawyers, less strict regulatory provisions and asking for (and granting) forgiveness. Interestingly, the Human Rights Watch report criticizes precisely these restorative elements of *gacaca*, notably infringement of the right to legal counsel or the questionable impartiality of judges. For instance, the authors report in an accusatory tone that the right to counsel was willingly omitted from *gacaca* by the government. International players had proposed a 'good' way of handling the issue but the Ministry of Justice did not even respond to their suggestions (2011: 29). In this plotline in which *gacaca* was not a restorative mechanism, the authors of the report insert the bad agent, the government, who willingly infringed upon defendants' right to legal counsel. However, one crucial element of any restorative justice process is – as Braithwaite explains – that the stakeholders in the juridical process are not lawyers and judges, but victims, defendants and the community (Braithwaite, 2002; Nickson and Braithwaite, 2013). With regard to peace processes more broadly, Zartman asserts that 'African conflict medicine', traditional conflict resolution mechanisms, have the potential to heal societies because they are rooted in symbolism and rituals that underpin the notion of local ownership (2000: 219–30). Local ownership was indeed a key goal of *gacaca*, through which unity and reconciliation should be achieved. Even though the state played an important role in *gacaca*, its reach and dominance in local *gacaca* processes was limited (Clark, 2014). In addition, the Human Rights Watch report neglects *gacaca*'s hybrid nature combining punitive and restorative measures by describing it only as punitive – with one exception. The authors list the five differences between contemporary and traditional *gacaca*, describing the former as:

> Fundamentally retributive or punitive in nature, with the exception of cases involving property crimes. *Gacaca* courts could impose prison sentences

ranging from short terms to 'life imprisonment with special provisions.' Reconciliation and restoration of social order remained objectives of contemporary *gacaca*, but they were secondary to the punitive process. (Human Rights Watch, 2011: 17)

This is a grave misconception. In fact, defendants could significantly reduce their sentence, even in Category One and Two cases, by pleading guilty and disclosing full information about the crimes, including naming others, locating and identifying bodies of victims and finally by showing remorse and/or asking for forgiveness. Defendants could also serve portions of their sentence through community work known as *travaux d'intérêt général* (TIG).

Another essential point of criticism that the report levels at *gacaca* is the accusation that the government sacrificed justice for the rapid resolution of cases. For instance, the Human Rights Watch report alleges that the infringement of the right to a lawyer was solely based on the fact that the government wanted to speed up trials (2011: 29) although, as explained above, the lack of legal representatives is a major element of restorative justice processes. The authors conclude that, from the very beginning, *gacaca* was built on compromises, which lies at the heart of the problem. In their view, these compromises – how to balance rights and the speed of trials – highjacked the rights of individuals, particularly those of defendants and as a consequence led to the infringement of the right to a fair trial.

## The Concluding Story: *Gacaca* and What Next?

Both Human Rights and Amnesty International conclude that *gacaca* was at best a mixed success since it failed to ensure important safeguards against violation of due process. The 'object of understanding' (the universal application of human rights) creates a hierarchy of legitimacy in which *gacaca* is rendered an illegitimate process because it does not follow the rigid legal rules of Western-style judicial practice. In Human Rights Watch's conclusion, the positive legacies of *gacaca* feature in a single paragraph (2011: 122). It is telling that, in a 150-page report, only two paragraphs are concerned with a solely constructive view of *gacaca*. However, in the subsection XI. Perspectives on *Gacaca*, the authors do acknowledge where the courts succeeded, which predominantly relates to revealing the truth about what happened and the fact that the existing cycle of impunity for ethnically motivated violence that had prevailed in Rwanda for decades and culminated in the genocide was put to an end through *gacaca*. However, the authors are careful to constrain these successes by using terms such as 'some survivors' or 'a number of people', whereas the negative points related to the infringement of rights are commonly wrapped in generalizing language. This strategy reinforces the report's methodological legitimacy, which depends on presenting human rights work as objective (Gready, 2010: 33), in particular through techniques of corroboration and certain report-writing standards (Cohen, 1996: 9; Gready, 2010: 33). The report concludes in generalizing terms that the government now faces a new challenge, which is 'to correct the grave injustices that have occurred through this process' (Human Rights Watch, 2011: 125).

This generalizing language suggests a strong evidentiary base for framing *gacaca* as a 'grave injustice'. However, when we take into account sources other than human rights reports, a somewhat different picture of *gacaca* emerges and the exclusion of meaning in the human rights reports through legal 'emplotment' becomes visible. Doughty argues, for instance, that *gacaca* was deeply contextualized and embedded in everyday life:

> public, participatory, routinized, and based on oral testimony – and this contextualization formed the basis of its situated relevance to people's efforts to shape forms of sociality. People used *gacaca* sessions to negotiate the micro-politics of reconciliation, which included debating definitions of 'genocide citizenship', guilt, innocence, exchange, and material loyalty. (2015: 419)

Importantly, Doughty acknowledges the sociality of *gacaca* as it was entangled with a process of social repair which, she argues, is intrinsically messy, unequal and sometimes even violent (2015: 421). It becomes evident here that, as Gready (2010: 39) argues, decontextualized human rights truths remake conflicts and histories in a single image. In the case of the Human Rights Watch report, the legal story with its bad agents and negative events remakes *gacaca* as a single image of failure and 'grave injustice'. However, meaning can only be attributed in terms of surrounding narratives that go beyond the linear and causal 'emplotment' of human rights reports. Wilson argues that instead of narratives and 'force fields of other meanings, what the reader gets is a pared down and frozen stream of action' (1997: 145). For instance, the human rights reports analysed here demonstrate, through their legal emplotment, how the government controlled and interfered in what was meant to be a process of popular participation in the quest for justice. Furthermore, the reports paint a picture of 'mob justice' that infringes core rights of the human rights corpus as outlined above. Human Rights Watch and Amnesty International do not take into account the diverse and complex ways of meaning-making of the *gacaca* process, for instance why citizens took part in the process or decided not to speak. Clark describes the different motivations for, and perceptions of, participation in *gacaca* as ranging from performing a duty to the state, to re-establishing community bonds through breaking the prevailing cycle of silence about the genocide (2014: 138–41). Therefore human rights reports impede the interpretation of meaning with their radical acts of exclusion.

The aim of this chapter was to deconstruct how human rights reports produced knowledge on the failure of *gacaca*. Both Human Rights Watch and Amnesty International tell a narrow, static story about *gacaca* that paints the courts as a deeply troubling community exercise that 'compromised justice' for the sake of speeding up genocide-related trials. The reports silence the many changes that *gacaca* brought on both an individual and a societal level. Many *gacaca* judges reported in interviews that *gacaca* has changed their social standing in the community and enabled them to continue their work in the justice system through the *abunzi* mediation committees. In particular, women were empowered through their work as *gacaca* judges, a role previously reserved for men (Karekezi, 2001: 78; Clark, 2010: 143). Others, however, reported on negative changes such as the difficulties of renegotiating trust, changing loyalties and reinterpreting guilt and innocence in a complex and charged social repair process. What becomes clear in assessing different studies is that *gacaca* was a complex social process that developed over time and changed community relations with time (e.g. Doughty, 2015; Clark, 2010; Palmer, 2014). The knowledge production on *gacaca* through human rights reports leaves gaps and silences that are important to illuminate given that such reports shape our understanding of the legacies of mass atrocities and genocide. The human rights reports tell a story that leaves little room for different interpretations or meanings attached to *gacaca* and therefore it is not a story of change but rather one of stagnation and failure rooted in the radical exclusion of context, subjectivity, sociality and material belonging.

## Works Cited

Amnesty International. 2002. *Gacaca: A Question of Justice*. Index AFR 47/007/2002. Available at https://www.amnesty.org/en/documents/afr47/007/2002/fr/ (consulted on 10 January 2018).

—. 2014. *Fair Trial Manual – Second Edition*. Index: POL 30/002/2014. Available at https://www.amnesty.org/fr/documents/pol30/002/2014/en/ (consulted on 10 January 2018).

Braithwaite, John. 2002. *Restorative Justice & Responsive Regulation*. Oxford: Oxford University Press.

Buckley-Zistel, Susanne. 2012. 'Between Pragmatism, Coercion and Fear: Chosen Amnesia after the Rwandan Genocide'. In Aleida Assmann and Linda Shortt (eds), *Memory and Political Change*. London: Palgrave Macmillan: 72–88.

Clark, Phil. 2010. *The Gacaca Courts: Post-Genocide Justice and Reconciliation in Rwanda*. Cambridge: Cambridge University Press.

—. 2014. 'Bringing the Peasants Back in, Again: State Power and Local Agency in Rwanda's Gacaca Courts'. *Journal of Eastern African Studies* 8.2: 193–213.

Cohen, Stanley. 1996. 'Government Responses to Human Rights Reports: Claims, Denials, and Counterclaims'. *Human Rights Quarterly* 18.3: 517–43.

Cowan, Jane K., Marie-Bénédicte Dembour and Richard A. Wilson (eds). 2001. *Culture and Rights: Anthropological Perspectives*. Cambridge: Cambridge University Press.

de Jonge, Klaas. 2010. *PRI's Gacaca research*. Bujumbura: Penal Reform International.

Dembour, M. 2001. 'Following the Movement of a Pendulum: Between Universalism and relativism'. In Jane K. Cowan, Marie-Bénédicte Dembour and Richard A. Wilson (eds), *Culture and Rights: Anthropological Perspectives*. Cambridge: Cambridge University Press: 56–79.

Donnelly, Jack. 2007. *International Human Rights*. Boulder, CO: Westview Press.

Doughty, Kristin. 2011. 'Contesting Community: Legalized Reconciliation Efforts in the Aftermath of Genocide in Rwanda'. Doctoral thesis, University of Pennsylvania. Available at http://repository.upenn.edu/edissertations/333 (consulted on 12 January 2018).

—. 2015. 'Law and the Architecture of Social Repair: Gacaca Days in Post-Genocide Rwanda'. *Journal of the Royal Anthropological Institute* 21.2: 419–37.

Dudai, Ron. 2006. 'Through no Fault of their own: Punitive House Demolitions during the al-Aqsa Intifada'. *Human Rights Quarterly* 28.3: 783–95.

Eltringham, Nigel. 2004. *Accounting for Horror: Post-Genocide Debates in Rwanda*. London: Pluto Press.

Gready, Paul. 2010. *The Era of Transitional Justice: The Aftermath of the Truth and Reconciliation Commission in South Africa and Beyond*. Abingdon: Routledge.

Human Rights Watch. 2011. *Justice Compromised the Legacy of Rwanda's Community-Based Gacaca Courts*. New York: Human Rights Watch.

Ingelaere, Bert. 2014. 'What's on a Peasant's Mind? Experiencing RPF State Reach and Overreach in Post-Genocide Rwanda (2000–10)'. *Journal of Eastern African Studies* 8.2: 214–30.

Jones, Nicholas. 2009. *The Courts of Genocide: Politics and the Rule of Law in Rwanda and Arusha*. Abingdon: Routledge.

Karekezi, Alice. 2001. 'Juridictions gacaca: lutte contre l'impunité et promotion de la réconciliation nationale'. In Eric Ntaganda (ed.), *Les Juridictions Gacaca et le processus de réconciliation nationale*. Butare: Editions de l'Université Nationale du Rwanda: 9–96.

Mutisi, Martha. 2011. 'The *Abunzi* Mediation in Rwanda: Opportunities for Engaging with Traditional Institutions of Conflict Resolution'. Available at http://www.accord.org.za/publication/the-abunzi-mediation-in-rwanda/ (consulted on 1 February 2018).

Mutua, Makau. 2002. 'Terrorism and Human Rights: Power, Culture, and Subordination'. *Buffalo Human Rights Law Review* 8: article 1.

Nickson, Ray, and John Braithwaite. 2014. 'Deeper, Broader, Longer Transitional Justice'. *European Journal of Criminology* 11.4: 445–63.

Palmer, Nicola 2014. *Courts in Conflict: Interpreting the Layers of Justice in Post-Genocide Rwanda*. Oxford: Oxford University Press.

Penal Reform International. 2009. *The Contribution of the Gacaca Jurisdictions to Resolving Cases Arising from the Genocide*. Kigali: Penal Reform International.

Ricouer, Paul. 1984. *Time and Narrative*. Vol. 1. Chicago, IL: University of Chicago Press.

—. 2004. *Memory, History, Forgetting*. Chicago, IL: University of Chicago Press.

Schabas, William. 2006. *The United Nations International Criminal Tribunals: the Former Yugoslavia, Rwanda and Sierra Leone*. Cambridge: Cambridge University Press.

Sikkink, Kathryn. 2011. *The Justice Cascade: How Human Rights Prosecutions Are Changing World Politics*. New York and London: W.W. Norton & Company.

Simms, Karl. 2003. *Paul Ricoeur*. London: Routledge.

Sokhi-Bulley, Bal. 2011. 'Government(-ality) by Experts: Human Rights as Governance'. *Law and Critique* 22.3: 251–71.

—. 2016. *Governing through Rights*. London: Bloomsbury Publishing.

Thomson, Susan. 2013. *Whispering Truth to Power: Everyday Resistance to Reconciliation in Post-Genocide Rwanda*. Madison, WI: University of Wisconsin Press.

Turner, Catherine. 2013. 'Deconstructing Transitional Justice'. *Law and Critique* 24.2: 193–209.

Waldorf, Lars. 2011. 'Instrumentalizing Genocide: The RPF's Campaign against "Genocide Ideology"'. In Scott Straus and Lars Waldorf (eds), *Remaking Rwanda: State Building and Human Rights after Mass Violence*. Madison, WI: University of Wisconsin Press: 48–66.

Wilson, Richard. 1997. 'Human Rights, Culture and Context: An Introduction'. In Richard A. Wilson (ed.), *Human Rights, Culture and Context: Anthropological Perspectives*. London: Pluto Press: 27–30.

Zartman, I. William. 2000. 'Conclusion: Changes in the New Order and the Place for the Old'. In I. William Zartman (ed.), *Traditional Cures for Modern Conflicts: 'African Conflict Medicine'*. Boulder, CO and London: Lynne Rienner: 219–31.

# Competing Narratives and Performances in Rwanda's *Gacaca* Courts

*Ananda Breed and Astrid Jamar*

This chapter will analyse *gacaca* court transcripts to evidence the wider context of changes in Rwanda post-1994 due to national and international pressures and pulls.[1] Through an analysis of three case studies, it will argue that the *gacaca* court process presented a type of optical illusion, distorting justice and undermining attempts to instigate a communally recognized fair trial system. The optical illusion has been enabled, we will argue, by a performative staging of jurisprudence and the manipulation of legal codes and 'law talk'. The Rwandan government launched *gacaca* in June 2002 and legally mandated Rwandans to participate actively in the *gacaca* courts from 2004 to 2012 for crimes committed during the 1994 Genocide against the Tutsi. The *gacaca* process aimed to establish truth and reconciliation, to reinsert victims and culprits back into society and to fight against impunity. Every citizen was required to attend the local-level courts to provide testimony and to serve as judge, witness (an individual called to give evidence during the trial by the complainant or defendant) and testifier (an individual from the community who comments during the trial) on a weekly basis. As part of the process, the local population elected *inyangamugayo*, or persons of integrity, to adjudicate crimes of genocide and crimes against humanity committed against Tutsi from 1 October

---

[1] The authors wish to thank Bert Ingelaere and the two reviewers for their insightful comments on earlier versions of this chapter.

1990 to 31 December 1994 (Official Gazette, 2004). In total, 15,300 courts ruled over nearly two million cases (see e.g. 'Rwandans Should Celebrate', 2012; Avocats Sans Frontières, 2010). *Gacaca* procedures were influenced by international norms, national law (specifically the *gacaca* Organic Law and public policy) and, more importantly, by the politics and social dynamics at local level. Between 2004 and 2012, this weekly *gacaca* ritual served as part of a national memory machine to produce Rwandanicity, or a unified Rwandan identity devoid of the ethnic identities of Hutu, Tutsi and Twa. We use the term 'Rwandanicity' following Frank Rusagara (2005) of the Rwandan newspaper *The New Times*, who described Rwandanicity as: 'an idea and philosophy that guided the people's conduct and perceptions. As an ideology, therefore, it is what the people of Rwanda understood themselves to be, what they knew about themselves, and how they defined and related to each other and their country as a united people (*Ubumwe*)'. Borrowing from J.L. Austin (1976), the legal utterances staged within the *gacaca* courts created a new national subjectivity.

Breed considers *gacaca* to be a performative event in that Rwandanicity 'was inculcated on a cell-to-district level and reinforced through the repeated portrayal of state power and the enactment of a "moral community" in performances of justice, forgiveness and reconciliation [...] The courtroom itself stages certain roles and scripts and is presented in a theatrical manner' (2014: 95). Similarly, Emil B. Towner analysed *gacaca* court transcripts, borrowing from Ernest Bormann (1972), who argued that 'Fantasy Theme Analysis enables researchers to understand how a group and its corresponding views of reality are formed by examining the group's communication, such as dramatic stories and themes shared between members' (Towner, 2015: 288). Our analysis of court transcripts explores the 'dialect and codes' of *gacaca* to illustrate how Rwandanicity has permeated the local, national and international social imaginary of post-'94 Rwanda. We use the term 'social imaginary' as used by Charles Taylor (2003) to describe the way a given people imagine their collective social life.

*Gacaca* law, policy and practices are linked through discourses of transitional justice and legalisms. However, there is a need for further examination of how the *gacaca* system has been consolidated, transformed, manipulated and enacted due to political and donor pressures, local level disputes, political rivalries or income (and potentially false accusations) generated from the auctioning of properties for reparation of genocidal crimes. In this way, *gacaca* can be understood as part of a machine that institutionalizes criminality and produces the image of a renewed Rwanda without addressing fundamental weaknesses within the system. James Ferguson uses the concept of an 'anti-politics machine' that institutionalizes an unproven system 'to capture something of the way that conceptual and discursive systems link up with social institutions and processes without even approximately determining the form or defining the logic of the outcome' (1990: 275).

Along with other peace-building and development initiatives noted in this section, the *gacaca* performances played an important role in consolidating the image of a new post-1994 Rwanda and anti-politics machine. *Travaux d'intérêt général* (TIG; community work) were organized in parallel with *gacaca* for defendants who pleaded guilty, and whose confessions had been accepted, to contribute to the reintegration of these prisoners and the reconstruction of the country and their neighbourhood. The *ingando* solidarity camps (civic education for returnees and ex-combatants),[2] *imihigo* (social contracts of performance) designed by each administrative entity,[3] *itorero* schools (a civic education programme teaching cultural values to wider Rwandan society)[4] and the *umuganda* (community work undertaken once a month) were also initiatives for the production of 'ideal' Rwandan citizens working for the sake of the country's development and supporting 'good values'. In relation to *ingando*, Jenifer Melvin observed the practices of the ruling Rwandan Patriotic Front (RPF): 'Particularly troubling are recurrent accusations of repression, intimidation and violence inflicted

---

[2] The National Unity and Reconciliation Commission (NURC) defines *ingando* as 'A civic education activity that has facilitated the smooth reintegration of former returnees, X-FAR, provisionally released prisoners back to their communities'. A place that provided 'forums to Rwandans to come to terms with their past by facing history, forging a common vision for a united future' (National Unity and Reconciliation Commission, n.d.).

[3] Performance contracts have been described by the Rwandan government as follows: 'Imihigo is the plural Kinyarwanda word of Umuhigo, which means to vow to deliver. Imihigo also includes the concept of Guhiganwa, which means to compete among one another. Imihigo describes the pre-colonial cultural practice in Rwanda where an individual sets targets or goals to be achieved within a specific period of time. The person must complete these objectives by following guiding principles and be determined to overcome any possible challenges that arise' (National Unity and Reconciliation Commission, 2007).

[4] The NURC defines *iterero* as a 'homegrown initiative inspired by the Rwandan culture that was formerly a traditional Rwandan school to instill moral values of integrity, and capacity to deal with one's problems' which 'has today been revived to promote values of unity, truth, culture of hard work and avoiding attitudes and mindsets that deter development all aimed at speeding up the attainment of Vision 2020, MDGS and EDPRS' (National Unity and Reconciliation Commission, n.d.).

upon members of political parties at the hands of the RPF and its proxies' (2012: 940). Similar observations led Purdeková to describe *ingando* as 'a state-organised rite that is permeated by and reflects wider social dynamics and power constellations, and is ultimately meant to serve grand social engineering purposes' (2011: 44). In their analysis, both authors draw parallels between the practice and policy models of all these reconstruction initiatives (including *gacaca*). They both emphasize the renewal of traditions that encourage participation, 'authenticity' and 'adaptation to the local' (see e.g. Purdeková, 2011: 5–6). These policy models have seduced the development community, which has provided strong financial support for the establishment of these renewed traditions. Several sources estimate the financial support to the national service of *gacaca* courts alone to be over US$50 million in total (excluding strong NGO support involved in the implementation of *gacaca*) (Jamar, 2016: 16).

More importantly, as Jamar argues, 'these initiatives are the cornerstone of the regime's legitimacy at the political level, holding together and inculcating a specific perception of Rwanda being destroyed by colonialism and the genocide, but then saved and renewed by the RPF' (2016: 110). This long list of reconstruction initiatives illustrates the sophistication of the planning in terms of social engineering for the sake of development post-'94. Several scholars have analysed these reconstruction policies enacted in response to the genocide; they underline how overzealous development policies entail frictions between aims and outcomes, as well as the risks of neglecting political dynamics (e.g. Holvoet and Rombouts, 2008; Hayman, 2008; Hayman, 2009; Hayman, 2010; Ansoms and Rostagno, 2012; Debusscher and Ansoms, 2013; Debusscher and van der Vleuten, 2012). With a focus on the enactment of *gacaca* law, we demonstrate how the law talk enacted by Rwandan and international politicians and the actual trials conducted by the Rwandan population are crucial performances in the wider staging of Rwanda post-'94; a renewed Rwanda portrayed as a resilient nation that has dealt with the socio-legal consequences of the genocide and is now unified and reconciled.

This chapter follows up on an earlier research project conducted by the authors entitled the '*Gacaca* Narratives Project',[5] complemented by fieldwork including participant observations of *gacaca* courts and *gacaca*-related meetings, interviews with state officials, NGO and donor representatives,

---

[5] The *Gacaca* Narratives Project was funded by the University of East London to analyse ten *gacaca* court trial transcripts, selected from more than 507 case files originally transcribed and documented through the *gacaca* monitoring programme of Avocats Sans Frontières between 2008 and 2009.

as well as reviews of policy and legal documents that frame and constitute the *gacaca* system.[6] Our focus on the *gacaca* transcripts and enactments not only constitutes an alternative research approach but also 'unmasks and destabilizes the process of making models' (Ingelaere, 2012: 391). Bert Ingelaere identifies 'the gacaca courts as a mainly imaginary model from empirically adequate representations based on the actual modernized gacaca practice' (2012: 391). Ingelaere observes that the commentary and representations of *gacaca* include numerical legibility, magic syllogism and speech performance. He uses these terms to describe the strategy of *gacaca* supporters who 'mask the absence of the actual and profound reference reality of the representation in question' based on numerical descriptions of *gacaca* or 'primarily based on law or law talk' (2012: 391).

We will provide a 'kaleidoscopic' reading of optical illusions, or a slight shift in perspective, to integrate the multiplicity of performances of the *gacaca* system through the *gacaca* legal script, law talk and actual trial cases through legal anthropology and performance studies to make visible competing narratives, stagings, discourses, experiences and readings of *gacaca* outside the predominant policy framework and the official rendering of *gacaca* courts. These visual metaphors illustrate how the material that we are exploring appears to shift when a different perspective is introduced.

## Law Talk: Performative Functions of the *Gacaca* Law

A scrutiny of the legal and policy frameworks and their re-enactments in the national and international policy arenas uncovers the multiple performative functions of *gacaca* law to project the image of a renewed post-genocide Rwanda. From the first law establishing the *gacaca* courts (*Official Gazette*, 2001) to the laws providing for and modifying their organization, competences and functioning (*Official Gazette*, 2004, 2007, 2008), to the law terminating *gacaca* courts and determining mechanisms for resolving issues which were under their jurisdiction (*Official Gazette*, 2012), the complex *gacaca* legal framework resulted from long negotiations between

---

[6] Ananda Breed conducted fieldwork in Rwanda from the beginning of the *gacaca* process in 2004 to the closing of the courts in 2012. Breed has researched the use of performance in relation to the sensitization and mobilization of the *gacaca* courts. Astrid Jamar conducted ten months of fieldwork in Kigali between 2008 to 2014, during which she interviewed 40 professionals involved in the implementation of *gacaca* courts within Rwandan authorities, NGOs and donor agencies. Jamar also worked with one national institution and two INGOs involved in the monitoring of *gacaca* courts.

national and international actors involved in the preparation, implementation and funding of *gacaca* (Jamar, 2016). Most of the academic literature addressing *gacaca* has focused on these legal frameworks (Drumbl, 2005; Corey and Joireman, 2004; Meyerstein, 2007). Ingelaere argues against the excessive use of legal frameworks using the term 'magical legalism' to evoke 'a theoretical model that is primarily based on law or law talk' rather than giving attention to real practice (2012: 8). In other words, three levels of understanding of the law are aggregated in performances of *gacaca* law: 1) the legal framework – what is actually written in the law; 2) law talk – utterances and enactments of what the law claimed to achieve; 2) magical legalism – a projected illusion of what the law has achieved. By reviewing the kaleidoscopic function of *gacaca* performance, this chapter describes how the legal framework becomes magical legalism through law talk.

From such an understanding, *gacaca* performances are taking places in speeches and public ceremonies that refer to the *gacaca* legal framework, as well as the re-enactment of the law in the actual trials (as described in the following sections). The utterances of such legal scripts in political ceremonies project the image of a judicial system that respects international standards in terms of the right to a fair trial, embraces Rwandan conciliation culture and fulfils key transitional justice aims. These scripts and performances are crucial elements of the consolidation of the *gacaca* model, its staging for international policy audiences and Rwandan national politics, as well as the actual process taking place in local communities, as we show throughout the chapter.

The preamble of the *gacaca* law states that *gacaca* was a Rwandan solution for a Rwandan problem: 'Considering the necessity for the Rwandan Society to find by itself, solutions to the genocide problems and its consequences [*sic*]' (*Official Gazette*, 2004). Most literature has translated *gacaca* from Kinyarwanda to English as meaning 'judgement in the grass'. Already, the mind conjures an image of a community gathering in an informal and rural setting where the most respected community members resolve disputes favouring social harmony and perpetrators' reintegration. *Gacaca* courts were conducted in such settings, but many *gacaca* proceedings were also conducted in highly politicized spaces including government buildings and memorial sites like the former Mouvement révolutionnaire national pour le développement palace in Ngororero district, where a massacre occurred (Avocats Sans Frontières, 2009).

President Kagame (2012) described *gacaca* as 'our traditional conflict resolution mechanism' adapted 'to respond to the challenges facing us' at the closing ceremony of *gacaca* courts:

*Gacaca* has empowered Rwandans in ways few could have envisaged. It has illustrated the liberating value of truth. When truth came out in court, from both the perpetrators and survivors of genocide, from witnesses and the community – freely, not at the prompting or tutoring of paid lawyers – it set everyone free and prepared the ground for the restoration of social harmony [...] We should all be pleased that today, Rwandans live and work together for their well-being and common good as we look forward to the start of another chapter in our nation's development.

However, numerous critics have stated that the traditional *gacaca* had little to do with the modern reinvented version and there has been criticism regarding the granting of judicial power to individuals who have not been 'legally trained' and whose decisions either found defendants innocent or condemned them to life imprisonment.

Both *gacaca* law and policy discourses link the implementation of the law to several goals, principally of justice and reconciliation, to create a 'new' Rwanda with a Rwandan approach. The Preamble of the 2004 Organic Law defines these goals as follows:

Considering the necessity to eradicate for ever the culture of impunity in order to achieve justice and reconciliation in Rwanda, and thus to adopt provisions enabling rapid prosecutions and trials of perpetrators and accomplices of genocide, not only with the aim of providing punishment, but *also reconstituting the Rwandan Society that had been destroyed by bad leaders who incited the population into exterminating part of the Society*; Considering the necessity for the Rwandan Society to find by itself, solutions to the genocide problems and its consequences; Considering that it is important to provide for penalties allowing convicted persons *to amend themselves and to favour their reintegration into the Rwandan Society without jeopardizing the people's normal life*. (*Official Gazette*, 2004; emphasis added)

The Preamble emphasized the societal aims of the judicial system to reconstitute Rwandan society. The legal framework strictly defined the categorization of crimes (Art. 9, *Official Gazette*, 2008); court procedures, particularly the guilty plea (enabling a reduction of sentence length and part commutation in community work when the plea is accepted by the court – Arts 12, 13, 16, *Official Gazette*, 2008); and the general sentence calculation framework (Arts 17–21, *Official Gazette*, 2008). There are contradictions and potential limitations to implementing a 'proceduralized' and reinvented tradition to achieve these ambitious societal aims. At the same time, the law talk performed in public ceremonies, as well as the staging and enactment of local communities sitting on the grass following judicial procedures, embodied a performance in which the accomplishment of competing societal goals and judicial and traditional dimensions become possible to envision. Thus, we note that in some cases and within certain courts and regions, there was a dichotomy between some of these competing aims. In reference to the metaphor of the kaleidoscope, the process and outcome of trials shifted depending on whether the emphasis at the time (based on donor aid, government initiatives or local-level processes) was on reconciliation, justice or other diverted aims. Such *gacaca* aims and purposes (those set by the legal framework and those developed as people engaged with the process) are not inherently conjoined and may even be in opposition to one another. The function of a kaleidoscope connotes someone as the viewer, someone who turns the cylinder and the object or subject of observation. We argue at various points in the chapter that the turning of the kaleidoscope or altering of vision, affect and meaning shifted between international donors, government officials and citizens who were mandated by law to participate in the *gacaca* process. The language used within *gacaca*, for instance, that of justice and reconciliation, created different patterns and outcomes at different points within the implementation of *gacaca.*

The closing ceremony of the *gacaca* courts in 2012 is an important example of the enactment of judicial efficiency and law talk. It demonstrates the success of the *gacaca* model through the official speeches by Kagame and other *gacaca* supporters. During the ceremony, President Kagame (2012) stated: 'the value and effectiveness of *gacaca* will be measured against the record of other courts, principally the International Criminal Tribunal for Rwanda (ICTR). The ICTR has tried about sixty cases, cost 1.7 billion dollars and left justice wanting. Yet, at significantly less cost, the *gacaca* process has had the highest impact in terms of cases handled, and has delivered justice and reconciliation at a much higher scale'. He further stated that the *gacaca* process 'has been a period when we sought to reunite our nation, inspire confidence in the administration of justice and hold each other accountable for our actions'. Similarly, Jan Pronk (2012), a former Dutch politician and fervent supporter of the *gacaca* process, stated:

> The judicial procedures have been implemented with dignity and honour. Gacaca has proven itself as an honest way to achieve justice, including acquittal when justified, and reconciliation. The system was not perfect. It couldn't be, if only because of the countless numbers of victims and perpetrators. Moreover, some questions will remain, for instance those concerning the relation between personal reconciliation and national reconciliation, and – more difficult – between forgiveness

and reconciliation. However, there is no doubt in my mind: the Gacaca proceedings have made an essential contribution to the rebuilding of the nation, based on justice, peace and non-discrimination.

These two statements by national and international politicians positively evaluate the capacity of the *gacaca* legal framework and its implementation to achieve reconciliation and societal aims. However, *gacaca* was entirely dependent on international funding and, consequently, international pressures effected the *gacaca* process, like the speeding up of trials in 2016 that led to possible corruption, mismanagement of court files and excessive strain on the *inyangamugayo*.

The following case studies are derived from personal observations and thick description or detailed accounts of fieldwork to note patterns of social and cultural relationships alongside court transcript analysis that will further interrogate the variance between law talk as noted above and the social dynamics at play within the changing evolution of society through the *gacaca* court system. The case studies differ in terms of the profile of the defendant, the type of crimes described and the defence offered. However, there are some commonalities related to the increase in judgement within the appeal leave courts and incrimination of witnesses into the court trials as defendants themselves. Additionally, there are different levels of perpetration that directly or indirectly signify the participation of actors/bystanders in the genocide. Often, there are variances concerning the intention to commit genocide.

## *Gacaca* as Ikinimicu

The trial of François Mbarute observed by Breed from 14 to 16 April 2014 was conducted in the district hall, adorned with tapestries of the Rwandan flag.[7] In the centre of the room above the table for *inyangamugayo* was a picture of President Paul Kagame. There were six *inyangamugayo* – two women and four men – and 70 attendees. Approximately 24 attendees participated during the trial and several took notes with pen and paper. Key discussions concerned the role of Mbarute during militia training and his presence at the Red Cross and the interrogation of key witnesses of the accused. One witness stated that the *gacaca* court proceedings were like *ikinimicu* (the Kinyarwanda term for 'theatre'), that Mbarute should tell the truth and say where the bodies were buried. Another community member stated that Mbarute was saving people and killing at the same time.

---

[7] Although *gacaca* officially ended in 2012, the appeal trials continued.

Mbarute was eventually sentenced to life imprisonment after several trials (including in courts of appeal) in different communities, although he had originally been nominated for a hero award for saving over 90 people during the genocide. In 2008, Mbarute was first sentenced to 15 years in prison under category two in Nyakabanda court, which was later transferred from Nyakabanda sector to Gikondo sector. Mbarute was then sentenced to life under category one in Gikondo court in 2009. In April 2010 he was judged for the killing of 15 persons at the Gacaca Court of Appeal of Nyarugenge District and sentenced to life imprisonment. The extreme variance between being deemed a hero at first and eventually receiving a life sentence illustrates the unstable perception of Mbarute in relation to shifting political dynamics and the overarching political climate that increasingly considered bystanders as culprits.

According to a *gacaca* coordinator, witnesses were advised not to provide testimonies in support of the accused as they would often find themselves incriminated. At the outset of his case, there was one accusation against Mbarute that had 98 discharging witnesses. However, because several of these had cases filed against them (or had been imprisoned), witnesses were reluctant to come forward. Although 50 individuals had provided their names in his defence, only three witnesses came forward to testify on his behalf. All three were cross-examined by the *inyangamugayo* and eventually had a case filed against them.

Contextual information is required to grasp the social dynamics at play. Initially perceived as a saviour, Mbarute held a position of authority at the sector level until 2007. He enforced a new government policy that outlawed people from occupying properties they did not own, such as the illegal occupation of homes that were originally owned by individuals who fled in 1994 or who were imprisoned. Thus, the sudden incrimination of Mbarute may have been an act of revenge or an attempt to prevent the continued implementation of the above-noted public policy. There are a number of additional factors that may lead one to question the accusation of Mbarute. First, it is highly unlikely that someone guilty of genocide crimes would remain in a government position up to 2007 without any record of previous accusations during the data collection phase. Second, accusations were placed against him late in the *gacaca* proceedings. Third, one of his key discharging witnesses, who had sheltered many of the survivors Mbarute had brought to her clinic, had been sentenced to 30 years' imprisonment.

In this case, discharging witnesses were incriminated during the process of the trial. The focus turned from the accused to those who provided witness accounts, thus highlighting the fact that the defendant *had already been framed as guilty* and anyone who might identify with him would likewise come under suspicion as an accomplice. Witnesses were asked detailed questions (often in a random sequence) about times of day, timelines of activities, the physicality of observations and descriptions of events.

The president of the court asked the witness about Mbarute's role in militia training and whether the witness had seen him kill, to which the witness declared that Mbarute was saving people and never killed anyone:

> President: Did you know the individuals whom Mbarute was charged with killing?
> Witness One: No.
> President: You made previous statements that Mbarute was amongst the gang that killed *Yusuf*. Why are you changing your statement?
> Witness One: I didn't make that statement previously.
> President: Who was training? Who was being trained?
> Witness One: Mbarute notified me that they were planning to kill my wife, so I went past where they were conducting the training. Mbarute was standing near the militia, but I cannot confirm that he was training with the militia.
> President: Treat the courtroom as the trainees. How was Mbarute holding his body?
> Witness One: The defendant was far away and I could not see any detail.
> President: If you were able to see the accused, then you must have been standing on the side of the trainees and thus, Mbarute must have been facing the militia as a trainer.
> Witness One: I am telling you what I know. I cannot lie.
> Mbarute: The training was conducted in the valley, while I was a bystander. The person leading the training was a lieutenant.

In this exchange, the president presented Mbarute as a trainer of the militia. The testimony was questioned, although previous documents may have been recorded falsely. An attendee noted that several community members had made the claim that Mbarute had used grenades and guns, to which Mbarute replied, 'This woman lies. For anyone who lives in the sector, they know her lies are commonplace'. The next witness provided a statement against the accused, that he had observed Mbarute at the Red Cross where Hutu and Tutsi were separated:

> Witness Two: I witnessed the accused at the Red Cross register names.
> President: Were the persons mixed who registered [*sic*]?
> Witness Two: They were mixed between Hutu and Tutsi. Mbarute registered their identity cards. He arrived in a white car, parked in front, and entered the Red Cross with another individual. Mbarute asked for identity cards.

Mbarute: I didn't enter the Red Cross. Why have you made that statement? [the witness does not respond].

Witness Two: He separated Hutu from Tutsi. He took these individuals by foot and they have never returned.

In this exchange, the case was made against Mbarute that he worked alongside the militia:

President: Mbarute was amongst a group of militia that went to kill Yusuf. Did you know that?

Witness Three: No, I didn't know that.

President: How did you come to be in ownership of a gun, and how were the Tutsi who were in hiding with you killed and buried?

Witness: Mbarute had put me in charge of guarding the Tutsi, to protect them. We were discovered and the Tutsi were killed. I was not killed because I had an identity card that said I was Hutu with the former political party, and that I was commanded to put down my gun and that is when the Tutsi were killed.

Speaker from the floor: How did you get the gun? Why did you let the others die if you were supposed to be protecting them?

President: Have you been put in prison for this?

At this point, Mbarute approached the bench with a letter from the president of a previous *gacaca* court who declared that the current witness was an *inyangamugayo*, or person of integrity. The president put the letter to one side and continued to interrogate the witness:

President: Why didn't you defend the Tutsi?

Speaker from the floor: The declaration of character from the previous court must be false, if the witness had a gun.

President: How did you get a gun?

Witness Three: I was a soldier.

Speaker from the floor: If he had a gun, then he is responsible for the killing.

President: Who asked you to surrender?

Witness Three: Those that came from the market. They had lots of guns.

Speaker from the floor: If the witness didn't protect the Tutsi who he was given by Mbarute to protect, then he must have killed them.

Mbarute: When I arrived, he was kneeling. I had come to protect, but they were dead.

Speaker from the floor: You must have killed together. Who did you kill with?

Witness Three: No one.
Speaker from the floor: Why didn't the previous court make a case against this man?

The proceedings continued to question how the gun was passed between Mbarute and the witness. During the progress of the trial, the witness was cross-examined and eventually declared to be a conspirator with the accused. Audience incriminations questioned how the witness could have survived as 'one who is hunted' (Tutsi). The secretary read out the court transcript and then the witness was asked to sign. Mbarute owned several properties that would be auctioned off for monies to be distributed amongst those who filed against the accused.

In this way, although the court might have looked like it was following court procedures, the eventual outcome of the case was predetermined. No witness was safe from incrimination. The courtroom itself was an example of *ikinimicu* or theatre (Breed, 2015: 206). One observer who had attended each of Mbarute's court trials stated, 'Think back to events sixteen years ago. Can you remember what happened with the detail in which the defendant and witnesses are being questioned? Then, listen to the accusers. They have their stories pre-scripted in full detail, including exact time of day. They are the ones who are lying. For those that can't quite remember, or may get some details wrong, those are the ones telling the truth'.[8] The quote illustrates the possible pre-scripting of *gacaca* court proceedings as a kind of *ikinimicu* in which the accused has already been framed as guilty. The observer stated that Mbarute had documents to fight his case, such as land dispute papers against one of the accusers, but that the *inyangamugayo* would not acknowledge the documentation. Another observer of *gacaca* stated, 'During the last couple of years, *gacaca* has been used as a political device versus for justice' (Breed, 2015: 203).[9] The Mbarute case is thus an example of competing narratives and different tensions in post-genocide Rwanda.

## Competing Narratives

Thus far, we have illustrated a case study against an individual. However, the next case study of Kanyemera Calixte that transpired during the Gacaca

---

Court of Appeal in the District of Huye, Southern Province on 20 August 2008, moves from individual to collective guilt. During the course of the trial, over 47 additional defendants were charged with category three crimes related to looting. Kanyemera Calixte was originally sentenced to pay 300,000 Rwandan Francs (RWF) or £350. Kanyemera was eventually ordered to pay 1,500,000 RWF (£1,561) by the end of the trial. During the original court hearing, the defendants were accused of the looting and destruction of four houses, two cowsheds, two latrines, six cows, four beds, three mattresses, four tables, one cupboard, two green pea granaries, a banana field and cooking tools. The owner was killed during the genocide and his son was the plaintiff.

During the trial, two of the defendants submitted written lists of additional people who participated in the looting of the houses. While there had been no accusations against these individuals previously, an additional 47 people were sentenced during the trial to make reparations ranging from 12,000 RWF (£14) to 3,900,000 RWF (£4,570). Considering the annual per capita income of Rwanda, evaluated at $370 or £250, it is obvious that these fines would severely affect the economic well-being of the condemned (from half a month's income to 18 years of income). Kanyemera stated that he had been unjustly imprisoned and that his property was seized and auctioned off for the payment of an interminable debt. Penal Reform International, an INGO undertaking the monitoring of *gacaca* courts, reported on the dangers of reparation:

> The net result is that a person who stole a great number of personal belongings could end up having to repay the same amount of money as a person who arrived last on the scene and took a bowl or some wood from the debris so as to be able to cook a meal. Decisions relating to property offences were usually expressed in monetary terms. Given that many Rwandans live in extreme poverty and that the sums ordered by way of compensation for loss of valuable property – such as houses and livestock – were often quite considerable, large numbers of those ordered to make repayments were unable to comply. In such cases, courts had two options: to confiscate property such as land or livestock, plunging people into even greater poverty; or order that repayment be made in the form of unpaid labour for the victim, which is contrary to international law and which at times has posed a serious social threat. (2010: 59)

Though the law prescribes category three crimes related to looting, and ordained reparations to address genocidal crimes, it is important to note the potential for ongoing structural violence and economic inequality due to the reparations that must be considered on a grand scale across Rwanda.

During the court trial, Kanyemera noted that no evidence had been provided. The judge or *inyangamugayo* responded that the statement could be interpreted as a minimization of the genocide. Several of the defendants noted that the accusations were the result of revenge, inter-familial issues and denunciations of individuals during other trials that resulted in the claims during the current trial. In this case, the defendants referred to local-level politics that are acted out through the *gacaca* court system. When asked why he had signed the minutes from the original *gacaca* acknowledging his acceptance of repayment for looted goods, Kanyemera stated that he had been coerced.

This case study also showed instances of protecting victims and variance in how genocide was carried out from region to region or hill to hill. One man was asked why he did not participate in the looting. He noted his efforts to protect Tutsi in his cell and the intentional decision not to stop looting so that he would not be threatened or identified as an enemy. Thus, the man intentionally committed lower-degree crimes like looting in order not to bring attention to himself as someone who was protecting Tutsi from being killed. Another person from the general assembly noted the primary objective of the community to protect their Tutsi neighbours, and that when they lost the battle against Interahamwe, or the young thugs who acted together to kill during the genocide, that the defending Hutu of Rukeri Hill were labelled as Tutsi and rejected by Hutu from other cells. While not exonerating the act of looting, the case study illustrates the complexity of how genocide and justice might be considered from hill to hill. This example shows that defendants fought back against the Interahamwe, but were also incriminated and sentenced to genocidal crimes due to looting that may extend issues of structural violence due to reparations.

The case study illustrates the competing nature of the public narrative or performance of *gacaca* (as previously noted through legal structures) with the alternative narratives or discourses outside the government narrative that emerged within the court trial itself. The primary point that we want to make with this example relates to the cumulative sentencing of witnesses turned defendants and varied counter-claims and accusations that emerged during the hearing, and to note the complexity of the case in terms of issues concerning structural violence and poverty alongside genocidal crimes. In order to address the possibility of future unrest in Rwanda, we feel it is important to emphasize the continued structural violence that may have been enacted through reparations on a national scale.

## Stories of Change

The transference of rape as a category one crime from the ordinary courts to the local-level *gacaca* courts demanded a particularly swift social and cultural change. A victim was identified under Article 34 of Organic Law No. 16/2004 of 19 June 2004 as 'anybody killed, hunted to be killed but survived, *suffered acts of torture against his or her sexual parts, suffered rape*, injured or victim of any other form of harassment, plundered, and whose house and property was destroyed because of his or her ethnic background or opinion against the genocide ideology' (*Official Gazette*, 2004). In 1998, the ICTR was the first international court to define rape as a crime against humanity. The jurisdiction of rape as a crime against humanity promoted gender-based justice on an international level, thus changing the stories related to accounts of genocidal crimes from testimonies related to sexual violence, which might historically and culturally have been perceived as shaming, to stories of incrimination that influenced global politics and policies on a national and international level.

The case of Mukaruziga Eugénie in the *Gacaca* Court of Appeal in the District of Ngororero, Western Province, on 2 December and 10 December 2009 illustrates not only the violence inflicted upon women, but also the role of women as perpetrators during the genocide. Mukaruziga stated: 'I was coming back from the church service. I was with the victims. We had a beer in Ntawuhamarumwe's pub, just in front of my house. We had not finished our drinks, when we heard noise. We went out and noticed it was Interahamwe. I went back home and left the three women at the pub. I heard Nyirangezahayo Immaculée was killed by Simbarirwa Jean Baptiste'.

The bench cross-examined the appellant:

President: What were the circumstances of the murder of Nyirangezahayo Immaculée?
Mukaruziga: She was shot by Innocent and Kaninja took her clothes off.
President: During this time, could people go to the church service?
Mukaruziga: Yes.
President: Why did you run away and leave the victims in the pub, whereas [*sic*] you were a killer? [inference based on why she did not kill them herself]
Mukaruziga: I did not want my children to witness killing. Moreover, I did not know these Interahamwe.

The president reminded the appellant that it was in her interest to give a sincere confession to benefit from sentence reduction and urged her to tell the truth. The appellant declared that she would give a sincere confession.

Mukaruziga stated, 'I was coming back from the church services with the victims and we shared a beer in a pub. When the attackers arrived, I went out and indicated to one of the interahamwe the victims who were inside the pub. The Tutsi were killed around 15h00'. Mukaruziga continued: 'I was part of the attackers who took the victim to the scene of the crime. Nduwumwami hit her with a stick and she fell down. Innocent then shot her. Kalinijabo took her clothes off and I took off her underpants to see how the sex of a Tutsi woman looked like'.

Several incidents shown in the transcripts provide a nuanced reading of genocidal crimes at a societal level. Initially, the appellant noted that she had drinks with the Tutsi victims at the local pub. Additionally, she stated that she did not know the Interahamwe and did not want her children to witness the killing. These incidents evidence social relations alongside violent acts. The transcript noted: 'I took off her underpants to see how the sex of a Tutsi woman looked like'. Leading up to the genocide, graphic cartoons were used to portray Tutsi women as sexual deviants who seduced Hutu men away from their Hutu wives. Thus, the inspection of the Tutsi woman illustrated the potential role of the media in demonizing the Tutsi as other, and the mythological narratives that surrounded the genocide. Overall, the case study of Mukaruziga illustrates the changing perceptions of gender-based violence in Rwanda and the pendulum swing from state intervention that originally integrated rape as a weapon of war during the genocide to the incrimination of rape as a crime against humanity post-1994.

## Conclusion

By drawing attention to the performances of competing narratives and variance within the *gacaca* system, we have illustrated how *gacaca* scripts were performed for different audiences with different effects and functions depending on micro- and macro-politics. During the closing ceremony for *gacaca*, Kagame stated that the *gacaca* process 'has been a period when we sought to reunite our nation, inspire confidence in the administration of justice and hold each other accountable for our actions' (Kagame, 2012). Addressing primarily an international audience to mark the closing of *gacaca* in 2012, this law talk (utterance of the *gacaca* legal system) produces a magic relation between reconciliation, administration of justice and accountability. In contrast, the enactment of the legal framework in the appeal court case of François Mbarute from 2014 evidences the ongoing process of *gacaca* and the changing perception of Mbarute from 'hero' to 'perpetrator' after the official closure of the *gacaca* court system. The *gacaca* performances played an important role in consolidating the image of a new Rwanda post-1994 as evidenced by Kagame's speech. However, numerous interpretations and competing narratives have been performed and negotiated within the *gacaca* system itself as evidenced by the case studies provided in this chapter.

A clear and common vision of what happened during the genocide is impossible to reach, and even less so through the *gacaca* process. We have used the metaphor of the kaleidoscopic lens to illustrate the diverse patterns we have identified from our observations of *gacaca* performances. The performativity of judicial and cultural safeguards provided the illusion of legitimate fair trials that were conducted following standard procedures, even if these procedures diverged widely from one court or region to another. The enactment of the legal scripts through official speeches created the illusion of an effective model despite emerging competing narratives. In the projection of such images, the legal procedures framed the stage in which the population performed, improvised and manipulated the model according to their respective personal stakes within what was permitted by the official *gacaca* script, what was ordained by law and the political context.

The outcome of the court trials' procedures presented in this chapter demonstrates how sentences were increased to life imprisonment at the appeal level. A *gacaca* coordinator noted that he had advised witnesses not to testify, due to the likelihood that they would have case files against them. Following the closure of the *gacaca* courts, local level dispute resolution was transferred to *abunzi* mediators. The *abunzi* were established as an organ providing obligatory mediation prior to submission of a case before the first degree courts through the Organic Law No. 31/2006 adopted in 2006. Martha Mutisi states: 'Like *gacaca*, the *abunzi* is inspired by Rwandan traditional dispute resolution systems which encourage local capacity in the resolution of conflicts' (2012: 41). She describes *abunzi* as a 'dramaturgical representation of reconciliation and community building' while also observing that 'deep seated reservations, divisions and frustrations remain latent' (42).

One person involved in *abunzi* training expressed concern that *inyanga-mugayo* competencies were being transferred to *abunzi*. He considered that: (1) the population was already confused about the roles of *abunzi* and *inyangamugayo*; (2) *abunzi* already had too much to deal with; and (3) being involved in auctions for the implementation of *gacaca* decisions for crimes against property seemed to be contradictory to their conciliatory role (Interview, Kigali, Rwanda, November 2012). In this way, the *abunzi* continued the dramaturgical framework of the *gacaca* system to maintain the government script and outward appearance of upholding justice and reconciliation, although alternative and competing narratives remained under the surface. Furthermore, it illustrates how the performative lens and its kaleidoscopic functions are relevant to understand the divergent interpretations of contemporary Rwanda and its numerous transformative policies.

We have argued that the legal and policy framework served as an overarching optical illusion to regulate *gacaca* practices that performed a government-ordained structure of justice, but that the actual court trials themselves involved various practices that were easily manipulated on all levels of enactment – in policy events from a political and international audience, to actual *gacaca* courts ruling at the local level – within each community. Thus, the *gacaca* courts differed widely from region to region in terms of procedure and participation. NGO monitoring reports show how the implementation of *gacaca* differed from one court or location to another. Through the performance of oral and procedural judicial safeguards, *inyangamugayo* were given the authorial 'upper hand' and procedures were not respected in numerous trials. While law talk magically projected the image of a new Rwanda that was dealing with the consequences of the 1994 genocide, a scrutiny of various enactments of the *gacaca* model in court trials provides nuanced narratives from Rwandan citizens who struggled and/or continue to struggle with the judicial and social consequences of the genocide.

## Works Cited

Austin, J.L. 1976. *How to Do Things with Words.* Oxford: Oxford University Press.

Ansoms, An, and Donatella Rostagno. 2012. 'Rwanda's Vision 2020 Halfway Through: What the Eye Does Not See'. *Review of African Political Economy* 39.133: 427–50.

Avocats Sans Frontières. 2009. 'Synthèse mensuelle – Observations des Juridictions Gacaca, Province de l'Ouest – Ex-province de Gisenyi, Novembre et Décembre 2009' [Monthly Summary – Monitoring of Gacaca Courts, Western Province, Ex-Province of Gisenyi, November and December 2009], (on file with author).

—. 2010. 'Monitoring des Juridictions Gacaca – Phase de Jugement – Rapport Analytique N° 5' [Monitoring Report of Gacaca Courts – Judgement Phase – Analytical Report 5] Available at http://www.asf.be/wp-content/publications/Rwanda_MonitoringGacaca_RapportAnalytique5_Light.pdf (consulted on 12 February 2019).

Bormann, E.G. 1972. 'Fantasy and Rhetorical Vision: The Rhetorical Criticism of Social Reality'. *Quarterly Journal of Speech* 58: 396–407.

Breed, Ananda. 2014. *Performing the Nation: Genocide, Justice, Reconciliation.* Chicago, IL: Seagull Books.

—. 2015. 'Aesthetic Play: Between Performance and Justice'. In Gareth White (ed.), *Applied Theatre: Aesthetics*. London: Bloomsbury: 194–209.

Corey, Allison, and Sandra F. Joireman. 2004. 'Retributive Justice: The *Gacaca* Courts in Rwanda'. *African Affairs* 103.410: 73–89.

Debusscher, Petra and An Ansoms. 2013. 'Gender Equality Policies in Rwanda: Public Relations or Real Transformations?' *Development and Change* 44.5: 1111–34.

Dubusscher, Petra, and Anna van der Vleuten. 2012. 'Mainstreaming Gender in European Union Development Cooperation with Sub-Saharan Africa: Promising Numbers, Narrow Contents, Telling Silences'. *International Development Planning Review* 34.3: 319–38.

Drumbl, Mark. 2005. 'Law and Atrocity: Settling Accounts in Rwanda'. *Ohio NUL Review* 31.41: 41–72.

Ferguson, James. 1990. *The Anti-Politics Machine: Development, Depoliticization, and Bureaucratic Power in Lesotho*. G – Reference, Information and Interdisciplinary Subjects Series. Minneapolis, MN: University of Minnesota Press.

Hayman, Rachel. 2008. 'Rwanda: Milking the Cow. Creating Policy Space in Spite of Aid Dependence'. In Lindsay Whitfield (ed.), *The Politics of Aid: African Strategies for Dealing with Donors*. Oxford: Oxford University Press: 156–84.

—. 2009. 'From Rome to Accra via Kigali: "Aid Effectiveness" in Rwanda'. *Development Policy Review* 27.5: 581–99.

—. 2010. 'Abandoned Orphan, Wayward Child: The United Kingdom and Belgium in Rwanda since 1994'. *Journal of Eastern African Studies* 4.2: 341–60.

Holvoet, N. and Heidy Rombouts. 2008. 'The challenge of monitoring and evaluation under the new aid modalities: experiences from Rwanda'. *The Journal of Modern African Studies*, 46.4: 577–602.

Ingelaere, Bert. 2012. 'From Model to Practice: Researching and Representing Rwanda's "Modernized Gacaca Courts"'. *Critique of Anthropology* 32.4: 388–414.

Jamar, Astrid. 2016. 'Transitional Justice Battlefield: Practitioners' Everyday in Burundi and Rwanda'. Doctoral dissertation in International Development, Brighton, University of Sussex.

Kagame, Paul. 2012. Speech at the Official Closing of Gacaca Courts Rwanda, 18 June. Available at http://paulkagame.com/?p=1355 (consulted on 12 February 2019).

Melvin, Jennifer. 2012. 'Beyond the Veneer of Reconciliation: Human Rights and Democracy in Rwanda'. *Opinion: Commonwealth Advisory Bureau*: 1–8.

Meyerstein, Ariel. 2007. 'Between Law and Culture: Rwanda's *Gacaca* and Postcolonial Legality'. *Law & Social Inquiry* 32.2: 467–508.

Mutisi, Martha. 2012. 'Local Conflict Resolution in Rwanda: The Case of *Abunzi* Mediators'. In Martha Mutisi and Kwesi Sansculotte-Greenidge (eds),

*Integrating Traditional and Modern Conflict Resolution Experiences from Selected Cases in Eastern and the Horn of Africa.* Durban: ACCORD: 41–74.

National Unity and Reconciliation Commission (NURC). (n.d.). 'Home Grown Approaches'. Available at http://www.nurc.gov.rw/index.php?id=81 (consulted on 12 February 2019).

—. (2007). 'Imihigo'. Available at http://www.rgb.rw/index.php?id=36 (consulted on 12 February 2019).

*Official Gazette.* 2001. *Gacaca Organic Law No. 33/2001 of 2001* (on file with author).

—. 2004. *Gacaca Organic Law No. 16/2004 of 19/06/2004* (on file with author).

—. 2007. *Gacaca Organic Law No 10/2007 of 01/03/2007* (on file with author).

—. 2008. *Gacaca Organic Law Organic Law No. 13/2008 of 19/05/2008* (on file with author).

— 2012. *Organic Law No 04/2012/OL of 15/06/2012* (on file with author).

Penal Reform International. 2010. 'The Contribution of the Gacaca Jurisdictions to Resolving Cases Arising from the Genocide'. Available at https://cdn.penalreform.org/wp-content/uploads/2013/06/Gacaca_final_2010_en.pdf (consulted on 12 February 2019).

Purdeková, Andrea. 2011. 'Rwanda's *Ingando* Camps: Liminality and the Reproduction of Power'. Refugee Studies Centre Working Paper.

Pronk, Jan. 2012. 'Address at the Closing of Gaca [*sic*] Courts Activities, Kigali, Rwanda, June 18, 2012'. Available at http://www.janpronk.nl/speeches/english/gacaca.html (consulted on 12 February 2019).

Rusagara, Frank K. 2005. 'Gacaca: Rwanda's Truth and Reconciliation Authority'. *The New Times* 16 May. Available at https://allafrica.com/stories/200505170174.html (consulted on 12 February 2019).

'Rwandans Should Celebrate Gacaca Legacy – Karugarama'. *The New Times* 17 June 2012.

Taylor, Charles. 2003. *Modern Social Imaginaries.* Durham, NC: Duke University Press.

Towner, Emil B. 2015. 'Transcripts of Tragedy and Truths: An Analysis of Rwanda's Genocide Trial Documents'. *Atlantic Journal of Communication* 23: 284–97.

# The Incorporation of Women in Rwandan Politics after 1994

*Louise Umutoni-Bower*

*The fruits of the struggle are not for women.*
Gisela Giesler

National liberation movements usually incorporate women during the period of struggle for liberation, but tend to exclude them after power is captured. This was the case for most movements of the first wave (1960s and 1970s) and second wave (1980s and 1990s) of national liberation. The gender backlash that follows liberation involves the active exclusion of women and is believed to occur during the critical period of transition from war to peace (Manchanda, 2001). The Rwandan Patriotic Front (RPF), which was formed in exile by Rwandan Tutsi refugees, provides an interesting case study because it not only included women during the struggle but appointed them to key positions during the period of transition after they came to power in 1994. This initial incorporation is believed to have been fundamental in ensuring that women continued to play an active role in Rwandan politics. This chapter explores the factors that undermined the occurrence of a gender backlash and allowed for women's incorporation in the post-liberation politics of Rwanda during the period of transition from 1994 to the first post-genocide elections in 2003. Women in Rwanda experienced unprecedented inclusion in decision-making after 1994, and have become the focus of numerous studies on post-conflict gender politics (Mageza-Barthel, 2015; Tripp, 2015; Burnet, 2008 and 2011; Wallace et al,. 2009; Kayumba, 2010; Powley, 2003 and 2005; Newbury and

Baldwin, 2000). The large proportion of women in parliament is usually cited as an indicator of this inclusion, and the last elections gave Rwanda the highest proportion of women in parliament in the world, at 64% (World Bank Database, n.d.; Inter-Parliamentary Union Press Release, 2003). Women have served in key ministerial positions – for example, Louise Mushikiwabo in the Ministry of Foreign Affairs or Agnes Binagwaho in the Ministry of Health – and can be found at all levels of government albeit to a lesser extent at the local level. Most of the literature on women in politics in Rwanda attributes women's incorporation to the quota system established through the 2003 Constitution. However, this fails to account for the incorporation that happened before 2003 and in particular during the transitional period. The RPF charted the way for women's inclusion between 1994 and 2003 by appointing women to half of the seats it was allocated in the Transitional National Parliament (Burnet, 2011). This initial inclusion in the transitional government brought the percentage of women in parliament up from 18% in the pre-genocide government to 25.7% (Powley, 2003). Women also took on some of the most challenging roles after the genocide; for example, Rose Kabuye was charged with running the city of Kigali, which was in complete disarray after the conflict. Women participated actively in peace-building and reconstruction efforts at both government and civil society levels. After the genocide, women's civil society organizations emerged as an important government partner in rebuilding the nation. By contrast, in pre-genocide Rwandan society, women were excluded from decision-making and participating in national politics. Only a handful of women were in government and women's civil society organizations, mostly formed in the late 1980s, were stifled and their work undermined (Mageza-Barthel, 2015).

Some scholars have cited the transitional period as that critical period in which women should seize their place at the decision-making table (Meintjes, 2001; Mama, 1995; Pankhurst, 2008). Mama (1995) suggests analysing the transition period for programmes which could provide the space or opportunity for women to realize their political ambitions. It is important to study the transitional period because it helps elucidate the conditions that undermined the occurrence of a backlash in Rwanda. Transition entails a period of change from one political regime or system to another, and often follows conflict (Holmes, 2014). It involves the restructuring of society and provides opportunities to renegotiate norms and ideas that govern society. The formative nature of this period determines the direction that the new government will take and many new governments use it to position themselves as reform-oriented regimes. It is important to observe this period of transition not only for the new elite discourse, but also the policies enacted which provide a window into the ideology that is at the heart of the new regime and its members (Mama, 1995). According to Mageza-Barthel, the 'normative framework and political imperatives after the genocide were important in shaping the options women had' (2015: 64).

Surprisingly, very little has been written on gender politics in Rwanda during the transitional period. The literature deals with the current position of women in government and contrasts this with their pre-1994 roles to show how profound the incorporation of women in post-genocide politics has been. The genocide marks a break in the history of the country, including gender relations. Transition is glossed over and is not afforded the critical engagement that would unearth some of the formative ideas that informed Rwanda's gender politics. The fact that, unlike many liberation movements, the RPF incorporated women during this critical period, is not interrogated, which limits our understanding of how and why women were included in the first place.

## RPF Ideology

Created in exile by the children of Rwandan refugees, the RPF made social equality and inclusion its core demand. The experience of exile had undermined the social and economic well-being of many, especially those in host nations that discriminated against refugees. As such, it is not surprising that the movement was birthed in Uganda, where Rwandan refugees had been systematically excluded and targeted for violence under the Milton Obote regime. Obote distrusted Rwandan refugees because a few of them had supported Idi Amin after he overthrew the Obote government in 1971 (Boyle, 2014; Reed, 1996). This was exacerbated by the fact that many Rwandan refugees joined Yoweri Museveni's National Resistance Army (NRA), which challenged Obote (Boyle, 2014; Prunier, 1998a). Between 1982 and 1983 the Ugandan government launched numerous attacks against Rwandan refugees, displacing between 20,000 and 40,000 (Boyle, 2014). Refugees were also deprived of their land and cattle and dismissed from positions in government (Reed, 1995 and 1996; Mushemeza, 2007; Prunier, 1998b). This drove many young Rwandans to join the NRA, to the extent that by the end of the conflict 3,000 of the 14,000 NRA soldiers were Rwandan (Boyle, 2014). Among the Rwandans who joined the NRA were Paul Kagame and Fred Rwigema, who were both members of RANU (Rwanda Alliance of National Unity), created in 1979 and later renamed RPF. RANU had started out as a refugee rights organization of only a few members from the Tutsi intelligentsia with a Marxist-inspired ideology that called for the abolition of the monarchy and establishment of a socialist state (Reed, 1996). By the mid-1980s RANU had adopted a new strategy that sought to broaden its reach and assumed nationalist goals. It decentralized its leadership and positioned itself as the voice of Rwandan refugees (Boyle, 2014; Reed, 1996). In 1987 it was renamed and its objectives expanded to include the grievances of all Rwandans (Boyle, 2014; Reed, 1996). The primary goal was the unity of all Rwandans and the social and political inclusion of every Rwandan. Political inclusion was particularly important for women, who had systematically been denied access to positions in government. According to one of the founders of the RPF, women's liberation was considered an important goal of the movement:

> We were tasked with analysing the objective conditions of our society to determine what problems needed to be addressed. During this process we observed that Rwandan women were at a great disadvantage. They were discriminated against in society and this oppression followed them to their own homes, where men who were disillusioned by dictatorship and lack of opportunity unleashed their frustration on their wives. We knew that women's liberation had to be a fundamental part of the movement. (founding member of RPF, Kigali, interviewed 30 March 2016)

The notion that women needed to be liberated as part of the movement's goals was not particular to the RPF and some have traced it to the movement's leftist origins (Kayumba, 2010). Women's liberation is usually considered an objective of many nationalist movements and has been declared a paramount goal of liberation by some of the most prominent movement leaders, such as Amilcar Cabral and Moa Zedong (Campbell, 2001). According to one RPF member, the decision to incorporate women was ideologically driven and it ascribed to leftist ideals of social equality for all, including women. This ideology was actively disseminated through the political schools set up to train political cadres in the RPF (Spens-Black, 2016).

Lapchick and Urdang (1982), who pioneered the research on women in southern African liberation movements, discovered a link between the socialist nature of national liberation movements and women's emancipation. Kittilson (2006), in discussing the conditions under which women are incorporated into political parties, argues that the political ideology of a movement provides an opportunity for women's inclusion. As such, if a movement is leftist then it is bound to be more open to women's incorporation. However, many leftist movements that subscribed to these principles did not fulfil their promises on women's incorporation, which resulted in a gender backlash (Lyons, 2004; Yuval-Davis, 1997; Giesler, 2004; Moore, 1988). For example, the South West Africa People's Organisation (SWAPO) is said to have used the rhetoric of its international backers without necessarily translating it into deeply rooted ideological commitments and policies

(Dobell, 1998). Moghadam (1997) attempts to explain this by distinguishing between nationalist movements that are modernizing in character and those that are patriarchal. The former believe in the liberation of women and consider women partners in the struggle, while the latter only see women occupying the traditional roles of caregiver and mother of the nation. Even when some women participate in the fighting, they are never portrayed as fighters, and the only imagery of them emphasizes their maternal function. This was seen in case of the National Union for the Total Independence of Angola (UNITA) and the People's Movement for the Liberation of Angola (MPLA), where women were shown in supportive roles or as the mothers of the nation and not as fighters (Campbell, 2001).

What makes the RPF different is that the ideology of the movement was maintained and carried on into post-liberation politics through the new elite discourse observed during transition. Moreover, women were immediately appointed to high-profile positions such as mayor of Kigali, minister of justice and members of parliament. Most of those appointed were women who had participated in the struggle, which has drawn criticism from those who consider this selective incorporation (Mageza-Barthel, 2014).

The RPF appointed women to half of the seats it was assigned in the Transitional National Parliament and put in place mechanisms that would facilitate women's participation in politics. These included creating a ministry of gender, organizing women's councils that ensured women's representation at all levels of government and instituting an electoral system with reserved seats for women in the national parliament (Burnet, 2008).

Rose Kabuye, the highest-ranking woman in the Rwandan military, stated that the RPF ideology created in exile was indeed influential in determining the nature of politics in Rwanda after 1994. This was especially the case in the area of gender, where the movement had to work to change gender norms:

We had a vision of what we wanted Rwanda to look like and knew what ideology we wanted to push. We knew that we would have to educate others on this new Rwanda we imagined and that leading by example would be the best way to do this. This is why the RPF took the lead on including women from the very beginning. (Rose Kabuye, Kigali, interviewed 15 April 2016)

These changes were felt at all levels of society as women were not only taking positions at the top, but also participating in local-level politics:

People could not believe that women were being appointed to high positions and many wondered whether they were capable to lead. Many were worried about how that would affect families. I heard stories of women mayors or local leaders who would sometimes get unexpected visits from constituents late in the evening seeking assistance and their husbands would answer the door expecting the visit to be for them only to realize that it's his wife they are looking for. (Rose Kabuye, Kigali, interviewed 15 April 2016)

Some have attributed the RPF's ideology on women's inclusion to the National Resistance Movement (NRM) influence and Museveni's support for women's issues after assuming power (Kayumba, 2010; Mageza-Barthel, 2015). The fact that women fought alongside men in the NRM was thought to have encouraged the RPF to include women in the struggle because they had proved to be capable combatants (Mageza-Barthel, 2015). Moreover, many of the members of the RPF had previously been part of the NRA/NRM and witnessed the incorporation of women into the movement. However, some interviewees stated that the NRM's influence was minimal and that its failure to fully incorporate women after liberation shows that the movement was never truly committed to women's liberation. The women's movement in Uganda is thought to have been a response to the backlash that women experienced after liberation. Women felt betrayed by movement leaders whose talk of women's liberation did not materialize as women were only marginally included (Tripp, 2000; Byanyima, 1992; Boyd, 1989). Tripp (2000: 69) cites Museveni's demoralizing speech on the role of women in post-liberation Uganda in which he opted to lecture women on the need to 'pull up their socks' if they wanted to have a say in decision-making. In addition, women had to actively lobby the NRM for inclusion since none were appointed to the first cabinet (Tripp, 2015). According to one interviewee, the discourse on women's inclusion did not go to the heart of the NRM's ideology and this might explain why it did not have a comprehensive strategy on how to include women:

> The NRM, I think, was driven by leftist ideas but did not necessary analyse the condition of women in their society and so did not have an informed strategy on how to incorporate women or address women's issues. (RPF Party Member 1, Kigali, interviewed 6 April 2016)

He added that what distinguished the RPF from the NRM was that women's liberation and incorporation was seen as a measure of the success of the movement. However, reviewing both the RPF's eight-point plan and the NRM's ten-point programme, it is difficult to argue that women's liberation was an explicit aim as neither document mentions women. The difference is in the post-liberation discourse and efforts on women's inclusion, with the RPF making women's political participation a vital part of its politics.

There are some who have questioned the intentions behind the decision by the RPF to include women and who argue that it was driven by necessity

(Kayumba, 2010). The argument is that the RPF could not afford to exclude women because it was a movement in exile with a meagre recruitment base of Rwandan Tutsi refugees. This perception was immediately rejected by RPF party members interviewed, who argue that if this were the case then they would have abandoned any attempts to include women after power was captured. One interviewee added that women did not always become members through being recruited but joined of their own accord:

> The idea that women were recruited because of numbers is not accurate. Women joined because they wanted to and were not sought out by recruitment teams. In fact, I remember a number of them coming to my home when they found out that I was part of the movement to ask about how to join and what they could do to help. Many were young university students and helped take care of the sick and injured soldiers because we could not send them to hospitals in Uganda. (RPF Party Member 3, Kigali, interviewed 11 April 2016)

Another interviewee added that women, like men, had suffered from exclusion and believed just as strongly in the need to fight for the right to return home. Women joined because they wanted to improve their circumstances and committed both effort and resources to ensuring this aim. They served in different roles and were especially praised for their role as mobilizers:

> At fundraising rallies, women were the majority and packed big halls, contributing as much as they could afford. Women joined the movement not because they were power-hungry, but because of conviction. They had more to gain from the success of the movement and were convinced of the goals of the movement. The zeal with which they carried out each task given to them was proof of this. (RPF Party Member 3, Kigali, interviewed 11 April 2016)

One female RPF member who joined the movement in the late 1980s described her experience of joining the movement:

> I was a student at Makerere University when I heard about the RPF from some other Rwandan students. I was excited to hear that people were actually speaking about going back home and I immediately joined the movement to try and contribute to the fight for our home. During school holidays I was able to attend training at the political schools, where we were trained in basic military training and the political ideology of the RPF. (RPF Party Member 4, Kigali, interviewed 18 March 2016)

This sentiment was shared by other RPF women interviewed and it was clear that they ascribed to the ideas preached by the movement. Their active participation positioned them as key players who could be not discarded after power was captured. Many fought alongside men and lost their lives on the battlefield. As one interviewee said, 'women bought their place in Rwandan politics through bloodshed' (female MP 1, Kigali, interviewed 23 March 2016).

## New Dominant Elite Discourse

Upon assuming power, the RPF embarked on a mission to change the dominant political elite discourse in Rwanda. The previous regimes had supported ethno-politics with ethnicity representing a political category (Mamdani, 2001). This changed after 1994: the use of ethnicity as a basis for political legitimacy was prohibited. According to Mageza-Barthel (2015), this new form of nationalism differed from that fought for at independence because it emphasized the commonalities among Rwanda's three ethnic groups by underlining their shared history, language and origins. Prunier (1998b) adds that discouraging the use of ethnic references was also useful in denying the opposition an ethno-political base for power. He argues that this was very important for the RPF, which was initially largely comprised of the minority Tutsi ethnic group. This is supported by Kayumba (2010), who states that, unlike ethno-politics, gendering politics was not considered a threat to nation building. The dominant elite discourse not only emphasized Rwandaness, it also privileged gender over ethnicity (Powley, 2003). This was possible because all traditional centres of power, such as the church and media, had been profoundly weakened by the genocide and their complicity in the violence. The Catholic Church exercised immense influence over the Rwandan population and had introduced Victorian ideals that emphasized the subordinate position of women in society. The media had gone a step further and popularized these ideas and cemented them in the general psyche. According to Manchanda (2001), such institutions determine whether the old ways are maintained or if there is room for new ideas. The weakening of these custodians of the traditional norms, including gender norms, made it possible to introduce new ideas. The ruling ideas were up for negotiation and the RPF, which had secured a military victory and ousted the previous regime, was in a position to determine what the new ruling ideas would be.

The dominant elite discourse of gendering politics can be observed in the speeches of politicians, such as those of the president:

My country's story begins with our four-year armed struggle from 1990 in which women and men shared a common purpose of ending the legacy of hatred, divisionism and exclusion. Our philosophy and practice was to demand the best of women and men – people in our movement succeeded or failed on the basis of their merit. (Paul Kagame, speech given at the international colloquium of women's leadership, empowerment, peace and security. Monrovia Liberia, 7 March 2009, cited in Kayumba, 2010)

According to Paxton and Hughes (2007), the nature of transition is important in the transformation of norms: change is likely in situations where the central government is overthrown through armed conflict, but political transformation is limited when conflict is resolved through power-sharing agreements because the old political institutions remain intact. Transition through victory and the overthrow of the central government creates more space for restructuring and reform of state institutions. Women tend to make gains from this sort of transition because of the opportunities for change. They are able to lobby the new government for women's rights and the creation of gender-sensitive laws. The new government, which is looking to secure a large support base, is usually willing to engage women in dialogue and is likely to be more open to change. The RPF, which was a movement from outside the country, brought with it new ideas and was eager to secure a sizable support base inside Rwanda. It was also composed of young and progressive people who were not afraid of change (Kayumba, 2010).

The dominant elite discourse was especially vital because it provided alternative ways of organizing access to power. It made women an acceptable political category that could be used to vie for positions in government. The term 'women' was seen as a homogenizing category that could include members from different ethnic groups and backgrounds. The result was that it de-ethnicized gender and made the category of women a stable social and political group around which women could mobilize (Kayumba, 2010). This had the negative effect of blurring the lines around the differences between women and made it difficult to determine which women were being incorporated. It is inaccurate to assume that women form a single category with the same experience of marginalization and exclusion. Women experience an intersection of oppression owing to their disparate backgrounds (Crenshaw, 1991). This is true for Rwanda, where you have women from exile (also differing in terms of the country of exile), genocide survivors, genocide perpetrators, women from different ethnic groups and so forth. Some argue that because of the nature of transition in which the RPF secured a military victory, many of the women initially included were from the movement (Burnet, 2011; Kayumba, 2010). This constituted a small segment of the exile community and was not representative of Rwandan women. The positioning of women in the post-conflict moment ensured that those women who had been mainstreamed into the struggle were retained whilst those who had been excluded during the pre-1994 government remained on the sidelines. An intersection of various experiences determined the positioning of women. Hutu women and Tutsi genocide survivors were at a disadvantage because there were no mechanisms in place to ensure their incorporation. The RPF made efforts to recruit women from disparate backgrounds, which also served to expand its support base. It put in place mechanisms such as the National Women's Council to encourage women's political participation at all levels of government. Such efforts were vital in ensuring that women were able to compete in elections from the cell level to the top, and were used to elect a lot of women to office in 1998 (Burnet, 2008).

Although efforts to insure grass-roots women's participation are important, some believe that they represent a top-down approach to women's incorporation. The National Women's Council is a government initiative created in line with the new elite discourse that favours gender politics. However, women's incorporation in Rwanda was not only top-down, as the next section will show. Women played a role in ensuring their participation in the post-genocide politics of the Rwanda.

## The Effect of Genocide and Civil War

The 1994 Rwandan Genocide against the Tutsi and the civil war in the northern part of the country had enormous effects on the social, political and economic fabric of Rwandan society. They left no area untouched and ushered in radical changes not previously seen in the history of the small East African nation. Gender norms and relations, which had remained relatively stable and were characterized by huge inequality, were altered and women emerged out of the private sphere to assume important roles in the reconstruction process. Some scholarship on women in post-conflict politics has argued that although conflict is particularly harmful to women and children, it can also result in potential 'gains' for women (Tripp, 2015; Bop, 2001; Manchanda, 2001; Meintjes, 2001; Byanyima, 1992; Goetz, 1995). This is based on the notion that conflict leads to the disintegration of social and political systems that thrived on gender inequality and provides opportunities for women to renegotiate their position in society (Goetz, 1995). According to Wallace et al. (2009), the loss of confidence in traditional society and institutions makes radical change possible. This argument is supported by the instance of increased representation of women seen in post-conflict African countries (Tripp, 2015). Many female African heads of state have arisen in post-conflict countries or have assumed power immediately after conflict, such as Catherine Samba-Panza in Central African Republic, Sylvie

Kinigi of Burundi and Ruth Perry and Ellen Johnson Sirleaf of Liberia (Tripp, 2015). Despite a reluctance amongst scholars to talk about the gains of conflict, Manchanda states that 'conflict opens up intended and unintended spaces for empowering women, effecting structural social transformations and producing new social, economic and political realities that define gender and caste hierarchies' (2001: 7). Nowhere is this more apparent than in the case of Rwanda, where women were suddenly thrust into the public sphere and became active in post-genocide politics. Three factors which were direct results of the genocide and conflict in Rwanda arguably made this change possible.

## Missing Men

The first factor that contributed to making women's incorporation possible is what has been termed the 'missing men' and refers to the large number of men killed, incarcerated or in exile after the genocide. Some have argued that the ratio of women to men increased significantly and some scholars went as far as to suggest that women represented 70% of the population in Rwanda after 1994 (Wallace et al., 2009; Izabiliza, 2003; Newbury and Baldwin, 2000). The statistic, first published by Human Rights Watch, has since been disputed, and greater weight has been placed on the number of female-led households that emerged after the genocide (Tripp, 2015). As of 1996, 34% of households were headed by women, who assumed roles that had previously been reserved for men (Newbury and Baldwin, 2000). One interviewee attributed this to mere necessity or subsistence:

> Women were very active after the genocide because they needed to adapt in order to survive. There was no one to do the tasks that had previously been done by men and women took on roles such as building houses, something that was originally considered an abomination. Women did not milk cows, but with no men to do it for them, they were forced to challenge cultural norms to ensure their survival and that of their dependants. (civil servant, Kigali, interviewed 28 March 2016)

This view was shared by many. Another interviewee, Jean-Paul Kimonyo, stated that one of the most surprising changes observed by those released from prison after the transitional period was the number of women participating actively in public affairs or doing so-called men's jobs.

This shift in gender roles had an impact on gender norms and explains why women went beyond merely providing for themselves and their families, which had been the initial concern, to actively participate in the reconstruction process. Many had witnessed the destruction of Rwandan society at the hand of institutions which were supposed to protect and preserve their well-being, and with these institutions in disarray, women saw an opportunity and a role for themselves in restoring their communities:

> Women immediately started to pick up the pieces of the society that had been torn apart by conflict. They were very effective in convincing those that had fled to neighbouring countries to return home, assuring them of their safety. They took in abandoned or orphaned children until the government was able to find homes for them. (gender specialist 1, Kigali, interviewed 11 April 2016)

According to Jolly Rubagiza, gender activist and director of the Centre for Gender Studies at the University of Rwanda, women were considered important players in the reconstruction process because of how actively they were involved in rebuilding Rwandan society after the genocide. She adds that there were no grounds on which women could be excluded, seeing that they had successfully carried out tasks that were initially believed to be beyond their abilities (Jolly Rubagiza, Kigali, interviewed 10 April 2016). It was even more important that they seized the opportunity to engage during the critical period of transition when the backlash is believed to commonly occur (Manchanda, 2001). This brief period of uncertainty provided women with the necessary window to participate in public affairs and because of their relentless commitment to rebuilding their communities; they were able to carve out a space for themselves in the post-genocide politics of the country:

> The challenges of national reconstruction provided good process opportunities for the Rwandan women to demonstrate their abilities and potentials, while providing equally good opportunities to Rwandan society and men, to gradually let go of the traditional prejudices and stereotypes previously cherished. (Kantengwa, 2004: 3)

In the past Rwandan women had been relegated to the private sphere with minimal public engagement in politics. In the period immediately before the genocide only three women were in government and it was widely perceived that women had no place in politics. Efforts to change this perception after 1994 faced some resistance as described above by Rose Kabuye. However, the unusual situation after 1994, which demanded that women take on new roles as the heads of households, challenged the idea that women had no place in public sphere. Women could delegate on issues in their communities and many rose to the position of community leader.

## Gendered Genocide

The second factor that helps to explain the incorporation of women after 1994 is related to the gendered nature of the genocide, as some have described it (Mageza-Barthel, 2015; Turshen and Twagiramariya, 1998; Baines, 2003). Attacks on women were not only ethnically based; they had an added dimension that emphasized the gender of the body on which violence was enacted, and the type of violence was determined by the gender of the victim. It is because of the Genocide against the Tutsi that rape was declared a crime against humanity (Mageza-Barthel, 2015). The politics of exclusion espoused by the Second Republic and the National Republican Movement for Democracy and Development (MNRD) government not only discriminated along ethnic lines but also excluded women:

> As a genocide survivor, I had lived through a period of exclusion from any form of politics because of both my gender and ethnicity. Even the women we thought were empowered, like Agathe Uwilingiyimana, were publicly humiliated and we saw how unsupportive they were to her. We did not imagine that there was room for us in politics. (member of parliament 2, Kigali, interviewed 18 April 2016)

According to Mageza-Barthel, women in Rwanda became 'a battle ground on which genocide was fought because they symbolized the Rwandan nation's construction' (2015: 8). Inscribed on women's bodies were ideas about nationhood that determined who was included or excluded. The fact that Tutsi women were perceived as a threat was further elucidated in the Hutu Ten Commandments, of which three were devoted to women. The infamous extremist-owned media outlets such as Kangura and RTLM disseminated the message that Tutsi women were a threat that needed to be eliminated, whilst emphasizing the need to protect Hutu women from the invading RPF forces, which they claimed were raping and killing Hutu women. Hutu women were also called upon to defend their families and men from so-called seductive and devious Tutsi women who were polluting the Hutu ethnic group through intermarriage. This pitting of women against each other further alienated them and undermined any attempt at mobilization to demand equal treatment or representation. Women who were seen as challenging the status quo were targeted, such as Agathe Uwilingiyimana, who after assuming office as prime minister became a victim of a tirade of attacks in the media and was one of the first people killed at the start of the genocide. The conflation of the private and public spheres seen in extremist media denied women the original safety of the private sphere. They were forced to engage either as victims or perpetrators in a conflict that they had played no role in creating.

The tendency to portray women in conflict strictly as victims was evident in the Rwandan genocide. Some scholars argue that women's perceived lack of complicity in the violence afforded them the moral grounds on which to base their demand for a role in the peace-building and reconstruction process (Mageza-Barthel, 2015; Tripp, 2015). However, women in Rwanda did participate in the genocide and about 2.3% of women were incarcerated (Holmes, 2008). Admittedly this is small in comparison to men and, as argued above, women were largely kept out of decision-making before 1994 and played almost no role in creating the conflict. Only three women were in government at the time but two of them, Agathe Ntamabyariro and Pauline Nyiramasuhuko, were strong proponents of the genocide. Nyiramasuhuko, who was the Minister of Women and the Family at the time, was a particularly keen participant in the violence and was known for initiating campaigns of rape and inciting the torture and killing of Tutsi women (Mageza-Barthel, 2015). As such, it is difficult to see Rwandan women as strictly innocent victims in the violence or to base their incorporation post-conflict on a perceived non-complicity. I would argue that the victimization and partici-pation of women in the genocide forced women to participate in the public domain. The politicization of women's bodies made gender an important category in the conflict. Unlike traditional wars in which only men partic-ipated, the genocide left no sphere of society untouched (Spens-Black, 2016). The public and private spheres were conflated and women were forced to straddle both in order to survive.

## Women's Civil Society Organizations

The third and final factor is the rise of women's civil society organi-zations and the increased influence of international actors. Post-conflict forms of intervention targeting reconstruction are a common occurrence and were particularly important in Rwanda, where the social, economic and political fabric was completely destroyed. The guilt-induced scramble by the international community to respond to the devastating effects of the genocide, which they had failed to halt, resulted in a much larger international presence than in most post-conflict contexts. Many of these interventions were targeted at supporting local efforts and were vital in strengthening local civil society. The international organizations that were active during this period included UNIFEM and UNDP, which supported women's organizations financially, through skill transfer, and supported the incorporation of women in decision-making (Mageza-Barthel, 2015). The

UNHCR's Rwanda Women's Initiative directly targeted government efforts and funded the Gender Ministry's running costs (Mageza-Barthel, 2015).

There was also a proliferation of local civil society actors, all of whom were eager to find solutions to the huge task of helping Rwandan society recover. AVEGA, for example, was created to support survivors of the genocide and joined the umbrella organization Profemme Twese Hamwe in unity and reconciliation efforts:

> Profemme was very active in reconstruction through its various member organizations, such as AVEGA, Duterimbere and Haguruka. Duterimbere, for example, was streamlined to provide support for income-generation activities through its small loans scheme. This was possible because, unlike most of the bigger financial institutions, Duterimbere's coffers were not sacked during the genocide. We also had unity and reconciliation programmes before this was adopted as an official government policy. (Profemme employee, Kigali, interviewed 1 April 2016)

It is imperative to note that women's organizations did not simply emerge out of the ruins of the genocide, but had existed before 1994. These included the 13 founding organizations of Profemme Twese Hamwe, whose members were active advocates for women's equality. However, their work was undermined by the MNRD government, which did not consider gender issues a priority (Mageza-Barthel, 2015; Powley, 2003). It was only after the genocide that they were able to effectively position themselves as key partners to the government in the reconstruction efforts. These organizations continued to advocate for women especially during the critical time of transition and have been credited with ensuring that more women were included in decision-making (Burnet, 2008). According to Powley (2003), this increased influence of women's organizations and their commitment to helping the most vulnerable in society made them the most active sector of civil society during the transitional period. The transitional government was quick to realize how vital these women's organizations were and sought their input on various issues:

> The problems we were trying to address were so many but we always made sure that women were at the centre of all our efforts. We were invited to dialogues with the government on women's empowerment and we tabled what we believed were the problems affecting women. (Profemme employee, Kigali, interviewed 1 April 2016)

Another factor that enhanced the presence of a women's civil society was the availability of funding through international aid efforts. International organizations have also been credited with pushing for women's inclusion in post-genocide Rwanda and ensuring that gender-sensitive policies were enacted (Tripp, 2015; Mageza-Barthel, 2015; Burnet and RISD, 2003; Burnet, 2008). This is based on the notion that international actors wield substantial influence in post-conflict countries whose governments rely heavily on international support, and are therefore more likely to adopt their policies to the demands or interests of these international actors. However, some have challenged the role of the international community in ensuring women's incorporation in Rwandan politics and argue that international efforts only served to complement the local efforts that were already in place. Jolly Rubagiza espoused this view in interview and questioned why the same degree of incorporation of women was not possible in other post-conflict countries where similar levels of international intervention were seen:

> The international community responded to government needs and policies that were already being implemented by the government. I would say that the policies adopted to incorporate women were home-grown. (RPF Party Member 1, Kigali, interviewed 6 April 2016)

In discussing the role of international actors, Jean-Paul Kimonyo voiced similar views and stated that international actors and norms such as those enacted at the UN women's meeting in Beijing in 1995 gave momentum to existing trends towards women's inclusion. I would add that the international norms such as those discussed in the Beijing Declaration and Platform for Action gave women the language necessary to better articulate their demands for gender equality and provided them with indicators with which to measure their success:

> The role of international actors cannot be disputed, but the level of influence was not huge. Gender inclusion in the 1990s was a hot topic internationally and culminated in the Beijing meeting in 1995. I believe that this external narrative fit a local context that was ripe for that sort of narrative. (Lecturer, University of Rwanda, Kigali, interviewed 23 March 2016)

The notion that post-conflict countries tend to be more inclusive of women, especially in the area of politics, is not undisputed. In fact, the end of conflict is generally characterized by a gender backlash with women forced back into the private sphere. Women are expected to resume their culturally accepted identity to signal a return to normality and peace is seen as a return to previous gender norms (Manchanda, 2001). In addition, the idea that conflict completely destabilizes gender norms is challenged by El-Bushra (2003), who argues that conflict does not necessarily alter gender norms but rather rearranges or adapts and reinforces patriarchal systems. In essence, the societies that arise out of conflict might claim to embark on various reforms but harbour the same patriarchal ideals and will adjust their methods of exclusion to fit the reigning ideas of the day.

However, women in Rwanda were largely included in post-genocide politics and conflict did serve to open the door to their public engagement and eventually to political inclusion. The important question to ask is why this backlash, common in many other post-conflict countries, did not happen in Rwanda. One factor that explains this is the unusual state that the country was in as a result of a genocide that victimized and criminalized a majority of the population. More importantly, one should not downplay the rapidity and zeal with which Rwandan women took up roles in the reconstruction process and positioned themselves as vital actors in decision-making. The period of transition is critical to determining whether women return to the private sphere or can secure a position for themselves in government. Rwandan women were pushed into the public sphere by necessity and as a result of conflict and were able to ensure their continued role in decision-making through active engagement in rebuilding their society. The vital question is whether this was enough to secure genuine political participation or whether women's inclusion in Rwanda remains largely top-down.

## Conclusion

The RPF is an interesting case study for scholarship on women and liberation movements. It provides a unique yet complex instance in which incorporation into power did happen for women after power was captured. As argued above, three factors during transition that made incorporation possible. The first is that women were incorporated in the movement while it was in exile, and played a significant role in the liberation struggle. The experience of exile forced women to undertake new roles as providers for their families, which compelled them to transcend gender norms and to participate in the public sphere. This had a profound effect on the gender norms and relationships among Rwandan refugees, and ultimately had an impact on how the movement conceived the role of women within it and in the post-liberation government.

The second factor is that the RPF was able to create a new elite discourse that favoured women's inclusion and discredited ethno-politics. During transition all aspects of Rwandan society were thrown into flux, which made it possible to transform the social, political and economic structures of the country. The traditional centres of power had disintegrated and norms that had hitherto gone unchallenged were up for negotiation; the time was ripe for new ideas. The RPF, which secured a military victory over the previous regime and ended the genocide, earned the freedom to create new, dominant ideas. It was in a position to determine the nature of politics in post-genocide Rwanda and in the reconstruction process. It brought with it new ideas about the role of women in society and sought to rebuild Rwandan society according to these ideas. This top-down form of incorporation was vital, especially to bring about change in the gender politics of Rwanda. However, it is not enough to ensure genuine women's participation; it must be coupled with women's own initiative to secure their position in decision-making.

The third factor highlights women's initiative to ensure their incorporation. Women played a vital role in the post-genocide reconstruction process and took on new roles and responsibilities. Genocide had drawn women out of the private sphere through their participation as victims or perpetrators. Women remained in the public sphere, in which they engaged in rebuilding their society either through civil society or through private initiatives. The effects of the violence forced them to take up new roles as the sole providers of their households. These new responsibilities allowed them to participate in decision-making and gave them a new sense of their capabilities. In doing so, they were also now in a position to challenge gender norms which they viewed as oppressive. The adaptive nature of transition made this possible as women were able to participate in the drafting of the new Constitution and ensured that their political position was secured through the legalization of quotas.

All three factors came to the fore in the period of transition, in which they combined to create a political climate that was conducive to women's political inclusion. The period after the genocide was characterized by a loss of trust in the old systems and customs, which provided a window of opportunity to renegotiate and transform customs and norms, including gender norms. The opportunity to rebuild and reform institutions made it possible to adopt new ideas. This convergence of external and internal factors following the genocide is unique to Rwanda, and is what undermined the occurrence of the gender backlash after the RPF took power.

## Works Cited

Baines, Erin. 2003. 'Body Politics and the Rwanda Crisis'. *Third World Quarterly* 24.3: 479–93.

Bop, Codou. 2001. 'Women in Conflict, their Gains and Losses'. In Sheila Meintjes, Anu Pillay and Meredeth Turshen (eds), *The Aftermath: Women in Post-Conflict Transformation*. London: Zed Books: 20–33.

Boyd, Rosalind E. 1989. 'Empowerment of Women in Uganda: Real or Symbolic'. *Review of African Political Economy* 16.45–46: 106–17.

Boyle, Michael J. 2014. *Violence after War: Explaining Instability in Post-Conflict States*. Baltimore, MD: Johns Hopkins University Press.

Burnet, Jennie E. and RISD. 2003. 'Culture, Practice, and Law: Women's Access to Land in Rwanda'. In L.M. Wanyeki (ed.), *Women and Land in Africa: Culture, Religion and Realizing Women's Rights*. New York: Zed Books: 176–206.

Burnet, Jennie E. 2008. 'Gender Balance and the Meanings of Women in Governance in Post-Genocide Rwanda'. *African Affairs* 107.428: 361–86.

—. 2011. 'Women Have Found Respect: Gender Quotas, Symbolic Representation and Female Empowerment in Rwanda'. *Politics & Gender* 7.3: 303–34.

Byanyima, W. Karagwa. 1992. 'Women in Political Struggle in Uganda'. In Jill M. Bystydzienski (ed.), *Women Transforming Politics: Worldwide Strategies for Empowerment*. Bloomington. IN: Indiana University Press: 129–42.

Campbell, Horace. 2001. *Militarism, Warfare and the Search for Peace in Angola*. Pretoria: African Institute of South Africa.

Crenshaw, Kimberle. 1991. 'Mapping and Margins: Intersectionality, Identity Politics and Violence against Women of Colour'. *Stanford Law Review* 43.6: 1241–99.

Dobell, Lauren. 1998. *Swapo's Struggle for Namibia, 1960–1991: War by Other Means*. Basel: Schlettwein Publishing.

El-Bushra, Judy. 2003. *Women Building Peace: Sharing Know-How*. London: International Alert.

Giesler, Gisela. 2004. *Women and the Remaking of Politics in South Africa: Negotiating Autonomy, Incorporation and Representation*. Uppsala: Nordic African Institute.

Goetz, Anne Marie. 1995. 'The Politics of Integrating Gender to State Development Processes: Trends, Opportunities and Constraints in Bangladesh, Chile, Jamaica, Mali, Morocco and Uganda'. United Nations Research Institute for Social Development Occasional Paper 2. Available at http://www.unrisd.org/80256B3C005BCCF9/(httpPublications)/8856EC9F7738F32A80256B670 05B6AD5 (consulted on 15 May 2016).

Holmes, Georgina. 2008. 'The Postcolonial Politics of Militarizing Rwandan Women: An Analysis of the Extremist Magazine Kangura and the Gendering of a Genocidal Nation-State'. *Minerva Journal of Women and War* 2.2: 44–63.

—. 2014. *Women and War in Rwanda: Gender, Media and the Representation of Genocide*. London: I.B. Tauris.

Inter-Parliamentary Union: Press Release. 2003. 'Rwanda Leads World Ranking of Women in Parliament'. Available at http://www.ipu.org/press-e/gen176.htm (consulted on 15 May 2016).

Izabiliza, Jeanne. 2003. 'The Role of Women in Reconstruction: Experience of Rwanda'. UNESCO. Available at http://www.unesco.org/new/fileadmin/MULTI MEDIA/HQ/SHS/pdf/Role-Women-Rwanda.pdf (consulted on 15 May 2016).

Kantengwa, Juliana. 2004. 'Women's Participation in Electoral Processes in Post-Conflict Countries: The Case of Rwanda'. Presented at panel discussion organized by IPU, the United Nations and the Permanent Mission of Norway, UN Headquarters, Room 2, New York.

Kayumba, Christopher. 2010. *Understanding High Presence of Women in Rwanda's Parliament: Paths to World's First Female Parliamentary Majority in Post-Genocide Rwanda*. Saarbrücken: LAP Lambert Academic Publishing.

Kittilson, Miki Caul. 2006. *Challenging Parties, Changing Parliaments: Women and Elected Office in Contemporary Western Europe*. Columbus, OH: Ohio State University Press.

Lapchick, Richard E., and Stephanie Urdang. 1982. *Oppression and Resistance: The Struggle of Women in Southern Africa*. Westport, CT: Greenwood Press.

Lyons, Tanya. 2004. *Guns and Guerrilla Girls*. Asmara: Africa World Press Inc.

Mageza-Barthel, Rirhandu. 2015. *Mobilizing Transnational Gender Politics in Post-Genocide Rwanda*. Farnham: Ashgate Publishing.

Mama, Amina. 1995. 'Feminism or Femocracy: State Feminism and Democratisation in Nigeria'. *Africa Development* 20.1: 37–58.

Mamdani, Mahmood. 2001. *When Victims Become Killers: Colonialism, Nativism and the Genocide in Rwanda*. Princeton, NJ: Princeton University Press.

Manchanda, Rita. 2001. 'Ambivalent Gains in Conflicts in South Asia'. In Sheila Meintjes, Anu Pillay and Meredeth Turshen (eds), *The Aftermath: Women in Post-Conflict Transformation*. London: Zed Books: 99–120.

Meintjes, Sheila. 2001. 'War and Post-War Shifts in Gender Relations'. In Sheila Meintjes, Anu Pillay and Meredeth Turshen (eds), *The Aftermath: Women in Post-Conflict Transformation*. London: Zed Books: 63–76.

Moghadam, Valentine M. 1997. 'Gender and Revolutions'. In John F. Foran (ed.), *Theorizing Revolutions*. London and New York: Routledge: 137–67.

Moore, Henrietta L. 1988. *Feminism and Anthropology*. Minneapolis, MN: University of Minnesota Press.

Mushemeza, Elijah D. 2007. *The Politics of Empowerment of Banyarwanda Refugees in Uganda 1959–2001*. Kampala: Fountain Publishers.

Newbury, Catherine, and Hannah Baldwin. 2000. 'Aftermath: Women in Post-Genocide Rwanda'. U.S. Agency for International Development Washington, Working Paper 303.

Pankhurst, Donna. 2008. *Gendered Peace: Women's Struggles for Post-War Justice and Reconciliation*. New York and London: Routledge.

Paxton, Pamela, and Melanie M. Hughes. 2007. *Women, Politics, and Power: A Global Perspective*. London: Pine Forges Press.

Powley, Elizabeth. 2003. 'Strengthening Governance: The Role of Women in Rwanda's Transition'. Available at https://www.inclusivesecurity.org/publication/strengthening-governance-the-role-of-women-in-rwandas-transition/ (consulted on 23 May 2016).

—. 2005. 'Rwanda: Women Hold Up Half the Parliament'. In Julie Balington and Azza Karam (eds), *Women in Parliament: Beyond Numbers*. Rev. ed. Stockholm: International IDEA: 154–63.

Prunier, Gérard. 1998a. 'The Rwandan Patriotic Front'. In Christopher Clapham (ed.), *African Guerrillas*. Oxford: James Currey: 119–33.

—. 1998b. *History of a Genocide: The Rwandan Crisis 1959–1994*. New York: Columbia University Press.

Reed, Wm. Cyrus. 1995. 'The Rwanda Patriotic Front: Politics and Development in Rwanda'. *A Journal of Opinion* 23.2: 48–53.

—. 1996. 'Exile, Reform, and the Rise of the Rwanda Patriotic Front'. *Journal of Modern African Studies* 34.3: 479–501.

Spens-Black, Hannah. 2016. 'Rwandan Women at War: Fighting for the Rwandan Patriotic Front (1990–1994)'. In Shirley Ardener, Fiona Armitage-Woodward and Lidia Dina Sciama (eds), *War and Women across Continents: Autobiographical and Biographical Experiences*. New York: Berghahn Books: 127–45.

Tripp, Aili M. 2000. *Women and Politics in Uganda*. Madison, WI: University of Wisconsin Press.

—. 2015. *Women and Power in Postconflict Africa*. New York: Cambridge University Press.

Turshen, Meredeth and Twagiramariya, Clotilde. 1998. *What Women Do in Wartime: Gender and Conflict in Africa*. London: Zed Books.

Wallace, Claire, Christian Haerpfer and Pamela Abbott. 2009. 'Women in Rwandan Politics and Society'. *International Journal of Sociology* 38.4: 111–25.

World Bank Database. n.d. 'Proportion of Seats Held by women in National Parliaments (%)'. Available at http://data.worldbank.org/indicator/SG.GEN.PARL.ZS (consulted on 15 May 2016).

Yuval-Davis, Nira. 1997. *Gender and Nation*. London: Sage.

# Rebranding Rwanda's Peacekeeping Identity during Post-Conflict Transition

*Georgina Holmes and Ilaria Buscaglia*

In 1994, Rwanda's positive nation brand as a model of development in Africa and exotic tourist destination was quickly replaced by images characterizing Rwanda as a land of transgressive and bloody violence, and Rwandans as uncivilized and driven by primal needs. In the international media, Rwanda was imaged as a failed state where the unimaginable horrors of tribal war and genocide had taken place. Since UN troops had been deployed in Rwanda at the time of the genocide and civil war to oversee the Arusha Peace Accords and later in the aftermath of conflict, Rwandans were not just depicted as perpetrators, survivors and victims of genocide but as a passive and helpless 'peacekept' community in need of international assistance. Yet, over the past 20 years, the government of Rwanda, led by the ruling Rwandan Patriotic Front (RPF), has embarked on an extensive country rebranding exercise to support President Paul Kagame's vision to rebuild and transform Rwanda into a middle-income state by 2020. Part of this strategy involves transforming Rwanda's image as a peacekept nation state into that of a proactive peacekeeper and contributor to UN and African Union peacekeeping operations. Indeed, in the 15 years since Rwanda first deployed 150 troops to Darfur in 2004, the post-conflict state has embarked on a rapid ascent to the top of UN troop contribution league tables.

Scholars have contended that mediatized narratives about Rwanda's domestic and foreign security policies facilitate implementation of the RPF's centralized state-building project, and have argued that official security narratives, promoted in policy discourse, state-owned media and via the social media of Rwandan officials and their supporters, legitimize and strengthen the powerbase of the RPF and military elites (Jowell, 2010; Holmes, 2014; Holmes 2018; Wilén, 2018; Purdeková, Wilén and Renteyns, 2018). Scholars have also identified how security narratives are used as a propaganda tool to restrict domestic public space and to discipline Rwandan citizens (Pottier, 2002; Straus and Waldorf, 2011; Burnet, 2012; Purdeková, 2011; Grant, 2015). Yet how mediatized security narratives serve to 'market' Rwanda as a competitive troop-contributing country (TCC) and peacekeeping provider, and inform Rwanda's broader rebrand after civil war and genocide, has not been considered.

Drawing on recent theorizing of 'nation branding', we examine how mediatized security narratives are used as part of the RPF's public diplomacy strategy to establish and stabilize post-conflict Rwanda's peacekeeping identity and brand image as a TCC. We do so by undertaking an analysis of media discourse published by the state-owned English-language national newspaper *The New Times*, and a 'twitter storm' that occurred after March 2017 in response to the Central African Republic (CAR) sexual exploitation and abuse scandal involving French peacekeepers and, one year later, in February 2018 in response to a second scandal involving Ghanaian peacekeepers in South Sudan.[1] Specifically, the chapter asks, how is the current RPF government using mediatized security narratives as a nation-branding tool after genocide and civil war? We argue that mediatized security narratives are used by the RPF to erase Rwanda's negative brand informed by the frameworks of victimology, poverty and violence, and to reposition Rwanda as an emerging strategic player in international peacekeeping. The RPF achieves this by 'niche building' and later mimicking the public diplomacy strategies of middle powers in order to present Rwanda as a catalyst and facilitator of contemporary peacekeeping policy and practice.

Two hundred print and online news and current affairs articles were obtained from *The New Times* archives at the newspaper's headquarters in

---

[1] Although state-owned radio and television are by far the most accessed and listened to media genres in Rwanda, we chose to examine *The New Times* discourse because of the accessibility of the newspaper's archives. A brief survey of news and current affairs programmes and articles published on Ighie (one of the main English-Kinyarwanda online news platforms), KT Press and the weekly newspaper *The East African*'s 'Rwanda Today' section shows that reports on Rwanda's engagement in peacekeeping are similar across the different news outlets. This may be because the news stories originate from the same sources and press conferences organized by the Rwanda Defence Force.

Kigali in March 2017 by a male Rwandan research assistant. The articles selected discussed peace, peacekeeping and the engagement of the Rwanda Defence Force (RDF) and the Rwanda National Police in peacekeeping and peacebuilding in Rwanda and overseas. The timespan of the research corpus was limited to the media discourse that had been archived by *Rwanda National Times* staff, and we were informed that earlier media discourse had not been collected and categorized. Additional archival research was undertaken in March 2018 by the authors to collect articles published online in 2017. Tweets were downloaded via the Twitter account of one of the authors in February 2018 and retrieved by searching for the hashtags #SomeoneTellFrance24, #SomeoneTellRfi and #TweetLikeRfi. The Twitter accounts of influential Rwanda Twitter users (the #RwOT community) were also identified over a two-year period between March 2016 and February 2018. Media texts and images were analysed using discourse analysis to enable the study of issue areas related to Rwanda's domestic and foreign security policies, and to identify key 'niche issue areas'.

We first briefly conceptualize 'nation branding' in the context of changing the nation state's image during post-conflict transition. We then undertake a discourse analysis of print and online news and current affairs articles published by *The New Times* to critically assess how Rwanda's peacekeeper brand identity evolved over a ten-year period between January 2008 and January 2018, and to identify three discursive phases in the development of Rwanda's TCC brand identity: start-up, consolidation and power-maximization. Using as case studies the CAR and South Sudan sexual exploitation and abuse scandal, we consider the RPF's attempts to stabilize the TCC's brand image in a changing global media environment wherein RPF-produced mediatized security narratives may be reappropriated by international actors (Holmes, 2013; Holmes, 2015). In doing so, we reflect on the precariousness of the RPF's TCC-branding efforts.

## Rwanda, Peacekeeping and Competitive Identity

Rwanda's commitment to peacekeeping links back to the failure of the international community to intervene during the Genocide against the Tutsi in Rwanda, when the world stood by as some 800,000 Tutsi and moderate Hutu were killed in 100 days. Belgian soldiers pulled out of Rwanda in the first week of the genocide after the murder of ten peacekeepers who had been protecting the moderate Hutu Prime Minister Agathe Uwilingyimana. Under the leadership of Canadian Lieutenant-General Roméo Dallaire, a small contingent of 400 peacekeepers with limited resources were unable to protect civilians. Rwanda's entry into peacekeeping in 2004, ten years after the genocide, marked a shift in identity from failed state and peacekept nation, to peacekeeping actor on the international stage. Today, Rwanda is among the world's top ten contributors of uniformed peacekeepers, deploying around 6,000 troops annually to complex peacekeeping operations including the UN/African Union Mission in Darfur (UNAMID), the UN Mission in the Republic of South Sudan (UNMISS) and the UN Multidimensional Integrated Stabilization Mission in the CAR (MINUSCA). In parallel with its efforts to establish gender parity in government, the RDF and Rwanda National Police are required to integrate more female uniformed peacekeepers, positioning Rwanda in the top five contributors of female police peacekeepers.

Peacekeeping also provides economic and political benefits to the Rwandan state, its ruling elite, the RPF and uniformed personnel. In support of the state's reconciliation initiatives, peacekeeping is considered to have assisted both the RDF and Rwanda National Police to develop cohesive security forces with shared institutional histories of deployment overseas (Jowell, 2010). Since its first deployment, Rwanda has accrued substantial financial gains from reimbursements, as well as significant combat experience, notably in high-risk missions such as MINUSCA in the CAR, when in 2013 Rwanda was among the first TCCs to deploy (Beswick and Jowell, 2014). Peacekeeping also enables the government of Rwanda to justify and sustain its large security forces.

As with other TCCs from West and East Africa, Rwanda has been labelled a 'new peacekeeper' (Wilén, 2018). De Waal defines 'new peacekeeping' as 'an extension of political bargain over position within a globalized hierarchy', enabling 'new peacekeepers' such as Rwanda to 'use their position to advance their political-business interests, including deploying their own soldiers as peacekeepers' (2015: 190). While de Waal observes how peacekeeping can be instrumentalized by TCCs to accrue more political and economic capital, it should be noted that peacekeeping is a competitive demand/supply-driven marketplace. TCCs provide human and logistical resources to the UN and rent out equipment such as medical facilities. Male and female peacekeepers provided by TCCs are assigned 'use-values' within the peacekeeping system, and within individual peacekeeping missions, and are expected to act in accordance with UN values and codes of conduct (Pruitt, 2016; Holmes, 2019). Therefore, Rwanda must compete with a range of peacekeeping providers in Africa, as well as elsewhere in the Global South, to ensure that the state maintains its annual contracts with the UN's Department of Peacekeeping Operations (DPKO).

As the dominant securitizing actor in Rwanda, the RPF-led government engages in 'securitization' – a discursive 'security construction' process, wherein narratives are edited to present a 'logically and theoretically coherent account' of how security and insecurity occurs and is managed (Wilkinson,

2010: 95). Bottom-up anthropological studies focus on everyday security issues to consider how official narratives produce, as Grant (2015) describes it, 'a highly securitized environment in Rwanda'. This research identifies the role which state-controlled media plays in securitizing and silencing Rwandan citizens by discursively producing and reproducing internal and external security threats, and by reproducing monolithic victim/survivor and perpetrator identities in the post-conflict era (Burnet 2012; Thomson, 2013; Guglielmo, 2015). Knowledge production is conceptualized as a one-way, top-down process controlled by the RPF. Accordingly, mediatized security narratives are regarded as a propaganda tool, produced with the deliberate intent 'to influence the opinions' and to restrict the practices of Rwandan citizens 'through the transmission of ideas and values' that will 'serve the interests of the propagandists', the RPF elite (Melissen, 2007: 16–17). Less attention is paid to how the RPF engages in new public diplomacy in an effort to counter negative branding – either due to the legacies of past conflict, or in cases where other states and/or international actors produce and circulate negative images to discredit the country and the regime (Szondi, 2007: 17) – and in particular how security narratives about peacekeeping are incorporated into Rwanda's nation-branding strategy. As Beswick and Jowell observe, and as we explore in this chapter, Rwanda's 'contribution to peacekeeping' has become 'part of the post-genocide story of Rwanda's place in the world and part of the RPF approach to nation-building' with a population left polarized by genocide and civil war (Beswick and Jowell, 2014: 3).

## Public Diplomacy and Nation Branding after Conflict

New public diplomacy constitutes the process whereby states engage in dialogue with a variety of foreign audiences and actors to further foreign policy objectives. Dialogue takes place in the new media environment, wherein states no longer cede control over the production and dissemination of political narratives, and is facilitated by Web 2.0 technologies such as social media platforms. For Cottle (2006), the 'new media ecology' constitutes an international web of intersecting mediatized public spheres that, while dominated by state-sponsored media institutions of great and middle powers (notably the US, UK and France), provides space for small powers like Rwanda and marginalized and/or subordinated actors to engage in dialogue. For Chadwick, 'political communication now occurs in complex, hybrid assemblages of older and newer media, as a diverse array of actors, ranging from large professional news organizations to elite politicians to engaged citizens, participating in an incessant struggle to shape public discourse and define the political agenda' (2017: 184–85).

Nation branding is conceptualized as a communications, reputation management and relationship-building process by which a state *'as a whole* presents and represents itself' to other states within the international system (Szondi, 2007: 9). It is also a positioning strategy whereby governments or consultancy firms employed by governments use 'branding to alter or change the behaviour, attitudes, identity or image of a nation in a positive way' (Szondi, 2007: 9). Anholt defines nation branding as 'competitive identity', observing that globalization and changing power dynamics within the international system compel states to respond more strategically to 'global public opinion and market forces' by adopting a 'brand-orientated approach to competitiveness' (2007: 19).

Although an externally facing brand-management process, effective public affairs at home are perceived to garner support for the newly created nation brand amongst the domestic workforce. Without the nation brand being 'lived out' and performed by the workforce, and embedded in 'the internal structures, processes and cultures' of state institutions and national organizations and businesses, the 'external promise to the marketplace has little meaning' (Anholt, 2007: 6). In this sense, citizens must operate as 'brand ambassadors' if nation branding is to be a success (Szondi, 2007: 17). As a concept, nation branding is distinct from 'destination branding', which seeks inward investment by attracting visitors and boosting tourism (Szondi, 2007: 9; Gudjonsson, 2005); 'place branding', which focuses specifically on 'the presentation and representation of government policy to other publics'; and 'country-of-origin branding', which 'promotes exports (outward direction) or attract investors or a skilled workforce (inward direction)' (Szondi, 2008: 271). However, all three activities support the building and sustaining of the nation brand, and may be used to create 'sub-brands' of the nation brand, such as industries in any relevant sector. The 'nation brand identity' is drawn from a 'set of associations which the brand strategist seeks to create or maintain' (Fan, 2010: 101). A 'strong nation brand' can differentiate states from their 'competitors' (Henrikson, 2007: 23), and a 'distinctive and economically sustainable brand strategy is essential' if states wish to 'compete effectively in the international marketplace' (Anholt, 2007: 20).

Nation branding is an important form of soft power for all states, but holds a particular use-value for states that are transitioning out of conflict, such as Rwanda. As Szondi observes in his comparative analysis of post-conflict Balkan states, such states 'rely on the moral, financial and political support of more developed regions or nations' and are required to transform the negative image of conflict which hampers inward economic investment (2007: 10). For post-conflict states like Rwanda undergoing regime change, nation branding can be used strategically to garner legitimacy for the new government. The aim, therefore, is to transform the state's existing image from an 'impediment or a liability' into 'a competitive asset'. Szondi observes a pattern across the states in his study which indicates that transitional states shift from addressing 'internal affairs at the beginning of their transition' to focus their attention on 'their external image' up to a decade later. Anholt notes that:

> for poor and developing places, the intense competition for international funds, technology and skills transfer, inward investment, export markets and trade makes a clear positioning, a well-defined sense of national economic, social and political purpose, and a degree of influence over national reputation, more and more essential. (2007: 20)

Niche-building is a key function of nation branding and is often used to describe the patterned behaviour of small and middle powers. Niche-building is the process by which states develop a foreign policy to accrue political and economic capital with greater efficiency (see Cooper, 1997; Alden and Vieira, 2006; Henrikson, 2007). In addition to supporting 'coalition-building and cooperation-building' (Cooper, 1997: 9), foreign policy is designed to strategically 'concentrate resources in specific [issue] areas' that 'are best able to generate returns' for the state. Using public diplomacy tools, states adopt 'policy positions' that 'sell' at home in 'the domestic public sphere (the sphere of public affairs)', 'abroad to foreign publics' and/or networks of international actors ('the sphere of public diplomacy') (Henrikson, 2007: 66). Supporting niche-building strategies, both public affairs and public diplomacy can therefore help stabilize or reposition states within the international system. Having outlined national branding and niche diplomacy, we now turn to examine how the government of Rwanda engaged in nation branding during its post-conflict transition.

## Nation Branding in Rwanda

Although the RPF government ensured that official narratives about the genocide and civil war were promoted within Rwanda, during the early stages of the transition out of conflict and once the international community officially recognized the genocide, the international media produced racist narratives which portrayed Rwandans in two categories: perpetrators, who were hypermasculine, barbaric and uncivilized Hutu men; and victims, typically identified as Tutsi women and children, with emphasis placed on the large numbers of women who experienced conflict-related sexual violence (see Thompson, 2007; Holmes, 2013; Cieplak, 2017). Rwanda as a country was no longer the beautiful 'Suisse de l'Afrique' [Switzerland of Africa], but a bloody land of horror, littered with rotting bodies and later skeletons and poverty-stricken, helpless women, men and children, as well as thousands of incarcerated Hutu perpetrators. On the borders of Rwanda, the refugee crises in eastern Zaire and Tanzania confirmed Rwanda's failed state status and the requirement for the international community to step in and rebuild the country. For the RPF, these racist stereotypes were the payoff for ensuring that the international media memorialized the genocide, as opposed to the civil war, which had been the dominant media narrative in 1994. During these early years, Kagame frequently spoke of the requirement of Rwandans to rise up and 'restore their dignity'. Yet strategic efforts to transform Rwanda's negative nation brand began in 2010, when the RPF had stabilized its political power base and was in a better position to focus on developing its external brand image. Just before the 2010 presidential elections, the *Guardian* reported that Kagame had appointed London public relations firm Racepoint to develop Rwanda's nation brand to attract inward investment. At the time, Racepoint's managing director was quoted saying, 'You used to Google Rwanda and the first thing you would see would be about genocide. Now we are feeding content and stories to journalists about the economy and culture. A lot of it is about images' (Booth, 2010). Leading up to the twentieth commemoration of the genocide in April 1994, the RPF government appointed London-based PR agency Portland Communications, founded in 2001, to assist in placing positive stories about Rwanda and to cover the commemorations in the international media. Portland Communications held briefing sessions with several British-based academics to discuss coverage of Rwanda. However, they had few connections with journalists on the ground and struggled to source personal-interest stories about Rwandans. Portland Communications was later dropped by the RPF government on the grounds that the PR agency did not understand Rwanda's complex politics and history. In December 2014, the Ministry of Trade announced that Rwanda was to embark on a 'made in Rwanda' brand to help address the trade deficit and develop Rwanda's manufacturing sector. At home, the government launched a 'Buy Local – Twigire' campaign (Government of Rwanda, 2014). More recently, in 2017 the government appointed The PC Agency to 'build its brand in the UK' at a time when RwandaAir had launched its first direct flight from London Gatwick to Kigali. The emphasis here was on developing Rwanda's destination brand. Paul Charles, founder and CEO of The PC Agency, commented in a press release announcing the deal that 'Rwanda now has the leadership team, the product and the infrastructure to attract premium travellers' (O'Donnell, 2017).

Nation branding is considered integral to implementing Rwanda's National Export Strategy (2011). The strategy observes that 'national branding consists of developing and communicating an image – both internally and externally

– based on a country's positive values and perceptions relevant to export development' (Government of Rwanda, 2011: 25). The strategy also highlights the requirement for Rwanda to engage in niche-building: 'small developing countries such as Rwanda face budgetary and operational challenges while forging their national brands abroad. As such, Rwanda will explore creative and cost-efficient ways to create, position and communicate Brand Rwanda' (Government of Rwanda, 2011: 25). That 'Rwanda's brand is not well established internationally and suffers from unwanted associations' is a priority concern for the RPF. The strategy continues: 'Rwanda often receives unfair press through questionable sources. In a competitive global market, this association can hinder product positioning in key exports [*sic*] markets. A positive brand must be established for Rwandan products internationally in order to convey the true spirit of Rwanda'. In response, the strategy proposes that 'Rwanda's global brand image' should be managed:

> impressions about a country's brand are formed in different ways including international media, events, academic literature, arts and culture, etc. Rwanda will develop a strategy for identifying the different channels through which these impressions are formed, as well as a strategy for aggressively managing its brand position in these channels. (Government of Rwanda, 2011: 25–26)

We agree with Beswick and Jowell (2014) that the RPF considers peacekeeping to be an important component of 'Brand Rwanda'. However, we also suggest that the regime recognizes the need to market Rwanda as a competitive TCC in order to secure contracts with the DPKO and accrue financial support and military assistance from donor states. Therefore, we argue that mediatized security narratives are a nation-branding and public diplomacy tool used by the RPF government to position Rwanda as a competitive TCC in the eyes of foreign publics, significant security actors within the UN, including the DPKO, and donor agencies that sponsor security-sector reform and peacekeeping capacity-building programmes.

## Rwanda's TCC Brand Identity

In the following discussion, we show how mediatized security narratives were used by the state-owned *The New Times* to create Rwanda's TCC brand identity from January 2008 to January 2017 and examine how the RPF evolved the TCC brand identity away from peacekept nation to discursively reposition Rwanda as an emerging strategic player in peacekeeping policy and practice. We identify three phases in the development of Rwanda's TCC brand identity: start-up, consolidation and power-maximization.

*Phase One: Start-Up (2008–2010)*

In earlier *The New Times* media discourse, news stories appear to be less strategically placed and public relations efforts less sophisticated. At this point, Rwanda was deploying to missions in the African region, notably the hybrid African Union AU/UN peacekeeping operation UNAMID. News and current affairs articles focus on explaining and justifying Rwanda's recent entry into peacekeeping and reporting on the increase of deployed troops to around 3,200 by 2009. Types of news story include the capacity-building security forces, announcing the deployment of troops and their return, reporting the deaths of troops and injuries sustained in the mission area, announcing when troops have been awarded medals of honour by the AU/UN, explaining logistical challenges for troops once deployed and providing informational briefings to Rwandan citizens on the conflict.

Rwandan peacekeepers are not expected to embody or 'live-out' a Rwandan nation brand, as Anholt suggests, and troops deployed to UNAMID are described as 'hybrid peacekeepers' rather than 'Rwandan peacekeepers', reflecting the RPF's focus on assimilating Rwandans into the AU/UN peacekeeping force (Musoni, 2007a). However, early security narratives are used discursively to construct and reproduce the new RPF-constructed national culture, as well as the institutional culture of the Rwanda Defence Force. In an article published on the RPF government's national 'Liberation Day', 7 July 2008, *The New Times* reports on how UNAMID Deputy Joint Special Representative (DJSR) Henry Anyidoho, who had led the contingent of Ghanaian peacekeepers in Rwanda at the height of the Genocide against the Tutsi, encouraged Rwandan peacekeepers to 'participate in the process of restoring normalcy' in Darfur and to 'do their jobs in a noble manner', thereby emphasizing the dignity of Rwandans. The article then cites Rwanda's Deputy Force Commander, Major General Karake Karenzi, who links the RPF's security narrative, explaining Rwanda's commitment to peacekeeping to prevent genocide ('Never Again'), with the importance of forging a new military culture as part of the process of national reconciliation. The article states: 'Referring to the tragic events of the genocide in Rwanda, he urged the Rwandan peacekeepers in UNAMID to ensure that they are different from those who carried out the genocide' and to 'build on what Rwanda has achieved since liberation 14 years ago' (Tumwebaze, 2008).

During this start-up phase, there is evidence of niche-building in the construction of security narratives that in later years become central to Rwanda's TCC brand identity. Niche areas focus on Rwanda's ability to contribute to delivering mission objectives at the operational and tactical levels, but also aim to distinguish Rwanda for its professionalism and capabilities, setting it apart from both its former negative image as a victim and peacekept nation, and from other competitive TCCs from the Global South, such as India, Pakistan and other African TCCs. Quotations from influential actors engaged in UN peacekeeping, or representatives of more powerful states, are used frequently to strengthen Rwanda's legitimacy as an effective and reliable TCC.

Six niche areas are identified. Niche Area 1 suggests that Rwanda is committed to regional peace and security. For example, in August 2009, it is reported that a 'delegation of senior US Military officers praised the achievements of the Rwanda Defence Force [...] saying that Rwanda is contributing greatly to restoration of security on the continent' (Musoni, 2009).

Niche Area 2 makes the case that Rwanda is committed to protecting civilians. In July 2009, Karake recounts his decision-making process as Deputy Force Commander of UNAMID, indicating that he chose to risk his troops' lives rather than 'abandon the populations' around RDF 'positions' (Tumwebaze, 2009a). In August 2009, the 'Americans' are claimed to have said that 'the RDF has proven to be a force committed to putting the interests of the people first' (Musoni, 2009). Niche Area 3 posits that Rwanda offers UN peacekeeping experienced, professional, disciplined and hardworking forces. In a February 2011 report on the UN Mission in Sudan (UNMIS), the Police Commissioner praises Rwandan police peacekeepers for their 'exemplary performance, professionalism, discipline and good conduct' and a direct link is made between the behaviour of Rwandan police officers and the willingness of the UN to deploy Rwandan uniformed personnel. The Commissioner continues that 'as a result of the above, the Rwanda contingent in UNMIS grew from five police advisors in February' (Tumwebaze, 2011). In July 2009, the RDF's performance is described as 'outstanding' (Tumwebaze, 2009b). UNAMID Deputy Force Commander and RDF Major General Karake also describes the RDF as 'not just a "textbook" military force' but 'a force both with field experience, gained over the years, gathered in different conflict settings and theatres of operation and a professional force that has had conventional military training' (Tumwebaze, 2009a).

Niche Area 4 suggests that Rwanda draws on its previous experience in post-conflict development and peacebuilding to support delivery of AU/UN mission objectives. For example, in July 2008, it is announced that Sudan People's Liberation Army (SPLA) representatives will visit Rwanda on a 'study tour' in order to 'gain experience of how [Rwanda] managed to transform its guerrilla force into a professional army' (Musoni, 2008). Niche Area 5 promotes the ability of Rwandans to work well in multicultural teams. In November 2010, General Nyamvumba remarks that 'We work with colleagues from other sections like human rights, civilians [*sic*] affairs [and] police', before observing the logistical challenges facing Rwanda (Tumwebaze, 2010). Finally, Niche Area 6 posits that Rwandans have good relations with local populations in the host country. In another move to demonstrate the value of Rwandan peacekeepers, *The New Times* emphasizes positive relations with host communities but conceals the tensions and difficulties which peacekeepers often encounter. In a July 2008 article, RDF Brigadier General Rutaha thanks 'the people of Sudan, especially the Darfurians, for contributing to the welfare of Rwandan peacekeepers in Darfur' (Tumwebaze, 2008).

Later, *The New Times* publishes more articles on the successes of deployed Rwandan military leaders and their increasing value to the UN. There are also efforts to transform Rwanda's status as a recipient of foreign intervention in the early 1990s and to discursively reposition Rwanda as integral to international peacekeeping. For example, in October 2007, the RDF's Chief of Defence Staff General James Kaberebe remarks that 'the RDF has achieved global prominence in a very short time because of its discipline, commitment and excellent leadership' (Musoni, 2007b). In another article, RDF Brigadier General Rutaha claims, 'Rwanda [is] now an important player on the international scene, contributing peacekeepers to missions in Haiti, Comoros, Ivory Coast, Liberia, Chad and Sudan' (Tumwebaze, 2008).

*Phase Two: Consolidation (2011–2014)*
During this phase, *The New Times* reporting becomes more sophisticated, and articles often draw on several or all of the niche areas identified above to consolidate the discursive positioning of Rwanda as an important security actor in international peacekeeping. Particular attention is paid to garnering support for the newly created TCC brand identity and brand image among Rwanda's peacekeeping workforce, and news stories announcing new deployments and troop rotations become an opportunity for the RPF to remind Rwandan peacekeepers of the need to 'live out' or perform Brand Rwanda. As Anholt describes, Rwanda's 'external promise to the [peacekeeping] marketplace has little meaning' unless the TCC brand identity is embedded in 'the internal structures, processes and cultures' of Rwanda's peacekeeping contingents (2007: 9). Troops are told to be disciplined during deployment. In May 2014 it is observed that 'The Rwanda Defence Force's distinguished reputation of discipline is largely why it is respected worldwide and must be jealously guarded by all means' (Karuhanga, 2012a). Rwandans are also repeatedly asked to ensure 'that the Rwandan flag continues to rise', emphasizing their function in enabling Rwanda to accrue political and economic capital through international peacekeeping. In September 2012, police peacekeepers deploying to Haiti are told to 'execute your duties professionally and strive to raise our country's flag high. Rwanda has earned itself

a good name on the international scene' (Tumwebaze, 2012). In February 2013, soon-to-be-deployed peacekeepers are 'challenged' by the Army Chief of Defence Staff to 'maintain a high degree of discipline in the execution of their daily activities' and to 'know his or her role to make sure that our flag continues to rise' (Kabeera, 2013). The flag metaphor operates on several levels, indicating that Rwanda is a young nation that has risen out of the ashes, and suggesting that Rwandans are working hard to elevate themselves and to restore their dignity following their shameful transgression during genocide and civil war.

Articles about battalion rotations also provide an opportunity for the RPF to reaffirm Rwanda's position as a 'key player' in international peacekeeping and within African regional security architecture. January 2014 marked Rwanda's first deployment to the CAR, to work alongside the French. Related news stories emphasize the RDF's willingness and ability to use force to protect civilians while building close relations with the local population, and Rwanda's commitment to peacekeeping is linked back to the failure of the international community to intervene during the 1994 genocide in Rwanda (Musoni, 2014).

Two more niche areas are added during this consolidation phase: Niche Area 7 emphasizes Rwanda's official support for gender equality and women's empowerment. Increasingly, journalists draw links between Rwanda's 'feminist' domestic and foreign policies when the UN calls for more female police peacekeepers in order to mobilize a female peacekeeping workforce. Articles emphasize the specific use-value of female peacekeepers as 'human rights ambassadors' providing assistance to women and children within the mission area (Asiimwe, 2012). Niche Area 8 positions Rwanda as a regional hub for peacekeeping training. For example, in May 2012, 50 'high-ranking military and civilian personnel from around the world' attended a UN course 'for senior leaders' (Karuhanga, 2012b). In August 2013, a regional 'peacebuilding course' was established by Rwanda Peace Academy in partnership with the UN Institute for Training and Research ('Peace Building Course', 2013).

*Phase Three: Power-Maximization (Late 2014 Onwards)*
Phase Three marks a significant transition period as the RPF seeks to transform Rwanda's TCC brand identity from a tactical/operational-level peacekeeping provider into an emerging strategic player in international peacekeeping. In October 2012, Rwanda had taken up its two-year non-permanent seat on the UN Security Council, which enabled the small African state and small power to exercise a greater voice at the UN. The ability of peacekeepers to 'live out' and perform the Rwandan TCC brand identity continues. Peacekeepers are Rwandan ambassadors who must showcase the best of the country.

However, throughout 2015 and 2016, Rwandan peacekeepers become even more regulated after French peacekeepers are accused of sexual exploitation and abuse in the CAR. Prior to deployment, police peacekeepers are 'urged to be a value-addition to safety, security and peacebuilding in CAR' and to 'maintain their professional conduct' ('Police Rotate', 2016).

All eight niche areas are mobilized in *The New Times* media discourse, but subtle changes in perspective hint at the shift in the positioning of Rwanda from peacekept nation to strategic security actor in international peacekeeping. There is now less focus on Rwanda operating in partnership with fellow post-conflict African communities such as the Darfurians. Rwandan peacekeepers are instead portrayed as their 'mentors and advisors' (Kagera, 2016), demonstrating Rwanda's leadership capacity at the operational level in peacekeeping. When Niche Area 7 is mobilized (Rwanda's commitment to gender equality and women's empowerment), Rwandan women are depicted as empowered security actors assisting passive female 'African' victims (Kagera, 2016). Building multilateral relationships with other TCCs and donor states such as the UK, the US and the Czech is are also prioritized. Reports focus on how Rwanda is providing more specialist functions to the peacekeeping marketplace, including a more advanced Level II Hospital to provide medical assistance to peacekeepers deployed in the CAR and more 'homegrown' initiatives such as hygiene campaigns that incorporate the distribution of 'made in Rwanda' hygiene bins – thereby enabling the RPF to promote Brand Rwanda exported products ('Police Rotate', 2016).

After 2015, the RPF begins to mimic the niche-building strategies that are often used by middle powers such as Canada and Australia, which emphasize 'entrepreneurial flair and technical competence' (Cooper, 1997: 9). This can be seen in the promotion of the 'Kigali Principles on the Protection of Civilians', a non-binding set of pledges which identify how to implement peacekeeping best practice. The Kigali Principles were drawn up at the High-Level International Conference on the Protection of Civilians held in Kigali, Rwanda on 28–29 May 2015. In *The New Times* media discourse, Rwanda is depicted as a 'catalyst' and 'facilitator' of peacekeeping policy and practice. As a catalyst, Rwanda is a generator of 'political energy around a particular issue' – namely, how to improve the protection of civilians. As a facilitator, Rwanda engages in the 'planning and hosting of meetings, setting priorities for future activity and drawing up rhetorical declarations and manifestos' (Cooper, 1997: 9). From mid-2015 onwards, articles increasingly depict external engagement with Rwanda, as more and more UN member states endorse the Kigali Principles, and by emphasizing the acclaim Rwanda has accrued during international conventions, notably the UK Defence Ministerial on Peacekeeping (September 2016) and the UN

Peacekeeping Conference in Vancouver, Canada (November 2017). Noting that 'nearly every speaker' in Vancouver 'who took the floor heaped praise on Rwandan peacekeepers for their professionalism', Rwanda, as a catalyst and facilitator, is discursively constructed as an emerging strategic player in peacekeeping: 'Rwanda has helped change the face of peacekeeping. Gone are the days when peacekeepers were there to be seen, patrolling in their armoured vehicles but crossed their arms and failed to protect civilians when needed' ('Rwandan Peacekeepers', 2017). Similarly, in December 2017, *The New Times* reports that Rwanda has 'become a strong advocate for reforming peacekeeping across the world. The latest effort is the Kigali Principles on the Protection of Civilians adopted in May 2015. More than 40 countries have adopted the set of practices designed to efficiently protect those at risk' (Habumuremyi, 2017).

## The Precariousness of TCC Brand Identities

So far, we have made the case that the RPF attempted to develop and evolve its TCC brand identity from operational/tactical level peacekeeping provider to emergent strategic player in international peacekeeping. Using as a case study three social media events that prompted a twitter storm among RPF elites, we now turn to briefly examine how the RPF government and its supporters seek to protect and stabilize Rwanda's TCC brand image in a changing global media environment. In particular, we focus on influential Rwanda Twitter users, identified as the #RwOT (Rwandese on Twitter) community. We define this group as an elite-intellectual online community of Rwandans, comprising mainly young women and men in their thirties. Tweeting in both English and Kinyarwanda, the community includes journalists, columnists, researchers and consultants, artists/musicians, degree-educated Rwandan-born citizens, returnees and family members of the elites in power.

As we have shown, distinguishing Rwandans as professional and disciplined troops is a central niche area of Rwanda's TCC brand identity. However, Rwanda's TCC brand image was threatened when on 28 March 2016 international news agency France24 used a photographic image of a Rwandan police peacekeeper in an online article reporting allegations of child abuse in the CAR, which had actually involved Moroccan and Burundian troops. In the image, the Rwandan flag was clearly visible on the left arm of the police peacekeeper. Yolande Makolo, President Kagame's communications director, was the first to point out the error that day, tweeting, 'I know they do it intentionally to disturb Rwanda, or to create confusion'. Her remark prompted a debate among Rwandans on Twitter as to the intentions of associating Rwandan peacekeepers with sexual exploitation and abuse. The debate ended quickly when France24 removed the image from the article the same day, and some Rwandan Twitter users thanked the agency.

A year later, on 22 March 2017, France24 tweeted the same image of the Rwandan police peacekeeper when reporting on the case of six French soldiers accused of sexually abusing children in the CAR. This led to several reactions from the #RwOT community. As an intellectual-elite group that frequently retweets and 'likes' social media from the official accounts of the President of Rwanda, the Rwanda Defence Force and the Rwanda National Police, this group often engages in dialogue with international actors, and appears to play a central role in delivering the RPF's new public diplomacy to, as the Rwandan government describes in Rwanda's National Export Strategy, 'aggressively manage' Rwanda's brand position on social media. Collectively, the #RwOT community share a deep sense of patriotism and the will to defend the image of Rwanda globally. The use of the Rwandan police peacekeeper image was not interpreted as an oversight by a French media corporation, but as an intentional attack on Rwanda. Ange Kagame, the daughter of President Paul Kagame, was the first to react on Twitter, followed by several #RwOT users who started the hashtag #SomeoneTellFrance24, in order to unveil the deliberate intention of France24 (and the French government) to undermine Rwanda's TCC image.

In response, #RwOT members began to tweet positive images of Rwandan peacekeepers protecting civilians. Rwanda National Police was the first to do so on 30 March 2017 via the official account @Rwandapolice. This included the image of a Rwandan female police peacekeeper sitting with Darfurian women and children in an internally displaced persons camp. Unarmed and holding a baby, she stands in direct contrast to the image of the sexually abusive, armed Rwandan male peacekeeper implied by France24. The image was retweeted and 'liked' more than 80 times, demonstrating significantly higher than usual engagement with @Rwandapolice generated social media.[2] A second image, which was tweeted 40 times, showed Rwandan peacekeepers hard at work in a challenging environment in the aftermath of Hurricane Matthew, which took the lives of some 1,000 Haitians and left 1.5 million in need of humanitarian aid in 2016. On the same day, a third image depicted Rwandan peacekeepers in the CAR on VIP escort duty. The combination of the three images aimed to restore the reputation internationally of Rwandan peacekeepers as compassionate, defending the most vulnerable civilians (women and children), but also as brave and trusted by

---

[2] According to an analysis undertaken between February 2016 and February 2018 using the online twitter analytics service. See https://socialbearing.com/search/user.

the UN. Several #RwOT users also took the opportunity to highlight French peacekeepers' misconduct in the CAR, and to explicate their interpretation of France's involvement during the 1994 genocide through the juxtaposition of images and cartoons. For example, one RPF supporter tweeted '#Rwandan peacekeepers are renowned for humanity & heroism #French peacekeepers for barbarism & cruelty #FactsofHistory'. France24 removed the image of the male Rwandan peacekeeper a few days later, blaming an automated process and lack of editing. France24 representative Sylvan Attal answered to the hashtag #SomeoneTellFrance24, tweeting: '#SomeoneTellFrance24: The picture was automatically published with an AFP wire. That was an unfortunate choice and we removed the post'. This time the #RwOT community was not satisfied and asked for an official apology. A petition generated on www.change.org was signed by 175 people. France24 did not apologize.[3]

On 26 February 2018, a news story published online by Radio France Internationale (@RFI) reporting that UN peacekeepers had been accused of sexual exploitation and abuse in South Sudan was accompanied by an image depicting Rwandan military peacekeepers, with the Rwandan flag clearly visible on their arms. This time the troops involved were Ghanaian police peacekeepers. Reactions from the #RwOT community were unanimous in accusing France of having a hidden agenda to tarnish Rwanda's TCC brand image, but also accusing RFI of unprofessionalism and ignorance. The hashtag #SomeoneTellRFI was used by #RwOT community members in tweets, accusing RFI of racism and suggesting that they should 'go back to school and learn flags' or 'stop thinking that all black people are the same', since they 'confused' Ghanaians with Rwandans. It was also suggested that RFI should 'refresh their photo gallery'. Other members of the #RwOT community used the hashtag #TweetLikeRFI ironically in tweets created to mimic the kind of error produced by RFI. For example, one paired the news of Ghanaian peacekeepers' alleged sexual misconduct with images of French peacekeepers. Another tweet discussing warm and sunny Kigali was paired with an image of the Eiffel Tower in the snow. In response, @RFI apologized and promptly replaced the offending image of Rwanda peacekeepers, thanking #RwOT members for their 'sense of humour'.

---

[3] See 'Someone Tell France24: French Prosecutors Want Central African Republic Child-Rape Case Dropped', at https://www.change.org/p/someone-tell-france-24-to-stop-using-rwanda-peace-keepers-images-on-french-troops-crime-articles?recruiter=17041031&utm_source=share_petition&utm_medium=copylink (consulted on 17 February 2018).

## Conclusion

Drawing on theories of nation branding and new public diplomacy, this chapter has examined how mediatized security narratives serve to 'market' Rwanda as a competitive TCC as one aspect of a broader nation-branding exercise after genocide and civil war. It has been argued that mediatized security narratives are used by the RPF to 'niche-build' in an attempt to transition the negative nation brand of a peacekept nation and reposition Rwanda as an emerging strategic player in peacekeeping. Reflecting on the importance of nation branding for the RPF government, we have analysed the print and online media discourse of the state-sponsored national newspaper *The New Times*. Three discursive phases were identified: start-up, consolidation and power-maximization. In the first two phases, the RPF aimed to transition Rwanda's unplanned nation brand following genocide and civil war in the 1990s from a liability into a nation brand of significant asset value – for both the UN and the RPF. This was achieved by mobilizing eight niche issue areas, which allowed the RPF to economize its resources by prioritizing foreign policy areas. In the third phase, we examined how the RPF mimicked the niche-building strategies conventionally associated with middle powers to position Rwanda as both a catalyst and facilitator of peacekeeping policy and practice. We then reflected on how nation branding is a precarious exercise that can become destabilized – not just by external actors, but by the elites in power themselves. In conducting this analysis, we make a significant contribution to understanding how the RPF seeks to accrue political and economic capital through engaging in peacekeeping (and narrating its engagement). We also contribute to understanding how elites that govern contemporary African states operate as agentive subjects in international relations and attempt to maximize power despite their often-marginal position within the international system.

## Works Cited

Alden, Chris, and Marco Antonio Vieira. 2006. 'The New Diplomacy of the South: South Africa, Brazil, India and Trilateralism'. *Third World Quarterly* 26.7: 1077–95.

Anholt, Simon. 2007. *Competitive Identity: The New Brand Management for Nations, Cities and Regions*. Basingstoke: Palgrave Macmillan.

Asiimwe, Bosco R. 2012. 'Women to Constitute 30 Percent of Police'. *The New Times* 1 June.

Beswick, Danielle, and Marco Jowell. 2014. *Contributor Profile: Rwanda*. IPI. Providing for Peacekeeping Project. Available at http://www.providingfor peaceeeping.org/2015/03/30/peacekeeping-contributor-profile-rwanda/ (consulted on 31 January 2018).

Booth, Robert. 2010. 'Does this Picture Make You Think of Rwanda?' *Guardian* 3 August. Available at https://www.theguardian.com/media/2010/aug/03/london-pr-rwanda-saudi-arabia (consulted on 31 January 2018).

Burnet, Jennie, E. 2012. *Genocide Lives in Us: Women, Memory and Silence in Rwanda*. Madison, WI: Wisconsin University Press.

Chadwick, Andrew. 2017. *The Hybrid Media System: Politics and Power*. Oxford: Oxford University Press.

Cieplak, Piotr. 2017. *Death, Image, Memory: The Genocide in Rwanda and its Aftermath in Photography and Documentary Film*. Basingstoke: Palgrave Macmillan.

Cooper, Andrew F. 1997. *Niche Diplomacy: Middle Powers after the Cold War*. New York: St Martin's Press.

Cottle, Simon. 2006. *Mediatized Conflict*. Maidenhead: Open University Press.

Fan, Ying. 2010. 'Branding the Nation: Towards a better Understanding'. *Place Branding and Public Diplomacy* 6: 97–103.

Government of Rwanda. 2011. *Rwanda National Export Strategy (NES)*. Available at http://www.minicom.gov.rw/fileadmin/minicom_publications/Strategies/National_Export_Strategy.pdf (consulted on 31 January 2018).

—. 2014. 'Rwanda Embarks on "Made in Rwanda" Brand'. Available at http://www.minicom.gov.rw/index.php?id=24&tx_ttnews%5Btt_news%5D=912&cHash=fc72f3dc09ab3c0c08a81faa2aee8b21 (consulted on 31 January 2018).

Grant, Andrea Mariko. 2015. 'Quiet Insecurity and Quiet Agency in Post-Genocide Rwanda'. *Etnofoor* 27.2: 15–36.

Gudjonsson, Hlynur. 2005. 'Nation Branding'. *Place Branding* 1.3: 283–98.

Guglielmo, Federica. 2015. 'Medicalizing Violence: Victimhood, Trauma and Corporeality in Post-Genocide Rwanda'. *Central African Studies* 7.2: 146–63.

Habumuremyi, Pierre-Damien. 2017. 'Rwanda Defence Forces: The Engine of Rwanda's Resilience'. *The New Times* 4 December.

Henrikson, Alan K. 'Niche Diplomacy in the World Public Arena: The Global "Corners" of Canada and Norway'. In Jan Melissen (ed.), *The New Public Diplomacy: Soft Power in International Relations*. Basingstoke: Palgrave Macmillan: 67–87.

Holmes, Georgina. 2013. *Women and War in Rwanda: Gender, Media and the Representation of Genocide*. London and New York: I.B. Tauris.

—. 2014. 'Gendering the Rwanda Defence Force: A Critical Assessment'. *Journal of Intervention and Statebuilding* 8.4: 321–33.

—. 2015. 'Negotiating Narratives of Human Rights Abuses: Image Management in Conflicts in Eastern Democratic Republic of Congo'. In Julia Gallagher (ed.), *Images of Africa: Creation, Negotiation and Subversion*. Manchester: Manchester University Press: 144–66.

—. 2018. 'Gender and the Military in Post-Genocide Rwanda'. In E. Bemporad and Joyce W. Warren (eds), *Women and Genocide: Survivors, Victims, Perpetrators*. Bloomington, IN: Indiana University Press: 223–49.

—. 2019. 'Situating Agency, Embodied Practices and Norm Implementation in Peacekeeping Training'. *International Peacekeeping* 26.1: 55–84.

Jowell, Marco. 2010. 'Cohesion through Socialization: Liberation, Tradition and Modernity in the Forging of the Rwanda Defence Force (RDF)'. *Journal of Eastern African Studies* 8.2: 278–93.

Kabeera, Eric. 2013. 'Rotation of Peacekeepers in South Sudan Kicks Off'. *The New Times* 16 February.

Kagera, Thomas. 2016. 'Cause of Humanity Drives Rwandan Peacekeeping Interventions'. *The New Times* 29 May.

Karuhanga, James. 2012a. 'Rallying Call for Professionalism in Darfur'. *The New Times* 14 May.

—. 2012b. 'Peacekeeping Course Opens in Kigali Today'. *The New Times* 21 May.

Melissen, Jan. 2007. 'The New Public Diplomacy: Between Theory and Practice'. In Jan Melissen (ed.), *The New Pubic Diplomacy: Soft Power in International Relations*. Basingstoke: Palgrave Macmillan: 3–27.

Musoni, Edwin. 2007a. 'Fifty RDF Peacekeepers Off for UN Mission'. *The New Times* 25 October.

—. 2007b. 'Gen. Kabarebe Salutes RDF on Darfur Mission'. *The New Times* 28 October.

—. 2008. 'SPLA Condemns Attack on Darfur Peacekeepers'. *The New Times* 28 July.

—. 2009. 'US Military Lauds Rwanda's Darfur Mission'. *The New Times* 11 August.

—. 2014. 'Rwanda Peacekeepers Arrive in CAR'. *The New Times* 17 January.

O'Donnell, Richard. 2017. 'Rwanda Chooses The PC Agency to Build its Brand in the UK'. Available at http://www.gorkana.com/2017/05/rwanda-chooses-the-pc-agency-to-build-its-brand-in-the-uk/ (consulted on 31 January 2018).

'Peace Building Course Opens at Rwanda Peace Academy'. *The New Times* 21 August 2013.

'Police Rotate Peacekeeping Contingent in CAR'. *The New Times* 11 October 2016.

Pottier, Johan. 2002. *Re-Imagining Rwanda: Conflict, Survival and Disinformation in the Late Twentieth Century*. Cambridge: Cambridge University Press.

Pruitt, Lesley J. 2016. *The Women in Blue Helmets: Gender, Policing, and the UN's First All-Female Peacekeeping Unit*. Oakland, CA: University of California Press.

Purdeková, Andrea. 2011. '"Even if I Am Not Here, There Are So Many Eyes": Surveillance and State Reach in Rwanda'. *The Journal of Modern African Studies* 49.3: 475–97.

Purdeková, Andrea, Nina Wilén and Philip Renteyns. 2018. 'Militarisation of Governance after Conflict: Beyond the Rebel-to-Ruler Frame – the Case of Rwanda'. *Third World Quarterly* 39.1: 158–74.

'Rwandan Peacekeepers Have Set the Bar Very High'. *The New Times* 17 November 2017.

Straus, Scott, and Lars Waldorf (eds). 2011. *Remaking Rwanda: State Building and Human Rights after Mass Violence.* Madison, WI: University of Wisconsin Press.

Szondi, György. 2007. 'The Role and Challenges of Country Branding in Transition Countries: The Central and Eastern European Experience'. *Place Branding and Public Diplomacy* 3.1: 8–20.

—. 2008. 'Public Diplomacy and Nation Branding: Conceptual Similarities and Differences'. Discussion papers in Diplomacy. Netherlands Institute of International Relations 'Clingendael'. Available at http://www.kamudiplo-masisi.org/pdf/nationbranding.pdf (consulted on 31 January 2018).

Thompson, Allan (ed.). 2007. *The Media and the Rwandan Genocide.* London: Pluto Press.

Thomson, Susan. 2013. *Whispering Truth to Power: Everyday Resistance to Reconciliation in Postgenocide Rwanda.* Madison, WI: University of Wisconsin Press.

Tumwebaze, Peterson. 2008. 'Rwandese Troops in Darfur Celebrate Rwanda Liberation Day'. *The New Times* 7 July.

—. 2009a. 'Karake Speaks on Darfur Experience'. *The New Times* 1 July.

—. 2009b. 'Karake Speaks Out on Darfur Mission'. *The New Times* 2 July.

—. 2010. 'Unamid Has Made Tremendous Progress, Says Force Commander Gen. Nyamvumba'. *The New Times* 11 November.

—. 2011. 'Rwandan Police Honoured in Sudan'. *The New Times* 6 February.

—. 2012. 'Rwandan Peacekeepers Leave for Haiti'. *The New Times* 27 September.

Waal de, Alex. 2015. *The Real Politics of the Horn of Africa.* Cambridge: Polity Press.

Wilén, Nina. 2018. 'Examining the Links between Security Sector Reform and Peacekeeping Troop Contribution in Post-Conflict States'. *Journal of Intervention and Statebuilding* 12.1: 64–79.

Wilkinson, Cai. 2010. 'The Limits of Spoken Words: From Meta-Narratives to Experiences of Security'. In Thierry Balzacq (ed.), *Securitization Theory: How Security Problems Emerge and Dissolve.* Abingdon: Routledge: 94–115.

# 'One Rwanda For All Rwandans': (Un)covering the Twa in Post-Genocide Rwanda

*Meghan Laws, Richard Ntakirutimana and Bennett Collins[1]*

The unity of the Rwandans is the expression of a historic will, an ancient and deliberate choice: the Rwandans have found themselves to be three (Hutu, Twa and Tutsi) and they have decided to be one (Rwandans). Since then, the nation of Rwanda was not an association of ethnic groups but an entity of citizens who had chosen to live together.

Servilien Manzi Sebasoni (2007: 10)

Why are the other Rwandans called Rwandan, and why are the Batwa called historically marginalized? [...] We are also Rwandan [...] we want to be Rwandan. We have the thirst to be Rwandan, but the poverty stops us. We want that our state makes it possible for us to be at the same level as other Rwandans.

Jean-Bosco (personal interview, 2016)

---

[1] The authors' names do not appear in any particular order. We want to avoid falling into the unsaid academic tradition of ranking based on contribution or where we fall in the alphabet, and instead make clear that this paper would not be possible without the teamwork and individual hard work of each author. The authors would like to thank the African Initiative for Mankind Progress Organization, the Third Generation Project, the University of St Andrews, Queen's University, and the Aegis Trust in their support of our research.

125

Pursuing reconciliation and building national unity after mass violence is a uniquely challenging task as victims and perpetrators – albeit rarely straightforwardly defined – must live side by side, and struggle to rebuild broken social networks, and reimagine their political and moral community (Purdeková, 2015: 5). Rwanda fits this description, for it is difficult to fathom the degree of disruption, devastation and social anomy the genocide produced both inside Rwanda and throughout the wider Great Lakes region. The 1994 Genocide against the Tutsi claimed the lives of an estimated 800,000 Rwandans,[2] produced millions of refugees, generated the chaotic return of hundreds of thousands of people and catalysed a continental war in the neighbouring Democratic Republic of the Congo (Reyntjens, 2009: 10–44). Brutal massacres were carried out on Rwandan soil by 'intimate enemies', many of whom were acquaintances, neighbours, friends and even family (Purdeková, 2015: 5). In its aftermath, the genocide heightened tensions between Hutu and Tutsi, and as time marched on, generated a complex web of new social identities related to heterogeneous experiences of marginalization, exile, ethnic and regional violence, and state-sponsored violence, as well as nationality, language and region of exile.

The post-genocide regime's response to this kaleidoscope of complexity is to promote the discourse of *ubumwe n'ubumwiyunge* – unity and reconciliation – twin concepts the government generally defines together. As a corollary, state authorities have implemented an ambitious social re-engineering project, which entails promoting a 'unifying' Banyarwanda identity, epitomized by the ubiquitous popular slogan – 'One Rwanda for All Rwandans' – and predicated on the current government's version of Rwanda's history. National unity is naturalized as 'a traditional value which must be reasserted, reinforced and taught to all Rwandans', while ethnicity is presented as a sinister, foreign construct associated with the political ideology of oppression and violence which caused the genocide (Office of the President of the Republic, 1999: 16). On this basis, the government seeks to 'de-ethnicize' political space (see Purdeková, 2008; 2015), and to eradicate the 'bad mentalities' of 'divisionism' and 'genocide ideology' that continue to circulate among *génocidaires*, genocide sympathizers and

---

[2] We use the figure 800,000 with some reservation, simply because it is the most commonly cited. The exact number of victims remains unknown, and estimates should be thought of as rough approximations based on census data. Estimates by NGOs and researchers typically range from 500,000 to 800,000 deaths while the government of Rwanda cited a much larger figure of nearly one million in its 2002 report. For a more detailed discussion of estimated death tolls, see Reyntjens (1997).

negationists.[3] 'Hutu', 'Tutsi' and 'Twa' are no longer recognized social categories, and public expression of ethnic identity outside the frame of the genocide is proscribed to replace atavistic substate loyalties with a progressive form of national belonging.

The government of Rwanda's unity and reconciliation project has attracted considerable interest among regional experts, journalists, democratic practitioners, and academics alike, and while the popular literature has tended to mark a clear difference between pre- and post-genocide Rwanda – attributing Rwanda's 'social transformation' and 'the cooling of sectarian passions' to President Paul Kagame's model of 'guided reconciliation' and 'honest governance' (Kinzer, 2007: 3; Crisafulli and Redmond, 2012; Soudan, 2015) – much of the academic literature sees the twin concepts of *ubumwe n'ubumwiyunge* as deeply politicized terms that serve to paper over divisions, and to disguise the monopolization of power by a small regime elite (Ingelaere, 2010; Purdeková, 2015; Reyntjens, 2013; Thomson, 2013). This literature has contributed enormously to our understanding of the dynamics of unity and reconciliation in Rwanda, from both top-down and bottom-up perspectives, but there are noteworthy gaps in the analysis. Chief among them is the tendency among scholars to reify the ethnicity dichotomy by focusing exclusively on the experiences of Hutu and Tutsi, while ignoring the perspectives of Rwanda's most marginal minority, the Batwa (Twa).[4] With few exceptions, the historical narratives and post-genocide experiences of the Twa elicit a mere footnote in the leading academic scholarship, mirroring the tendency of Rwandan governments, both past and present, to render the Twa invisible.

---

[3] The government has adopted various legal measures to criminalize the public expression of ethnicity, and to eradicate divisionism and negationism. The 2001 Law criminalizes 'the use of any speech, written statement or action based on ethnicity' to curtail 'discrimination and sectarianism'. Further to this, the 2003 Constitution proscribes 'ethnic, regional, racial or discrimination of any other form of division', and prohibits political parties 'from basing themselves on race, ethnic group, tribe, clan [...] or any other division which may give rise to discrimination', to ensure that they 'reflect the unity of Rwandan people' (Title II, Ch. 1, art. 33; Title III, art. 54). Article 13 of the Constitution further prohibits 'Revisionism, negationism and trivialisation of genocide' as outlined in the 2003 Law 'Repressing the Crime of Genocide, Crimes against Humanity, and War Crimes', and the 2008 Law 'Relating to the Punishment of the Crime of Genocide Ideology'.

[4] Following British academic conventions, the stem 'Twa' is used here interchangeably with *batwa* (plural) and *mutwa* (singular). 'Twa' is a form of the word 'Tua', which is the most widespread term in local Bantu languages covering the autochthonous peoples of Central Africa. 'Tua' means 'hunter-gatherer' or former hunter-gatherer autochthonous people.

Yet the Twa are profoundly impacted by post-genocide reconstruction and development processes. In line with its unity-building agenda, the government of Rwanda discourages the public expression of Twa identity, and has eliminated ethnic indicators from all formal decrees and policies. In its place, the 2003 Constitution introduced the quasi-official and ambiguously defined category of 'historically marginalized people' (HMP). While the HMP label is widely interpreted as a moniker for 'Twa', many government officials and civil society organizations suggest it applies to 'all Rwandans left behind by history', including women, people with disabilities, genocide survivors and religious minorities (Beswick, 2011: 502). Based on interviews and focus groups conducted in Rwanda between March 2014 and March 2016, as well as personal testimony provided by three Twa civil society leaders, this chapter sheds light on the ways in which Twa perceive, experience and enact *ubumwe n'ubumwiyunge* on the ground. As a component of this, we also examine popular perceptions of the HMP label within the broader framework of unity-building and reconciliation. This snapshot of Twa interactions with government policy and practice shows that many Twa feel excluded from participation in post-genocide politics and decision-making, especially concerning efforts to foster national pride, unity and reconciliation. Equally, our findings illuminate both the unpopularity of the HMP label among individual Twa, and the continued relevance of Twa identity and culture at a community level.

## Becoming 'Historically Marginalized': A Historical Overview of the Situation of Twa in Rwanda

Few historians disagree that the semi-nomadic Twa were the first inhabitants of the Great Lakes region of Africa. Oral traditions common to all three ethnic groups in Rwanda concur in identifying the Twa as autochthonous peoples who lived in the equatorial forests near the great marshes on the borders of central Rwanda and survived for centuries as hunters and foragers (Vansina, 2001: 36). The forests were their homelands, providing the Twa with sustenance and medicine, and containing burial grounds and sacred sites for religious practice and ancestral connection. Their low-impact lifestyle and use of forest resources allowed the Twa to sustain their unique culture and way of life for millennia (see Klieman, 2003). Likely beginning in the eighteenth century, the Twa were gradually pushed out of their ancestral lands by agriculturalists who converted forests into farm land, pastoralists who created pasture for grazing cattle and European colonizers who encroached on these lands for the purpose of lucrative resource extraction and the creation of commercial plantations. Large-scale deforestation, conflict leading to violence and, more recently, conservation and the creation of national parks, meant that as early as the mid-nineteenth century, the majority of Twa were unable to survive as hunters and foragers, and were integrated into mainstream society at the lowest level, with pottery providing their primary occupation. Some Twa also provided important services at the (Tutsi) royal court in Rwanda as dancers, musicians, spies, secret messengers, warriors and even assassins and court executioners (Lewis and Knight, 1995: 25–37). In general, a pattern of avoidance emerged between Twa and the wider population primarily because of the antediluvian association of Twa with gluttony, barbarism and moral indecency – degrading stereotypes that persist today.[5] Though it is unclear how much the 'pygmoid race myth' contributed to these stigmas for the Twa of Rwanda in particular, it is abundantly clear that dwarfish forest peoples across the continent were seen as the lowest form of human under Eurocentric racial ideology (Klieman, 2003: 1–20). As recently as the 1990s, the remaining forest-dwelling Twa in Volcanoes National Park and Gishwati-Mukura National Park in the north-western corner of Rwanda, and Nyungwe National Park in the south-west of Rwanda were expelled without consultation, compensation or reparation, despite many tireless attempts to defend their homelands against encroachment. Owing to their sustainable use of forest resources, the Twa did not leave evidence of land exploitation and/or

---

[5] Well before the arrival of Europeans in Rwanda, labour involving direct contact with the earth was considered impure according to Rwandan court culture. The most esteemed labour involved the earth in the most mediated fashion, pastoralism. Agriculture entailed working and tilling the land, but with tools, whereas hunting, foraging and pottery-making, the most common occupations of the Twa, implied the most extreme forms of moral indecency and impurity because they necessarily involved a direct connection to the earth. Early written sources also suggest that the association of the Twa with 'gluttony' derives from their consumption of mutton. The taboo against eating mutton was, and still is, extremely strong in Rwanda because sheep are valued for their pacific qualities, as they historically accompanied cattle herds and were thought to exert a moderating influence. The Rwandan proverb 'One must not mix sheep and goats' speaks to this precedent, and was used in part to justify the practice of segregating Twa during meals. Eating and or drinking in the presence of Twa was publicly proscribed: Twa were expected live apart, collect water downstream and remain on the fringes of society. Although many of these practices have ceased today, particularly among city dwellers, they are sometimes permitted to continue in rural areas, and negative and damaging stereotypes of Twa as gluttonous, greedy, unkempt, impure and 'animal-like' persist unabated (Taylor, 1992: 38; Lewis, 2000: 14).

agricultural and industrial development, which enabled colonial adminis-
trations and post-independence governments to claim the land as 'vacant'
from a Eurocentric legal framework. On this basis, the Twa were denied land
claims and rights over the forested areas they customarily used (Huggins,
2009: 9–10). They now constitute the poorest and most vulnerable people
in Rwanda, comprising a mere 33,000 individuals, approximately 0.003%
of Rwanda's total population of nearly 12 million (CAURWA, 2000: 8). As
in the past, the Twa remain a marginalized minority that faces unique
challenges and uncertainties related to landlessness, high unemployment
and underemployment, poverty, limited access to education and health care,
social discrimination and acute political marginalization. Women and girls
deal with multiple and intersecting forms of disadvantage and dislocation,
and suffer from extremely high rates of gender-based and sexual violence
relative to their non-Twa counterparts (see Ramsay, 2010).

Despite the government of Rwanda's sustained efforts to advance the socio-
economic position of Twa/HMP by way of national policies, such as compulsory
nine-year basic education, community-based healthcare insurance and
promotion of economic cooperatives, Twa communities lack direct political
representation, and are conspicuous in their absence from the government's
*ubumwe n'ubumwiyunge* project – a key focus of government programming.
They are perceived as tangential to the causes and consequences of the
genocide, and therefore tangential to Rwanda's post-genocide reconstruction.
Yet Twa communities were dramatically affected by the volatile events
of the 1990s. They were often victims of the Interahamwe, the extremist
Hutu militia, which targeted Twa as sympathizers of the Rwandan Patriotic
Front (RPF), and more generally, 'friends of the Tutsi', based on widespread
perceptions of a historical connection between the pre-colonial (Tutsi) royal
court and Twa families who provided services at court (Lewis and Knight,
1995: 26–27). Some were mistaken for Interahamwe, while others were killed
for their 'Tutsi' features. Many also died as collateral victims of the carnage.
An estimated 30% of the Twa population perished during the 100 days of
violence (CRIN, 2006: 5).

As mentioned above, in the post-genocide period, the government removed
Twa identity from public policy and discourse as a means of de-emphasizing
ethnicity in political spaces, and introduced the non-ethnic HMP label in
2003. Article 80 (2) of the 2003 Constitution, revised in 2015, requires that
the president appoint eight senators to represent 'historically marginalized
groups'. At present, only one of 26 senators identifies as HMP. Moreover, the
term was never officially defined, and the current Constitution does not clarify
the groups to which it applies. Most Rwandan civil society organizations
interpret the term as an 'inclusive category', encompassing 'all Rwandans

disadvantaged throughout history'. At present, however, the Twa are the only people that uses the HMP category as a method of collective identification because, unlike other marginalized groups (i.e. women, peoples with disabilities, genocide survivors and children) that have formed organizations to lobby on behalf of their specific needs, the Twa cannot legally refer to their identity, which complicates efforts to address their particular situation.

The Rwandan government refuses to use the indigenous label in Rwanda on the grounds that all Rwandans are native to the region. There are legitimate and historical reasons for this, especially because the Twa are not the first people to claim indigenous status. The leaders of Rwanda's first (1962–1973) and second republics (1973–1994), Grégoire Kayibanda and Juvénal Habyarimana, respectively, used the concept of indigeneity in a racialized sense to distinguish between the 'native-born' Hutu majority and the 'Hamitic' Tutsi minority, depicted as 'foreign invaders' of a different racial stock. These manipulations undoubtedly stoked racial tensions, and contributed to the genocide in 1994, which in turn was preceded by waves of anti-Tutsi violence in 1959, 1963 and 1973. A localized reading of the terms *abasangwabutaka* and 'indigenous' thus rouses memories of Rwanda's violent past.[6] Yet there are also more practical reasons for denying Twa claims of indigeneity. As NGOs and human rights activists begin to connect Twa discourses to the global indigenous rights framework, they open up the possibility of internationally recognized human rights claims. The government sees this as unacceptable because it involves 'meddling into the affairs of Rwanda' – a country where much of the historical conflict is attributed squarely to external, and namely, European intervention. Conveniently, however, government rhetoric also serves to deny the Twa a special status to address marginalization and pursue land claims. The UN Independent Expert on Minority Issues and the UN Human Rights Council have repeatedly condemned the government's thinking. Most recently, in May 2016, the UN Review Committee on Rwanda's Compliance with the Convention on the Elimination of all Forms of Racial Discrimination proclaimed that 'without the adoption of specific measures protecting them, the Twa risked extinction', and urged the Rwandan administration to address the acute poverty and discrimination which Twa face in health, employment and education. The government's response was predictable: Rwandan ambassador François Xavier Ngarambe replied that 'the government did not consider any group of Rwandans as distinct from others' (United Nations Human Rights Office

---

6 See Adamczyk (2011: 181–84) for an excellent discussion of the debates surrounding the concepts of 'Autochthonry' and 'Indigeneity' in post-genocide Rwanda.

of the High Commissioner, 2016). As such, 'members of formally marginalized communities had now, thanks to inclusion policies, access to health,
education and employment services without discrimination'.

## Twa Perceptions of Rwanda's Nation-Building Project

Given the recent shift in the legal and political framing of Twa identity,
how effective has the government's approach been in terms of transforming
systems of classification and social practice at the individual level? How
do Twa perceive, understand and enact Rwandan national identity on the
ground? Do Twa feel Rwandan? Do they feel integrated into Rwandan society,
socially, politically and economically? Furthermore, how do they relate to
the HMP label as a component of the government's wider national unity
and reconciliation project? Do they see this label as a positive step in terms
of combatting discrimination, and specifically targeting the needs of Twa
communities? Or do they see it as a means of further stigmatizing Twa as a
backward people 'left behind by history'?

To begin to answer these questions, we conducted 20 semi-structured
and informal focus groups with approximately ten to 15 participants per
group. Focus groups were conducted in Kinyarwanda and then translated
into English by our research assistants. In general, we found informal focus
groups to be the most appropriate method of data collection because they
allow for multiple voices to be heard, and more easily incorporate important
cultural practices, such as traditional song and dance, which create a relaxed
and open environment for conversation. It was also difficult to isolate
individuals for interviews. Often, other village members would interrupt the
interview or join in with their own observations. That said, an additional
20 people were interviewed individually in Kigali, but these interviews
were prearranged and participants were carefully selected based on their
standing within their respective communities. Interviews were conducted
in French or English. We were also able to conduct structured focus groups
with ten of Rwanda's 45 university-educated Twa, and draw from the survey
findings on Twa perceptions of the HMP label published in Collins and
Ntakirutimana's (2017) policy brief.[7]

Our combined research findings suggest that government-led projections
of national unity and reconciliation do not necessarily correspond to the
realities of Twa on the ground. Many participants shared experiences of
ongoing marginalization, exclusion and discrimination in the realms of

---

[7] Questionnaires were written in Kinyarwanda, and translated by Richard
Ntakirutimana.

education, employment and daily social life. For example, in a focus group discussion with five young, university-educated Twa, two individuals shared experiences of discrimination in education and employment. François, a 25-year-old Twa, recounts his experience as both student and teacher:

> You know, when I was teaching, there was a teacher. He was teaching with me. He said, 'Did you know that this one is a Twa?' [lowers voice, laughter] Because, he don't know that also, me, I am a Twa. I said, 'Oh! Is it true?', because being a Twa is shameful I tell you. In Rwanda, it is shameful. You cannot say this. I am telling you the truth [...] If they know you are Twa, it will be a very big problem.

His colleague, 26-year-old Emmanuel, shared a similar experience:

> Me, I am advisor of 300 students [...] The students, they think that I am one of them [...] They think that I am Tutsi or Hutu. They don't know I am Twa [...] Then I converse with my fellow Twa, a girl that is Twa. When I converse with her, another girl talked to me, 'Are you converse with Twa? You start making relationship with Twa?' I told her, 'Also me, I am Twa'. Then I told my colleagues, 'Also me, I am Twa'. When you are saying that, they say, 'You are lying. It is not possible'. [...] So, that job I was getting because they don't know me [...] Everything which is bad belongs to Twa [...] So, I am telling you, when someone knows you are Twa, he does not give that kind of job you want.

In addition to describing daily experiences of discrimination, many participants associated the HMP category with increased dislocation and marginalization. Part of this stems from the confusion surrounding the label's origins and use. Nowhere were we able to locate the origins or official meaning of the term, and we found no evidence during our fieldwork that Twa were consulted before the term was adopted, or sensitized on its meaning and use. When asked why the Twa are called HMP instead of Twa, 28-year-old Philibert responded: 'We don't know the reason. You can't guess the reason. There is no reason. Why not just find a new name for people who committed genocide? Why the government only just create a new name for Mutwa?' When asked how she learned about the HMP label, one middle-aged Twa woman, Fidela, answered: 'I heard the term from the other population. One day, when walking – walking to find food, I found people calling me HMP. I do not know where it came from'. Fellow participants in her focus group nod in general agreement. The results of Collins and Ntakirutimana's (2017) questionnaire analysis further confirm this confusion. Looking at the responses to the question 'Do you know the meaning of HMP?', 67% of respondents either 'did not know' or were unsure of the term's meaning.

The 20% of respondents who claimed to have knowledge of the term did not provide a clear, singular interpretation (Collins and Ntakirutimana, 2017: 4). For example, the following is a sample of answers which Collins and Ntakirutimana received in response to a question that asked respondents to define 'Historically Marginalized People':

A.  A word cursed by god.
B.  A word showing that people should not have a seat at the table.
C.  An English word that means 'Twa' [response to reading the Kinyarwanda version of HMP].
D.  A word that implies a person has been discriminated against for a long time.
E.  A word showing that a person is physically short.
F.  Impoverished.
G.  Twa.[8]
H.  Left behind.[9]

Answers A, B and F imply a negative interpretation of the HMP label. Answers D and H offer more sterilized and 'official' definitions of the term, even if the interpretations are quite literal. Answer G, repeated six times by respondents, suggests a common view that HMP is synonymous with Twa, challenging the interpretation of Rwandan civil society, and international governmental and non-governmental organizations, that HMP is an umbrella term that includes multiple groups. Answer C is perhaps the most telling as it unveils a view that the HMP label is something alien, unfamiliar and perhaps decidedly 'un-Rwandan'.

Despite this confusion, few participants displayed indifference towards the label, and many expressed open disdain for its continued use. Several respondents expressed pride in their identity as Twa, emphasizing that Twa are a peaceful and 'happy people' who avoid politics, and have always been victims of violence but never instigators (interview, Philibert, 2016). Twa participants contested and challenged the adoption of the HMP label in a number of ways. While some expressed a desire to be fully integrated into Rwandan society, and to be referred to simply as 'Rwandan', others wished to preserve their Twa identity and culture, and did not see this as incompatible with their Rwandan identity. Likewise, when asked: 'how would you preferred to be called?', 59% of Collins and Ntakirutimana's respondents answered, 'Twa', while only 19% answered 'HMP', 8% answered 'both' and 6% answered

---

[8] 'Twa' was the response given by six participants, indicating that the label helps to identify them as an ethnicity.

[9] This response was given by two participants.

'Rwandan' (2017: 2). In contrast, a select number of respondents expressed a preference to identify as 'Indigenous' or 'First peoples', tying their identity as Twa to the broader, transnational indigenous rights movement to encourage the government of Rwanda to recognize their rights to ancestral lands and natural resources, and their political status as a 'people' with a distinct identity and culture. Again, participants who espoused this perspective did not see their identity as indigenous Twa as incompatible with Rwandan national pride and identity.

The vast majority of participants in our research also expressed a positive view of the government's efforts to de-emphasize ethnicity and reduce social stigma in the post-genocide period. They were equally encouraging of the government's efforts to support HMP communities to achieve economic sustainability, and wished to see the government continue to engage with community leaders, activists and youth to improve the livelihood and well-being of Twa in Rwanda.

## Testimonies from Three Twa Civil Society Leaders

As a corollary, we couple the results of our past fieldwork with the following personal testimonies from three Twa community leaders and activists (one of whom is a co-author of this paper): Richard Ntakirutimana, Delphine Uwajeneza and Justin Sebanani. All three activists work for the African Initiative for Mankind Progress Organization (AIMPO), one of several grass-roots organizations in Rwanda that focuses on the development of the Twa.[10] These testimonies provide key insights and a greater sense of context to the dominant narratives on unity and reconciliation created and enforced by the government, for their narratives and life histories allow us to observe how community activists of Rwanda's most marginal minority perceive and represent their own lived experiences of violence, dislocation, discrimination and personal triumph, as well as their interactions with government policy and practice.[11]

---

[10] All three contributors are proficient in English, and chose to give their testimony in English rather than French or Kinyarwanda. This follows the broader 'anglicization' of the Rwandan state and society, when English was adopted by the government as the official language of instruction in 2008 to increase foreign investment, economic development and technology transfer. See, for example, Samuelson (2010).

[11] Moreover, we recognize, as three authors one of whom is Twa and two white and Western, that it is essential to give space to the voices and stories that are overlooked and under-represented in the academy.

## Richard's Story

I was born in Uganda in 1988. My great-grandfather lived in the court of the Mwami. In 1959, he went into exile together with Tutsi and the king because he was among the persons who was dancing for the king. In 1995, my grandfather and his family came back to Rwanda after the liberation war of 1994.[12] At that time, I was seven years old. I started my primary school at Rwisirabo primary school in 1996. Later on, I moved from Rwisirabo to Kizirakome primary school closer to my home after a new primary school was constructed. It was so difficult to me [*sic*] at that time because I was the only person from my family, not even just my family, but from my community, who was Twa and a student. I faced discrimination when I was in primary school. However, I was so proud and a very strong student. I was good in mathematics and science. The head of the school used to ask the students a question related to science or maths. Only the first pupil who answered the question correctly had the chance to go home early. Sometimes the head would slap the pupils. At the time, I was always the first person to answer the question and go home. Pupils could even fear to say in the class 'UMutwa aragikoze sha', meaning that Mutwa has done it. During the primary leaving examination, I was the first person in our school, which very unbelievable to me to be the first one at school. This has caused the mayor of the district to come to see me. I was proud and very happy.

Although it was very difficult to me to join secondary school, this was a dream to me. The Rwandese Community of Potters (CAURWA) at the time was paying school fees for the Twa children. I went to Kigali to CAURWA's office with my father. CAURWA provided me with a mattress, books and school fees. The person who welcomed me first at secondary school was the child who used to call me 'Mutwa'. That time it was completely different. He treated me very well, as his brother with full respect and love. I felt excited to meet my friends. We came to the same place and they help me to get beds and so on until I got familiar with everything. The situation of discrimination changed dramatically at secondary school. But to me, it

---

12 Rwandans use a variety of terms to describe the four-year civil war between 1990 and 1994, which ended in the Genocide against the Tutsi. The terms used to frame discussions of 1994 are sometimes revealing in terms of indexing ethnicity, and estimating one's support of the current RPF leadership. The official term used by the government of Rwanda to describe the civil war is 'the liberation war' or 'the liberation struggle', to emphasize the RPF's 'liberation' of the Rwandan people from a corrupt Hutu dictatorship in 1994. Rwandans 'show gratitude' for the sacrifices of Rwandan Patriotic Army soldiers on 4 July during the annual National Liberation Day celebrations (Mutesi, 2017).

was because of the good government which was teaching students to work together not discriminating against each other. The rules and regulations at schools were not tolerant of any discrimination based on colour, ethnic identity, etc.

I am among Twa students who received a university scholarship from the Ministry of Local Government. The scholarship was fruitful to me and has changed my life because it gave me a bachelor's degree. I used this degree to get funding for my Master's degree in Human Rights and Democratization at the University of Pretoria. I received my degree in December 2017, and became the first Mutwa man in Rwanda to have a Master's. I am very proud of this. The security and peace brought by the RPF government have become a point of departure for Batwa/Historically Marginalized People to receive sunlight like other Rwandans. I am keeping strong now. When I pass by people, what they say is, 'Look at that educated Twa', which is good for me because everything is possible when there is equality for everyone.

## Delphine's Story

My name is Uwajeneza Delphine, and I am a Historically Marginalized Person, formally known as Mutwa. I am 30 years old and the mother of three children. I was born in 1988, before the genocide.

My father, mother and uncles studied in hard conditions where other children used to beat them at school for being Twa. My uncles retired from school early because of being afraid of other children. I remember one day my mum told us how her classmates took her school uniform and put it in water. When my mum came, she asked why they took her clothes into the water. 'We don't want you here. You are Mutwa. You must go and make pots', replied her classmates. She was poor, and she made pots after school in order to get something to eat. However, even with these struggles, my parents continued in school. This is why they encouraged us to continue no matter how hard [the] situation is. When I joined the school too, my teacher beat me every day. In addition, he always told me that he must beat me because no one should come and save me. He terrorized me as well when I was in nursery school. I was the only Twa in our community because my parents studied and they knew how important education was, but to other Twa families, it was nothing.

After the Genocide against the Tutsi in 1994, I was six years old. I went into Primary One. The children kept saying to me and my three brothers that we are Batwa, and Batwa don't have knowledge. What we know is making pots only. They sometimes beat us at school, but we didn't stop studying. For me, I studied with the goal of buying a car and one day I had a dream of going to my village in my own car with my parents. But the others pointed fingers at me and told me that no Mutwa should study. They ordered me to leave. There was so much discrimination in my village. Even if we were intelligent, they didn't care. We tried to put on clean clothes and they said that even if we put on those clothes, we are still Batwa, 'Do you understand how bad those people are?'

When I arrived in secondary school, the other children said that everyone who does bad things is Mutwa. This caused me to become angry because I felt like I am alone and the worst in our society. I tried so hard in order to finish the school. After my schooling, I started my work in 2012, but I didn't think about marrying a man who is not Mutwa because I saw what happened to my aunt. Her fiancé took her [to meet his] family and they said that they can't have her as their daughter-in-law because she is Mutwa. They say that Batwa are the ones who steal, shout and disobey. They say we are dishonest and have other bad behaviours. This is the reason the man refuses to marry my aunt. I too choose to live only with Mutwa because I saw many bad things happen to those in my community. I was very sad because I couldn't do anything for them.

After getting a job, I told people many times that I am Mutwa, and I am proud of being Mutwa. I saw many cases where people violated my community, but because my community is voiceless, nothing happens. Some authorities come and take their cows and give it to other people. They also built bad houses, which makes me unhappy. This is the reason why I went to study law and become a judge. I need to show those who discouraged me that Twa are also able to do what they do, and through my advocacy work with AIMPO, I will continue to raise my voice to help those who still are still seeing discrimination and marginalization, and advocate for punishment for those who are doing this. Thank you so much.

## Justin's Story

When I was growing up and saw other people, especially our neighbours, call us Batwa, I didn't know it had to do with our ethnicity. I took it as an insult for someone who looked ignorant, stupid, or any person who is vulnerable. For example, during my education, anyone who didn't perform well in class was told that they looked like they came from a Batwa community, and this was after the genocide until 2006 when I was prepared to finish my primary school. I remember that Tutsi and other powerful Hutu farmers brought their cows to graze in our gardens, which grew potatoes, sorghum, beans, etc., and we weren't allowed to claim reimbursement for our crops because we would have risked being beaten by them as well as by the authorities, since they were often related.

Because of hard times, I didn't want to continue my studies in secondary school. I didn't see any of my extended family finishing primary school and there wasn't any Mutwa encouraging me to continue studying. I was discouraged from studying and sometimes I wanted to drop out of school completely, but it didn't happen in the end because of my mum's courage. She always told me that I needed to support the family, and by chance I succeeded in passing the national exam in order to finish my secondary school. I finished my secondary schooling and got a full university scholarship from the Ministry of Local Government through a programme that helped Batwa students who finished secondary school move on to studying a Bachelor's degree. I finished my studies in the Faculty of Social Sciences, in the Department of Development Studies.

I started talking about my history to show the change that happened for me and my family compared to before. I got a great chance to start volunteering with AIMPO, an organization that fights for the rights and interests of the HMP Batwa community to which I belong, after my time at university. So, this has given me hope that my childhood dream to develop my community will become a reality, as I took the first step to reach my goal.

Through volunteering, I've learned a lot but I was, and still am, interested in advocating for vulnerable people in my community across the country through our radio programme that we started at AIMPO to raise awareness about the challenges facing Batwa communities. Basically, one of the AIMPO team goes with a radio journalist to a Batwa community and during the show we [staff from AIMPO] discuss the issues faced by that particular community. We use the time to show the relevant local authorities what issues there are and how to improve them. The radio programme is having an impact on the communities we engage with. I'm already proud of being part of this programme but it's even better to see results.

Because of the many field visits and surveys that I carried out with AIMPO, we found that there are so many Batwa around the country who are still struggling from poverty, landlessness, homelessness, illiteracy and more. I can say that there is a little bit of improvement made on living conditions thanks to the government. But we can't say that it has been enough. Government, donors and NGOs should emphasize Batwa issues and take them on as an exceptional case in order to help the Batwa reach the standard of living that other Rwandans enjoy now.

Let us work together on Batwa issues in order to rehabilitate and integrate us into Rwandan society. So long as we continue to treat the Batwa as just other 'poor people', our problems will not be solved. It is not a case of opposing what the government has done for us, like distributing livestock [cows] to Batwa households or giving us homes, because the problems are not just cows or houses. Why aren't Batwa children given free education? Why do Batwa with undergraduate and graduate degrees have such difficulty finding jobs? Why aren't communities given or, at least, loaned land? All of these are the key issues that must be taken into consideration in order to improve the livelihoods of the Batwa.

For me, seeing all Batwa children attending school is a major change to the situation as it was before the genocide. The problem is that even if these children try to integrate into society like others, there will always be the challenge that we have no land to call our own.

## Concluding Remarks

Stepping back, the Twa are not confined to the borders of Rwanda. Rather, the Twa of Equatorial Africa,[13] and the Great Lakes region in particular, share comparable narratives of discrimination and marginalization, owing to their forest-dwelling lifestyles and/or physical characteristics. In this sense, it is important to point out that their marginalization in Rwanda is by no means isolated, and this chapter makes no attempt to exceptionalize the Twa of Rwanda. Rather, we aim to reveal the gap in the post-genocide era in relation to policy and academic discourse that centres on the narratives, histories and well-being of the Twa. With the exception of a handful of academic papers produced over the past 24 years, the Twa have received only a footnote in the abundance of analysis surrounding the 1994 Genocide against the Tutsi and resulting fascination with Rwanda's past. It is of the utmost importance that Twa narratives are not only brought into future papers on the Banyarwanda, but also that Twa voices are given the space and opportunity to speak for themselves.[14] Doing so would provide fuller and more complex narratives of the Banyarwanda, as Twa histories intersect with those of the Hutu and Tutsi.

The government's use of the term 'Historically Marginalized People', though, as a way of avoiding divisive terminology and as a possible means of identifying and integrating the Twa via positive discrimination, needs to be revisited. Without nuance and consultation with the Twa, socio-economic assistance, like knowledge production, will likely continue to show few

---

[13]  There are various forest peoples known as 'Twa' across Equatorial Africa.

[14]  Given the many barriers to accessing platforms of privilege within the academy and the specific expertise and knowledge found within Twa communities, we recommend that practitioners and academics adopt a community-collaborative methodology to produce Twa-designed and Twa-accessible outputs.

positive results, while straining relations between the Twa and their non-Twa neighbours who view such HMP programming as wasted resources. More than this, this label without official qualification continues to raise the quintessential question: How have the Twa been historically marginalized? To answer this, we call for the chance and space for Twa communities to explain their histories. From their ongoing struggle with the derivatives of the Pygmoid race myth to their roles in the Tutsi monarchy, to their history of dispossession from ancestral lands, to their intergenerational practices of *intwawa* music and dance and pottery, we must begin to fit the missing pieces into the large discussion of unity and reconciliation amongst the Banyarwanda.

## Works Cited

Adamczyk, Christiane. 2011. '"Today I Am No Mutwa Anymore": Facets of National Unity Discourse in Present-Day Rwanda'. *Social Anthropology* 19.2: 175–88.

Beswick, Danielle. 2011. 'Democracy, Identity and the Politics of Exclusion in Post-Genocide Rwanda: The Case of the Batwa'. *Democratization* 18.2: 490–511.

Collins, Bennett, and Richard Ntakirutimana. 2017. 'Am I Twa or HMP? Examining the Relationship between the Twa and the Historically Marginalized People Label'. Policy Brief produced as part of the Aegis Trust's Research, Policy, and Higher Education Programme and funded by the UK Department for International Development.

The Committee on the Elimination of Racial Discrimination, United Nations Human Rights Office of the High Commissioner. Consideration of reports submitted by States parties under article 9 of the Convention Eighteenth to twentieth periodic reports of States parties due in 2014, Rwanda. CERD/C/RWA/18-20 (12 December 2014). Available at https://tbinternet.ohchr.org/_layouts/treaty-bodyexternal/Download.aspx?symbolno=CERD/C/RWA/18-20&Lang=en (consulted on 21 February 2019).

Communauté des Autochtones Rwandais. (CAURWA). 2000. 'Enquête sur les conditions de vie socio-économique des ménages bénéficiaires de la Communauté des Autochtones Rwandais'. Kigali: CAURWA.

CRIN. 2006. 'Minorities under Siege: Pygmies Today in Africa'. Available at https://www.yumpu.com/en/document/read/23510308/minorities-under-siege-pygmies-today-in-africa-irin (consulted on 5 February 2019).

Crisafulli, Patricia, and Andrea Redmond. 2012. *Rwanda, Inc.: How a Devastated Nation Became an Economic Model for the Developing World.* New York: St Martin's Press.

Huggins, Chris. 2009. 'Land Rights and the Forest Peoples of Africa: Historical, Legal and Anthropological Perspectives.' Forest Peoples Programme.

Ingelaere, Bert. 2010. 'Peasants, Power and Ethnicity: A Bottom-Up Perspective on Rwanda's Political Transition'. *African Affairs* 109.435: 273–92.

Kinzer, Stephen. 2008. *A Thousand Hills: Rwanda's Rebirth and the Man Who Dreamed it.* Hoboken, NJ: Wiley.

Klieman, Kairn A. 2003. *The Pygmies Were Our Compass: Bantu and Batwa in the History of West Central Africa.* Portsmouth, NH: Heinemann.

Lewis, Jerome. 2000. 'The Batwa Pygmies of the Great Lakes Region.' Minority Rights Group International Report. Available at: http://minorityrights.org/ wp-content/uploads/old-site-downloads/download-150-Batwa-Pygmies-of-the-Great-Lakes-Region.pdf (consulted on 21 July 2016).

Lewis, Jerome, and Judy Knight. 1995. *The Twa of Rwanda: An Assessment of the Situation of the Twa and Promotion of Twa Rights in Post-War Rwanda.* Chadlington: World Rainforest Movement and International Work Group for Indigenous Affairs.

Mutesi, Mireille. 2017. 'Happy Liberation Day Rwanda … Soar Higher!' *The New Times* 4 July. Available at http://www.newtimes.co.rw/section/read/215443 (consulted on 9 October 2017).

Office of the President of the Republic of Rwanda. 1999. 'The Unity of Rwandans'. Report produced by the Committee for Studying the Issue of the Unity of Rwandans. August. Available at https://repositories.lib.utexas.edu/bitstream/ handle/2152/4918/2379.pdf?sequence=1 (consulted on 14 May 2015).

Purdeková, Andrea. 2008. 'Building a Nation in Rwanda? De-ethnicisation and its Discontents.' *Studies in Ethnicity and Nationalism*, 8.3: 502–23.

—. 2015. *Making 'Ubumwe': Power, State, and Camps in Rwanda's Unity-Building Project.* Oxford and New York: Berghahn Books.

Ramsay, Kathryn. 2010. 'Uncounted: The Hidden Lives of Batwa Women.' *Minority Rights Group International, Briefing.* Available at http://minorityrights.org/ wp-content/uploads/old-site-downloads/download-804-Uncounted-the-hidden-lives-of-Batwa-women.pdf (consulted on 23 July 2016).

Republic of Rwanda, Law No. 47/2001 of 2001 on 'Prevention, Suppression and Punishment of the Crime of Discrimination and Sectarianism [Rwanda]', 18 December 2001, available at: https://www.refworld.org/docid/4ac5c4302.html. (consulted on 16 March 2018).

République Rwandaise, Ministère de l'Administration locale, de l'information, et des affaires sociales. 'Dénombrement des victimes du génocide. Rapport Final'. Kigali, November 2002.

Reyntjens, Filip. 1997. 'Estimation du nombre de personnes tuées au Rwanda en 1994'. In S. Marysee and Filip Reyntjens (eds), *L'Afrique des grands lacs. Annuaire 1996–1997.* Paris: D'Harmattan: 179–86.

—. 2009. *The Great African War: Congo and Regional Geopolitics, 1996–2006.* New York: Cambridge University Press.

—. 2013. *Political Governance in Post-Genocide Rwanda.* New York: Cambridge University Press.

Samuelson, Beth. 2010. 'Language Policy, Multilingual Education, and Power in Rwanda'. *Language Policy* 9.3: 191–215.

Sebasoni, Servilien Manzi. 2007. *Le Rwanda: reconstruire une nation.* Kigali: Imprimerie Papeterie Nouvelle.

Soudan, François. 2015. *Kagame: The President of Rwanda Speaks.* New York: Enigma Books.

Taylor, Christopher. 1992. *Milk, Honey, Money: Changing Concepts in Rwandan Healing.* Washington, DC: Smithsonian Press.

Thomson, Susan. 2013. *Whispering Truth to Power: Everyday Resistance to Reconciliation in Post-Genocide Rwanda.* Madison, WI: University of Wisconsin Press.

United Nations Human Rights Office of the High Commissioner. 2016. 'Committee on the Elimination of Racial Discrimination examines report of Rwanda' (29 April 2016). News and Events, Summary Report. Available at https://www.ohchr. org/EN/NewsEvents/Pages/DisplayNews.aspx?NewsID=19908&LangID=E (consulted on 21 February 2019).

Vansina, Jan. 2001. *Antecedents to Modern Rwanda: The Nyiginya Kingdom.* Madison, WI: The University of Wisconsin Press.

*Interviews*
Emmanuel, graduate student, Kigali, February 2016.
Fidela, farmer, Nyagatare District, October 2015.
François, graduate student, Kigali, February 2016.
Jean-Bosco, hotel worker, Musanze District, March 2016.
Philibert, NGO worker, Kigali, February 2016.

*Testimonies*
Ntakirutimana, Richard. Executive Director, AIMPO.
Sebanani, Justin. Program Manager, AIMPO.
Uwajeneza, Delphine. Deputy Director, AIMPO.

# Part Two:
# Changing People

# Writing as Reconciliation:
# Bearing Witness to Life after Genocide

*Catherine Gilbert*

Twenty-four years have passed since the 1994 Genocide against the Tutsi in Rwanda, and during that time a significant corpus of testimonial literature has been published, written primarily by Rwandan women genocide survivors.[1] This has been accompanied by a growing number of fictional accounts, edited collections of testimonies and documentary and cinematic responses to the genocide.[2] Yolande Mukagasana is well known as the first survivor to publish a full-length testimony, *La Mort ne veut pas de moi* [*Death Doesn't Want Me*], just three years after the genocide in 1997. A second testimony, *N'aie pas peur de savoir* [*Don't Be Afraid to Know*], appeared shortly afterwards in 1999, which repeated and expanded upon the information contained in her first testimony.[3] Fifteen years later, Mukagasana published a new testimonial

---

[1] To the best of my knowledge at the time of writing, a total of 20 women have published testimonial accounts. The majority of these have been written in French, with a smaller number in English and German.

[2] For two of the most recent studies of these bodies of work, see Brinker (2014) and Hitchcott (2015).

[3] Both of these testimonies were written in collaboration with Belgian journalist and author Patrick May. Mukagasana has also published a collection of testimonies and photographs with Greek-Belgian photographer Alain Kazinierakis, *Les Blessures du silence* [*Wounds of Silence*] (2001), as well as a collection of stories, *De bouche à oreille* [*Word of Mouth*] (2003).

narrative focusing on life after the genocide, *L'Onu et le chagrin d'une négresse* [*The UN and a Negress's Shame*], which appeared with Éditions Aviso in 2014.[4] Similarly, genocide survivor Annick Kayitesi-Jozan published her first testimony, *Nous existons encore* [*We Still Exist*], in 2004. After a hiatus of 13 years she then published a second testimony, *Même Dieu ne veut pas s'en mêler* [*Even God Doesn't Want to Get Involved*], with Éditions du Seuil in 2017. While other Rwandan women have published more than one text, including Esther Mujawayo and Scholastique Mukasonga,[5] what is particularly striking about the two women addressed in this chapter is the fact that there was such a long gap between the publications of their testimonies.

Why this decision to return to writing after so many years? In order to offer an initial response to this question – which I believe requires far greater analysis – this chapter will focus on Mukagasana's *L'Onu et le chagrin d'une négresse* and Kayitesi-Jozan's *Même Dieu ne veut pas s'en mêler* to investigate what has changed in their approach to writing – whether they still perceive writing as a 'need' or 'duty', as a form of 'healing' or a means of seeking justice, notions which were all expressed in their earlier testimonies. Both these narratives oscillate between the past and the present, intertwining painful memories of the past with reflections on these women's active roles in post-genocide society, both in Rwanda and in the diaspora. In particular, their engagement with processes of justice and commemoration offer insights into the changing roles these women are playing and the type of legacy they are building for future generations. Through close analysis of their narratives, this chapter will interrogate the ways in which their thinking about reconciliation in Rwandan society has changed, seeking to identify shifts in understanding of the role of writing in the post-genocide context.

---

[4]   At the time of writing, Aviso's website is advertising its 'Spécial 20ᵉ commémoration du génocide contre les Tutsi rwandais', showcasing Mukagasana's *L'Onu et le chagrin d'une négresse* alongside books focusing on the Bisesero massacre by French-Vietnamese author Bruno Boudiguet and French author and journalist Serge Farnel. See http://www.aviso-editions.fr (consulted on 3 March 2018). Numerous other titles primarily concerned with France's role in the genocide are advertised further down the page.

[5]   Esther Mujawayo has published two full-length testimonies, *SurVivantes* [*Survivors*] (2004) and *La Fleur de Stéphanie* [*Stéphanie's Flower*] (2006), both co-authored with Souâd Belhaddad. Scholastique Mukasonga has written two autobiographical texts, *Inyenzi ou les Cafards* [*Inyenzi or the Cockroaches*] (2006) and *La Femme aux pieds nus* [*Barefoot Woman*] (2008), and is now a well-known literary author published with Gallimard's prestigious Collection Blanche, having gone on to write a number of novels and collections of short stories. For an analysis of Mukasonga's fictional writing, see Hitchcott (2017).

Both intimate and condemning, these texts, written by women who have dedicated years of their lives to fighting for the rights of survivors of crimes against humanity, demonstrate a desire to preserve and mobilize the memory of the genocide, providing a clear indication of how testimonial writing in the diaspora is evolving and how its potential in facilitating reconciliation might be harnessed.

## A Return to Writing

Mukagasana and Kayitesi-Jozan have had very different life trajectories, but their return to writing and insistence on continuing to bear witness – their refusal to be silent/silenced – indicates a shared need to *re-prendre la plume* [take up the pen again] in order to confront the continued injustices survivors face in Rwanda and across the diaspora. They both revisit old wounds that will never be fully closed, and their candid narratives reveal that the pain and guilt of surviving has not lessened in any way and that they must continue to struggle to find ways of living with the devastating memory of the genocide. Moreover, they both foreground their ongoing fight for justice, their commitment to helping other survivors and their hopes and fears for future generations of Rwandans.

Born in 1954, just a few years before the 'social revolution' of 1959 and Rwanda's independence from Belgium in 1962, Yolande Mukagasana had already experienced the waves of massacres that swept across the country in the 1960s and 1970s. *L'Onu et le chagrin d'une négresse* revisits this period in greater detail than her previous two testimonies, tracing the United Nations' historic involvement in the country prior to the 1990s. Her testimony emphasizes Rwandans' continued disillusionment with an international justice system founded on a Western-centric understanding of human rights that has repeatedly let their country down. In 1994, Mukagasana lost her husband, Joseph (who had been orphaned in the killings of 1963), and her three children, Christian, Sandrine and Nadine. Mukagasana managed to flee to Belgium, where she lived for the next 16 years. Tired of fighting for justice in a country that is supposedly one of the founders of universal human rights, she returned to live in Rwanda to continue her work with survivors, a choice she describes in the following terms: 'Maintenant je suis rentrée, j'ai besoin de vivre et de mourir dans mon pays. Je n'ai pas rencontré beaucoup d'humanité en Europe. J'avais besoin de l'Afrique et l'Afrique avait besoin de moi' (2014: 196).[6]

---

[6] 'Now I have returned, I need to live and die in my country. I didn't come across much humanity in Europe. I needed Africa and Africa needed me'. All translations are my own.

For Mukagasana, it was already clear during the genocide that she would tell her story if she survived. In *La Mort ne veut pas de moi*, Mukagasna recounts that during the 11 days she spent hiding under the sink at a neighbour's house,[7] she finds an empty cigarette packet on which she notes the dates of her family members' deaths in order to keep a written record (1997: 126–27). In her early testimonies, she expresses a *devoir de mémoire* [duty of memory] towards those who died, confirming at the end of *N'aie pas peur de savoir* that: 'Oui, c'est devenu cela, ma vie. Me battre pour la mémoire de mon peuple' (1999: 295).[8] She expresses a similar sense of duty in her recent testimony; however, this sense of duty now appears to have far broader implications, as Mukagasana also calls on other survivors to respond to an historic duty of memory. In the chapter 'Message aux rescapés' [Message to survivors] she urges other survivors to tell their stories:

> Nous devons écrire notre histoire comme des Africains et comme des êtres humains, personne ne doit nous imposer l'écriture de notre histoire. Écrivons-le nous-mêmes. L'écrire pour nos enfants, nos petits-enfants et nos générations. Nous devons recoudre l'histoire en amont et en aval du génocide où la mémoire est le centre pour vivre notre passé et marcher droit vers l'avenir. (2014: 247)[9]

It is no longer a case of simply recounting what happened during the genocide, of testifying to those lives lost, but of bearing witness to decades of historical injustice and taking control of their own memory, both for the present and for the future.

Annick Kayitesi-Jozan belongs to the younger generation of survivors that Mukagasana seeks to invoke. She was just 14 years old when the genocide broke out in April 1994. She survived with her older sister, Aline, who was badly injured, but her younger brother, Aimé, and her mother, Spécioza, were both killed. Her father and younger sister had died a few years prior to

---

[7] The neighbour, Emmanuelle, was a Hutu who helped Mukagasana to hide and eventually had to flee with her. Mukagasana now considers Emmanuelle as one of 'les justes du Rwanda' (2014: 257) [the just of Rwanda]. The stories of these 'justes' have only recently begun to emerge, for example with the recent collection of testimonies compiled by Belgian scholar Jacques Roisin (2017).

[8] 'Yes, that is what my life has become. Fighting for the memory of my people'.

[9] 'We must write our history as Africans and as human beings, nobody should impose the writing of our history on us. Let's write it ourselves. Write it for our children, our grand-children and our future generations. We must reweave our history around and beyond the genocide, where memory is the key to understanding our past and moving towards the future'.

the genocide, in 1988, during a fire in a hotel in Brussels where they were staying while Nana received treatment. After the genocide, Annick and Aline were evacuated to Burundi and then to France, living with two foster families before Kayitesi-Jozan eventually moved to Paris to pursue her studies in political science and psychology. She is now the mother of two young children, Cyaka and Cyeza. While she has returned to Rwanda several times to look for the bodies of her family members and to participate in the *gacaca* trials, Kayitesi-Jozan remained resident in France until 2015, when she moved with her husband and children to Uzbekistan.[10]

In her first testimony, Kayitesi-Jozan emphasizes that her desire to testify, her decision to write, was driven both by an individual need and by the fact that so many survivors – particularly survivors of sexual abuse – continue to be silenced: 'Ce besoin de témoigner est d'autant plus intense que nombre de rescapés, de filles violées [...] sont condamnés au silence' (2004: 245).[11] However, in her later testimony, *Même Dieu ne veut pas s'en mêler*, her sense of duty is much more oriented towards her children: 'J'écris ce livre pour eux [...] Cette histoire n'est pas un conte. Je dois leur raconter la vie avec ses morts' (2017: 13).[12] This orientation towards future generations is one of the unifying themes running across both Mukagasana's and Kayitesi-Jozan's recent testimonies and, as the following analysis will argue, is a crucial aspect in their rethinking of the reconciliatory role which writing can play in post-genocide Rwanda.

## A Life of Testimony

What is immediately clear in these recent testimonies is that the return to writing is just one activity for these women who have devoted their lives to bearing witness and to fighting for justice for other survivors. Mukagasana is heavily involved with the Commission nationale de lutte contre le génocide [National Commission for the Fight Against Genocide] in Kigali, while Kayitesi-Jozan has collaborated with the Association des étudiants et élèves rescapés du génocide [Genocide Survivors Students Association] and has conducted research in Rwanda on genocide orphans and child perpetrators. I have elsewhere argued that this commitment to helping other survivors

---

[10] Her husband, Raphaël Jozan, is head of the Tashkent regional office for the Agence Française du Développement.

[11] 'This need to bear witness is even more urgent because many survivors, young girls who have been raped [...] are condemned to remain silent'.

[12] 'I am writing this book for them [...] This story is not a fairytale. I must tell them about life with its deaths'.

constitutes a form of 'altruism born of suffering' (see Gilbert, 2018b), a phenomenon that Ervin Staub and Johanna Vollhardt observe occurring when 'those who have suffered from violence reclaim meaning and turn towards others, becoming caring and helpful', particularly in the case of those who have experienced 'persistent, intentional victimisation'. They speak of this experience resulting in 'an alternative "survivor mission" [...] referring to a deep commitment by victims of violence to prevent further suffering' (2006: 267–68). For Mukagasana in particular, this 'survivor mission' is an ongoing duty in her life. She considers herself to be 'une des privilégiés des rescapés du génocide contre les Tutsi' while 'D'autres survivants du génocide au Rwanda vivent dans un désespoir sans fin' (2014: 267).[13] It is therefore her duty both to help those in need and to prevent the perpetuation of further violence: 'Il est de mon devoir de venir aider ceux qu'elle [la souffrance] a laissés faibles et qui ne penseraient qu'à se venger' (2014: 256).[14]

For Mukagasana, this mission to bear witness began almost immediately after the genocide and has given a sense of purpose to her life: 'j'ai compris que j'ai eu besoin de vivre pour le témoignage. J'ai eu besoin de vivre pour faire vivre les miens tant que je vivrais' (2014: 177).[15] It is also important to understand from Mukagasana's words here that bearing witness to the genocide is never a completed act. This is a vital aspect of testimony that is often overlooked in the Western psychoanalytic model, which centres around the rhetoric of healing and a tendency to focus on the restorative properties of narrative. In light of Judith Herman's three fundamental stages of recovery, which she identifies as 'establishing safety, reconstructing the trauma story, and restoring the connection between survivors and their community' (2001: 3), I have elsewhere argued that the creation of narrative is a step towards forging links and creating social bonds within a community of survivors; the telling – and retelling – of the survivor's story is central to working through her trauma and giving meaning to her experiences (Gilbert, 2018a). While I still believe this to be true, we must be careful when using notions such as 'healing', to which Herman – and Western psychiatry more broadly – adhere strongly. Placing the emphasis on 'healing' suggests that survivors will ultimately reach a stage where they are 'healed', which in turn suggests an end to testimony, with no more need

---

[13] 'one of the privileged survivors of the Genocide against the Tutsi'; 'other survivors of the genocide in Rwanda live in a state of endless despair'.
[14] 'It is my duty to help those who have been weakened by suffering and who think only of vengeance'.
[15] 'I understood that I needed to live in order to testify. I needed to live in order to give life to my loved ones, as long as I live'.

to tell the story. I don't discount the notion of healing, but what I believe these later testimonies written by Rwandan women show is that healing is not the primary goal, nor indeed even a possibility. They convey a different meaning to the women's survival that is grounded in an ongoing fight for justice and recognition.

In his preface to Annick Kayitesi-Jozan's first testimony, *Nous existons encore*, French philosopher André Glucksmann describes her story as a sort of celebration: 'Trouvez ici un hymne à la joie. Pas à la joie de vivre, trop naïve et trop aveugle par les temps difficiles. Un hymne à la joie de survivre. Une joie plus forte, conquise de haute lutte et réveillée à chaque victoire sur les désastres' (2004: 14).[16] In this manner, Glucksmann presents Kayitesi-Jozan's narrative as a 'success story', her survival a triumph of the human spirit over extreme suffering, over the 'cataclysme humain' [human cataclysm] of genocide (2004: 9). Kayitesi-Jozan herself suggests a sense of completion upon writing her first testimony: 'Moi aussi je dois parler, écrire, me souvenir. Ne serait-ce qu'une dernière fois. Avec l'espoir d'un autre jour [...] Une dernière fois, revivre l'enfer des Tutsis. Une dernière fois, me souvenir. Je me souviens. *IBUKA!* (2004: 27–28).[17] Nevertheless, the return to writing after 13 years suggests, rather, an incompletion, that her act of testimony and duty of remembrance will never be finished. Henry Greenspan argues that repeatedly retelling the story is part of the 'processual' nature of the act of testimony which is never 'finished' but always points beyond itself. According to Greenspan, the very use of the word *testimony* 'suggests a formal, finished quality that almost never characterizes survivors' remembrance' (2010: 3). In his repeated interviews with Holocaust survivors,[18] Greenspan observes that every time a survivor recounts his or her story, it does not become fixed but changes and grows with each retelling, just, I would argue, as the survivor's sense of self and relation to the world changes and grows. The

---

[16] 'You will find here an ode to joy. Not the joy of living, too naive and too blind for these difficult times. An ode to the joy of surviving. A stronger joy, gained through hard-fought struggle and awakened with each victory over disaster'.

[17] 'I too must speak, write, remember. Even if it's just one last time. With the hope of another day [...] One last time, reliving the hell of the Tutsi. One last time, remembering. I remember. *IBUKA!*' I chose this quotation for the epigraph to my recent monograph, which points towards the ways in which Rwandan women's testimonies (published before 2014) help rebuild a sense of self for the individual and the community, and how the act of writing is part of the process of moving from surviving to living. See Gilbert (2018a).

[18] Rather than interview a large number of survivors once, Greenspan's preferred method is to interview a small number of survivors multiple times throughout their lives.

Annick Kayitesi-Jozan who experienced the genocide at the age of 14 and who bore witness ten years later at the age of 24, is very different to the mother writing in 2017. I suggest that written narratives need to be understood and interpreted alongside and in light of the lives of the individuals who write them, taking into account the stage of life during which the individual is writing and considering the act of writing as one component of a broader life's work.[19] As my analysis in the next section will show, writing her story in the present is for Kayitesi-Jozan a way of 'working through' a fragmented past and reconciling herself to living with the weight of the dead and the guilt she feels at having found happiness in being a mother.

## Reconciling a Fragmented Life

Kayitesi-Jozan's *Même Dieu ne veut pas s'en mêler* fluctuates between the past and the present, with short chapters dated 1988 to 2015. Strange coincidences, such as the birth of her son exactly 20 years to the day after the fire that killed her father and sister in 1988, result in the memories of different events sliding into each other throughout the narrative. For example, the sirens of the ambulance when she goes into labour become confused with those rushing the burnt bodies of her father and sister to hospital. The narrative opens with a memory from 1994 recounted in the present tense, the inescapable 'temps du génocide' [tense of the genocide].[20] Kayitesi-Jozan recalls standing by the kitchen window watching her captors, Adolphe and his wife Nicole,[21] play with their young twins outside:

> Adolphe est rentré du 'travail'. Combien de personnes a-t-il fait tuer aujourd'hui? Il n'a pas de sang sur les mains. Il n'a jamais de sang sur les mains. Nicole lui sourit. Il s'allonge à ses côtés. Ils rient. Le soleil décline, les derniers rayons balaient la toiture en tuiles rouges. Pendant un court

---

[19] This, I would argue, is a crucial direction for the study of testimony and memory work more broadly. While, in *The Future of Memory* (2010), Antony Rowland suggests the need to focus more on the reception of testimony as well as taking into account critical interpretations of a broader range of literary texts, including written and oral narratives by both survivors and perpetrators (115), the lives and activities of individuals beyond the content of their testimonies are too often overlooked.

[20] The slippage between present and past tense is referred to by Souâd Belhaddad in her preface to Esther Mujawayo's *SurVivantes* as 'le temps du traumatisme' (2004: 11–12) [the tense of trauma].

[21] Adolphe and Nicole were colleagues and friends of her mother before the genocide.

instant, j'ai une vision. Je ne suis pas morte. Je n'ai pas vraiment changé. J'ai toujours 14 ans. Je n'ai pas quitté la cuisine. Pourtant je sens que le temps a passé. Mes enfants me regardent. Ils sont deux. (2017: 13)[22]

The image of a happy family is juxtaposed with the violent backdrop of the genocide and Kayitesi-Jozan's experience of being forced to work as a *bonne* [servant] for this family and to await her own death. This is a recurring, haunting memory for Kayitesi-Jozan which is stirred up, for example, by the sight of her own children playing outside during a family holiday, and she feels trapped in this past identity. The constant imposition of this memory, of this past self in the present, echoes Dominick LaCapra's notion of post-traumatic 'acting out' in which 'tenses implode, and it is as if one were back there in the past reliving the traumatic scene' (2001: 21).

However, for Greenspan, repeated telling of the story in this manner can also be indicative of the survivor's 'mastery over the memories to be recounted' (2010: 181). As such, recounting and retelling painful memories become a way of 'working through' the past. In LaCapra's words: 'Working through is an articulatory practice' in which 'one is able to distinguish between past and present and to recall in memory that something happened to one (or one's people) back then while realizing that one is living here and now with opening to the future' (2001: 21–22). Kayitesi-Jozan's acknowledgement of the passing of time in the passage above, and the repositioning of her self in the present with her two children, certainly suggests that she is writing in this manner – fusing past and present – in order to understand and work through the impact of her painful memories of the past on her present life.

Throughout her narrative, Kayitesti-Jozan revisits certain traumatic episodes that were recounted in detail in her first testimony, such as the death of her mother, whose blood she was forced to scrub off the floor, and of her friend Victor who was hacked with machetes in front of her and left to die behind the chapel.[23] Victor's death has become part of her, something that will remain with her forever: 'Quand on entend quelqu'un agoniser aussi

---

[22] 'Adolphe has come home from "work". How many people has he killed today? He doesn't have blood on his hands. He never has blood on his hands. Nicole smiles at him. He lies down beside her. They laugh. The sun is sinking, its last rays touching the red-tiled roof. For a short instant, I have a vision. I am not dead. I haven't really changed. I am still 14 years old. I haven't left the kitchen. Yet I feel that time has passed. My children are watching me. There are two of them'.

[23] Interestingly, she does not refer to the sexual abuse she suffered in her first foster family in France, who took advantage of her vulnerability, which formed a central part of her first testimony.

longtemps, soit on part avec lui, soit il reste en nous pour toujours' (2017: 104).[24] The memory of the dead is experienced physically, as a constant weight on the survivor. While not something an individual can ever 'heal' from, carrying the weight of the dead is something that Kayitesi-Jozan has had to come to terms with in order to continue living:

> J'accepte que jamais maman n'aura de sépulture, et je comprends que jamais je ne serai en paix [...] Je me dois d'être sa tombe, aussi longtemps que ses os traîneront quelque part sur ces collines. Vivante, elle m'a portée dans son ventre, elle m'a nourrie de son sein, elle m'a portée sur son dos, elle m'a aimée. Morte, je la porterai, dans mon ventre, sur mon dos. Partout, tout le temps. (2017: 113)[25]

While Kayitesi-Jozan has learned to live with this weight of the memory of the dead, her greatest fear is that she will in turn transmit it to her children. The legacy of the genocide that she is passing on to her children is her primary concern throughout the narrative, particularly as her children are of an age where they are beginning to ask questions and Kayitesi-Jozan is faced with the impossible task of telling them about her past and Rwanda's history. When her daughter, Cyeza, asks her what happened to her parents, Kayitesi-Jozan tells her, 'Ils sont morts à la guerre' (2017: 118) [they died in the war]:

> Ma mère n'est pas morte d'une guerre, mais d'un génocide. Les mots justes? Ma mère ne faisait pas la guerre. Son assassinat et celui d'un million de Tutsis collent à la définition que donne le dictionnaire: 'Crime contre l'humanité tendant à la destruction totale ou partielle d'un groupe national, ethnique...' Crime contre l'humanité! Cyeza a 3 ans. Comment traduire crime contre l'humanité à un enfant de 3 ans? (2017: 119)[26]

---

[24] 'When you hear someone in agony for so long, either you die with him, or he stays in you forever'.

[25] 'I accept that my mother will never have a tomb, and I understand that I will never be at peace [...] It is my duty to be her tomb, as long as her bones are scattered somewhere on these hills. Alive, she carried me in her belly, she nourished me from her breast, she carried me on her back, she loved me. Dead, I will carry her, in my belly, on my back. Everywhere, all the time'.

[26] 'My mother didn't die in a war, but in a genocide. The right words? My mother wasn't at war. Her murder and that of a million Tutsi matches the dictionary definition: "Crime against humanity aimed at the total or partial destruction of a group on the basis of their nationality, ethnicity..." Crime against humanity! Cyeza is three years old. How do you explain crime against humanity to a three-year-old child?'

In this intimate exchange, Cyeza surprises her by responding: 'Ze suis triste, maman. Ze voulais connaître tes parents. Ze voulais tellement connaître ta maman' (2017: 120).[27] That her daughter already feels the weight of this loss and sadness is extremely distressing for Kayitesi-Jozan: 'Je suis restée les yeux ouverts, incapable de saisir ce qui me terrifiait le plus. Le génocide, le souvenir ou la conséquence qu'il fait à ma fille' (2017: 121).[28] For Kayitesi-Jozan, then, the act of writing can be seen as an individual attempt to reconcile past, present and future, seeking to come to terms with the painful memories of the past and to anticipate the impact they will have on the younger generations so as to protect them from similar experiences.

The difficulty Kayitesi-Jozan experiences in finding the right words to explain what happened to her children is compounded by the question of language, particularly with her older child, Cyaka: 'Le problème avec mon fils, c'est qu'il ne parle pas le kinyarwanda [...] Pourtant, c'est seulement dans cette langue que se trouvent les mots qu'il demande à entendre' (2017: 18–19).[29] While a life in exile may ensure that her children are able to grow up in safety, it may prevent them from truly getting to know their mother's culture.[30] For Kayitesi-Jozan, her children have become her reason for living. Nevertheless, their curiosity about her past also forces her to re-confront her most painful memories and the complex sense of guilt she feels at having survived her loved ones in 1994. She confesses to feeling a profound sense of shame and expresses a fear that she herself will become a burden to her children: 'J'ai honte d'être mère [...] Ma fille est un cadeau que je ne mérite pas, à moins que ce ne soit l'inverse, je suis un fardeau qu'elle ne mérite pas' (2017: 74–75).[31] These feelings of guilt and fear contribute to what Mukagasana describes as the 'ambiguïté' (2014: 202) [ambiguity] that will always be part of the condition of being a survivor and that complicates reconciliation on both an individual and a community level.

---

[27] 'I am sad, Mummy. I want to know your parents. I really want to know your mother'.

[28] 'I remained wide-eyed, incapable of grasping that which terrified me the most. The genocide, its memory or the consequence it was having on my daughter'.

[29] 'The problem with my son is that he doesn't speak Kinyarwanda [...] Yet the words he demands to hear exist only in this language'.

[30] Informal conversations with survivors in the Rwandan diasporic community in the UK nevertheless suggest that children of survivors develop a strong interest in the experiences of their parents and play a leading role in many of the commemorative activities in the diaspora, even if they themselves were born after the genocide.

[31] 'I am ashamed to be a mother [...] My daughter is a gift that I don't deserve, unless it's the opposite: I am a burden that she doesn't deserve'.

## Justice and Reconciliation

Yolande Mukagasana has had to live with the same sense of shame and guilt expressed by Kayitesi-Jozan, and constantly questions the ability of an outsider/reader to grasp these complex emotions experienced by the survivor: 'Qui comprendrait que tu as honte d'avoir survécu seul sans les tiens? Qui comprendrait ton sentiment de culpabilité? [...] Qui comprendrait l'importance de la mémoire?' (2014: 199–201).[32] As a mother who lost her children during the genocide, Mukagasana's narrative evokes the weight of continually living with the dead in the present, with the phrase 'je vis avec mes morts au milieu des vivants' (2014: 181)[33] repeated on several occasions throughout the narrative.[34] However, for Mukagasana, the question of reconciliation takes on a more political focus. While Kayitesi-Jozan's testimony draws the reader into the intimate realm of the family, Mukagasana's narrative adopts a much more accusatory tone, her primary focus being a vitriolic attack on the United Nations. In particular, she expresses a profound disillusionment with the Western model of justice imposed on Rwanda and on the survivors of the genocide, which she claims 'nous aura laissé des blessures que rien ne pourra panser' (2017: 79).[35]

Mukagasana retraces the years of her childhood and youth during the 1950s and 1960s, evoking the violence against the Tutsi during the Hutu revolution and in the post-independence era, as well as going further back to tell the story of her grandmother's disillusionment with first the German and then the Belgian colonizers. Unlike her earlier testimonies, *L'Onu et le chagrin d'une négresse* is much more politically engaged as Mukagasana seeks to establish the long view of history and colonialism that created the

---

[32] 'Who would understand that you are ashamed at having survived without your loved ones? Who would understand your sense of guilt? [...] Who would understand the importance of the memory?'

[33] 'I live with my dead among the living'.

[34] Similarly, Kayitesi-Jozan writes: 'Les morts vivent parmi les vivants et les vivants parmi les morts' (2017: 218) [The dead live among the living and the living among the dead].

[35] 'has inflicted wounds upon us that nothing will heal'. Similar questioning and language in used Patrick Nsengimana's testimony, published in the same year as Mukagasana's *L'Onu et le chagrin d'une négresse*: 'Que l'on me laisse parler. Qui essuiera mes larmes? Qui m'apaisera? Qui comblera le vide laissé par les miens? L'abcès doit crever. Pour que la blessure puisse être pansée' (Nsengimana, 2014: 19) [Let me speak. Who will dry my tears? Who will comfort me? Who will fill the emptyness left by my loved ones? The abscess must burst. So that the wound can be dressed].

conditions that ultimately led to the genocide. In the opening pages of her second testimony, *N'aie pas peur de savoir*, Mukagasana all but apologizes to her French reader for her limited knowledge of politics. However, in her later narrative, she insists on the importance for survivors of becoming politically informed:

> Chers frères et sœurs survivants, moi, je me suis réconciliée avec la politique, essayons d'y entrer. Je me suis rendue compte que pour changer les choses, nous devons entrer en politique. Ceux qui ne se sentent pas capables devraient absolument le faire. Nous ne sommes pas fait [*sic*] uniquement pour mourir. Nous sommes faits aussi pour vivre pleinement comme les autres. (2014: 214–15)[36]

Mukagasana adopts an overtly political tone, openly condemning the role of the UN and its constituent organizations such as the UN Refugee Agency (HCR) and the International Criminal Tribunal for Rwanda (ICTR). Throughout her text, Mukagasana uses scathing, and at times abusive language to show her disgust with what she describes as a 'système criminel' (2014: 40) [criminal system].

In condemning the UN, she seeks justice not for herself but for other survivors who have been wounded by the international justice process. She repeatedly stresses that her life is no longer her own – 'Ma vie à moi ne m'appartient pas' [my life doesn't belong to me] – but is dedicated to 'la lutte pour la reconnaissance du génocide' (2014: 181).[37] She is particularly critical of the role of the ICTR, which she describes as 'Un beau tribunal international, dont les salaires des juges sont en eux-mêmes une insulte à la pauvreté des victimes du génocide' (2014: 75).[38] Given the profound sense of betrayal Mukagasana associates with the ICTR, she is deeply committed to the Rwandan justice system, notably the *gacaca* courts, which are heavily criticized by the West:

> Enfin, par un espèce de réflexe politique, la justice rwandaise a été critiquée comme étant celle des vainqueurs. Cette critique m'a paru odieuse, lorsque l'on sait que les parties civiles sont les rescapés, lesquels ont en général

---

[36] 'Dear brother and sister survivors, I have reconciled myself with politics, let's try to engage with it. I realized that we must engage with politics in order to change things. Those who don't feel capable should absolutely do it. We were not made simply to die. We were also made to live full lives like other people'.

[37] 'the fight for the recognition of the genocide'.

[38] 'a flashy international tribunal where the judges' salaries are in themselves an insult to the poverty of the genocide victims'.

perdu leurs familles dans le génocide. Comme si dans un génocide, il y avait des vainqueurs et des vaincus! (2014: 88)[39]

She emphasizes that Rwanda has had to face the unprecedented challenge not only of punishing the guilty but also of rehabilitating and reintegrating them into Rwandan society. Through her writing, Mukagasana urges survivors and perpetrators alike to engage in the justice and reconciliation processes, for it is this engagement and commitment to building a better future that ultimately gives meaning to her own survival: 'S'il vous plait, trouvez la force de protéger tous les enfants, même ceux des criminels, y compris les enfants des assassins de mes propres enfants. Je lance un appel aux jeunes du monde entier. Refusez de grandir dans un monde de violence [...] Rendez ma survie utile' (2014: 194).[40]

Mukagasana herself attended a number of *gacaca* trials. She recognizes that the system is problematic given its reliance on perpetrator confession, but she nonetheless remains 'convaincue que les Rwandais se sortiront de leurs problèmes et serviront de référence au monde et surtout aux autres Africains' (2014: 93).[41] Kayitesi-Jozan's experience of the *gacaca* is less positive, having attended Adolphe's trial in 2002:

> Dans la salle d'audience, en ce mois de mai, la foule était immense, les familles des accusés sont venues en nombre. Moi, je suis accompagnée d'une dizaine de rescapés de ma ville, serrés dans un coin [...] Le procès a duré une petite journée. Les juges ont estimé que, de nos deux vérités, celle d'Adolphe était préférable pour la nation. Ils ont ordonné la libération sur-le-champ des accusés. (2017: 189–90)[42]

---

[39] 'Of course, their political reflex has been to criticize the Rwandan justice system as being that of the winners. I find this criticism odious, especially when you know that the civil parties are survivors who, for the most part, have lost their families in the genocide. As if in a genocide there can be winners and losers!'

[40] 'Please, find the strength to protect all the children, even those of the criminals, including the children of the assassins of my own children. This is an appeal to young people around the world. Refuse to grow up in a world of violence [...] Make my survival count for something'.

[41] 'convinced that Rwandans will solve their own problems and will serve as a model to the world and especially to other Africans'.

[42] 'In the courtroom, in this month of May, the crowd was enormous, the families of the accused had come in large numbers. As for me, I was accompanied by a dozen or so survivors from my town, all squeezed into a corner [...] The trial didn't even last a day. The judges decided that, of our two truths, Adolphe's was preferable for the nation. They ordered the immediate release of the accused'.

This passage brings to light the tensions that exist between reconciliation at the personal and national level, where the government's goal of national unity does not always coincide with the needs of individual survivors.[43] For Kayitesi-Jozan, the trial was an intimidating and painful experience, where the accused refused to tell her where her mother's body is buried. The possibility of finding her mother's remains disappears with the death of Adolphe in 2009, another painful change of circumstance that Kayitesi-Jozan must come to terms with: 'C'est fini, je n'enterrai pas maman, aucun de *mes quelqu'uns'* (2017: 191; emphasis original).[44] As Phil Clark notes in his detailed study of *gacaca*, 'Public confession may aid survivors' catharsis through increasing their knowledge of exactly what happened in the past and opening the way for apology, reparation and even survivors' forgiveness of perpetrators' (2010: 197); on the other hand, 'The uncertainty of the details of a person's death can hamper a survivor's ability to reconstruct that event in his or her mind and to shape it in such a way as to move beyond grief to a less stricken state of being' (2010: 197). It is unclear whether Clark uses this phrase deliberately, but the notion of a 'less stricken state of being' encapsulates the differentiation between the Western concept of 'healing' and survivors' reality of attempting to move beyond a state of survival and to find ways of living with their painful past.

Boubacar Boris Diop writes in his endorsement on the back cover of Mukagasana's *L'Onu et le chagrin d'une négresse*: 'Au fil des ans, Yolande Mukagasana reste inconsolable mais sa douleur a fini par lui donner un authentique sens du dépassement'.[45] As Mukagasana herself observes, 'La souffrance que j'ai endurée m'a laissé une force que je ne pensais pas avoir' (2014: 256).[46] She concludes: 'Je ne pourrai jamais recommencer ma vie, je continuerai ma survie car ma vie, je ne peux la recommencer. Je la vis autrement' (2014: 241).[47] This implies a shift away from the Western understanding of 'healing' from trauma towards a 'living with' – a 'vivre autrement' – that the survivor develops over the years and which is

---

[43] A discussion of national reconciliation processes is beyond the scope of this chapter. For a recent study of Rwanda's policy of National Unity and Reconciliation, see Purdeková (2015).

[44] 'It is over. I will never bury my mother, nor any of my loved ones'.

[45] 'Over the years, Yolande Mukagasana remains inconsolable, but her pain has ultimately given her an authentic sense of moving beyond'.

[46] 'The suffering that I have endured has given me a strength I didn't know I possessed'.

[47] 'I can never begin my life again, I will continue in my survival because I can't begin my life again. I am living it differently'.

strengthened through her commitment to carrying the memory of the dead, to seeking justice for other survivors and to building a more humane world for future generations. Kayitesi-Jozan evokes a similar sentiment in an interview with Patrick Simonin on the chat show *L'Invité*, following the publication of *Même Dieu ne veut pas s'en mêler*: 'Les morts font partie de ma vie et ils me donnent le courage de me lever parce que j'apprécie d'être en vie [...] Mais en même temps ça me rappelle que c'est un combat de tous les jours, qu'on doit lutter contre la haine, qu'on ne doit pas laisser la haine nous envahir. Et je vis avec ça tout le temps'.[48] In a short testimony published in the special issue of *Les Temps Modernes* marking the twentieth anniversary of the Genocide against the Tutsi, young survivor Didacienne Uwaysabye also describes living after the genocide as a 'combat' (2014: 27).[49] In this context, writing becomes a crucial tool for survivors in the ongoing struggle to 'work through' and find a way of 'living with' the weight of the past, and in reconstructing themselves and their communities as part of LaCapra's 'opening to the future'.

---

[48] 'The dead are part of my life and they give me the courage to get up because I appreciate being alive [...] But they also remind me that every day is a struggle, that we must fight against hatred, that we can't let hatred take us over. And I live with that all the time' (interview with Patrick Simonin, 25 September 2017, available at https://www.youtube.com/watch?v=q0j43isTRhg (consulted on 18 March 2018)). This echoes Madelaine Hron's discussion of Christian testimonials in which forgiveness and reconciliation are only made possible through a 'letting go' of hatred and anger (see the chapter '*Imbabazi, Kwicuza* and Christian Testimonials of Forgiveness' in this volume). Significantly, however, religion is not a key theme in Kayitesi-Jozan's writing. She declares: 'Je ne suis pas croyante. J'ai cessé de l'être. En partie. Une part de moi espère que le mal sera sanctionné. Si ce n'est pas par les hommes (j'ai bien compris depuis un moment qu'ils en sont incapables), au moins par une force supérieure' (2014: 57) [I am not a believer. I have ceased to be one. Partially. A part of me hopes that evil will be punished. If not by men (and I have long understood that they are not capable of it) then at least by a higher power].

[49] It is worth noting that many publications of this nature are intended to coincide with significant date-based commemorations. While not considered explicitly in this chapter, this question certainly requires further investigation. Both authors under consideration in this chapter have published books in key commemorative years (2004, 2014). This is perhaps more to do with the publishers' strategies rather than a reflection of when the women themselves choose to write, although it is significant that three chapters in Kayitesi-Jozan's recent narrative address the twentieth anniversary commemoration – particularly as this is the year that her children first take part in the commemorative activities – which appears to be a factor in her decision to return to writing.

## Conclusion: Writing for the Future

The most crucial change in both Kayitesi-Jozan's and Mukagasana's recent testimonies lies in their ever-deepening commitment to the younger generations and anticipating how these future generations will remember, be affected by and respond to the genocide. Mukagasana writes that 'je vois les enfants qui naissent au Rwanda et j'ai peur. Ma vie ne m'appartient plus, sinon je m'arrêterais. C'est aussi pour eux et grâce à eux que je continue' (2014: 187).[50] She hopes her writing will serve as a useful legacy to the younger generations: 'Je ne serai plus là tout à l'heure, demain ou après demain. Mes livres publiés, j'espère qu'ils aideront les générations futures' (2014: 184).[51] It is this commitment to future generations that has become her purpose for living and ultimately renders her survival 'utile' [useful]. Her testimony also functions as a call for an ethical engagement on the part of other survivors and of the young generations to invest in the future: 'Vous allez un jour faire des enfants, vous avez le devoir de leur préparer un monde dans lequel ils se sentiront bien. Aujourd'hui, cet appel est pour vous et ce que je vous raconte aussi est pour vous' (2014: 240).[52] Kayitesi-Jozan reflects on the ways in which her children engage with – and are potentially damaged by – the memory of the genocide. In particular, she talks of her son's first experience of commemoration, which will inevitably become an annual ritual in his life: 'Cyaka a "fait" sa première commémoration, comme on dit sa première communion' (2017: 223).[53] While she does not want to burden her children with the painful memory of the genocide, she nonetheless recognizes that she needs to find the courage to tell them about their history and about her own experiences, which are an integral part of their cultural heritage. Both women, in their writing, recognize that the younger generations will play a crucial role in commemorative and reconciliatory practices at the personal, community and national levels, and that their participation in these practices must be free from the burden of hatred and anger so as to facilitate the rebuilding of society.

---

[50] 'I see the children being born in Rwanda and I am afraid. My life no longer belongs to me, otherwise I would stop. It is for them and because of them that I carry on'.

[51] 'Soon I will no longer be here, today or the day after. I hope that my published books will help the future generations'.

[52] 'One day you will have children, you have the duty of preparing a world for them in which they will be safe. Today, I appeal to you and my story is also for you'.

[53] 'Cyaka "took" his first commemoration, just as we talk about a first communion'.

As Rwandan psychiatrist Naasson Munyandamutsa[54] observes, 'Le contexte de violence extrême a mis en faillite les valeurs fondatrices de notre société',[55] destroying the familial 'chaîne de transmission' (2005: 84) [chain of transmission]. Munyandamutsa suggests that narrative plays a crucial role in rebuilding intergenerational links that facilitate the transmission of memory and the reconstruction of both the individual and the community:

> Renouer les liens générationnels suppose la capacité de mobiliser la mémoire du passé dans une dynamique d'appartenance [... L'individu doit] se structurer autour de la mémoire des siens disparus, qui ont constitué le fondement de sa vie, qui lui ont légué un dispositif capable de découvrir l'humain dans l'homme et de chercher à le découvrir envers et contre tout, contre toute conviction triviale. C'est à cette condition que le récit est possible. (2005: 87)[56]

This is reflected in Rwandan women's testimonies as they strive to mobilize and transmit the memory of the genocide and reforge links between the generations, which, as Kayitesi-Jozan's narrative indicates, poses a unique set of challenges for Rwandans living in the diaspora. There is an urgent need for deeper examination of the impact of the genocide in diasporic communities,[57] particularly in terms of both the potential harm and the constructive possibilities that the memory of the genocide can have on the

---

[54] It is significant that Naasson Munyandamutsa is referenced by both Kayitesi-Jozan and Mukagasana as the only Rwandan psychiatrist practising in Rwanda (Kayitesi-Jozan, 2017: 175; Mukagasana, 2014: 265). Munyandamutsa passed away in March 2016.

[55] 'The context of extreme violence has left the foundational values of our society bankrupt'.

[56] 'Rebuilding generational links requires the capacity to mobilize the memory of the past in a dynamic of belonging [...] The individual must build herself around the memory of her disappeared loved ones, who constituted the foundation of her life and who handed down to her a set of values capable of recognizing the human in man and of seeking to recognize it against all odds, against any trivial conviction. It is on this condition that the narrative can be told'. Again, this echoes Madelaine Hron's discussion of Christian testimonials of forgiveness in her chapter in this volume, where it is only through admitting the humanity of the perpetrators that forgiving them is made possible, a process of 'humanization' that is also essential for reconciliation.

[57] A few studies are starting to emerge focusing on specific diasporic communities. For example, a team of Rwandan and Finnish social psychologists have recently published findings on the trauma inflicted by the genocide on the Rwandan diaspora in Finland (Banyanga, Björkqvist and Österman, 2017). A

children of survivors, who are often actively engaged in commemorative practices in Rwandan communities. Numerous youth initiatives and organizations are emerging both in Rwanda and across the diaspora, working actively to transmit the memory of the genocide, promote reconciliation and fight against further violence. In the UK, for example, the Rwandan Youth Information Community Organisation (rYico) is extremely active in educational and commemorative activities.[58] In 2013, rYico published a volume of testimonies, *Keeping Memories: Rwandans in the UK*, which is dedicated to 'those who died, those who lived and those who are building a future for Rwandans'.

Finally, this looking to the future and the place which the legacy of the genocide will occupy in that future echoes current discussions in the field of memory studies around what has been termed 'anticipatory memory'. As Claire Colebrook points out, 'To remember is never simply to retain and recall a past, but always to do so from the point of view of a present that anticipates a future' (in Craps et al., 2017: 10). While anticipatory memory is currently referred to primarily in the context of climate change and environmental catastrophes, Stef Craps notes that it also plays into the 'never again' imperative associated with Holocaust remembrance: 'Just as the memory of the Holocaust can allegedly help prevent future genocide, so the proleptic memory of climate catastrophe can perhaps function as a spur to action that would prevent the anticipated catastrophe from actually coming to pass' (2017: 488).[59] Just as Mukagasana calls for a longer view of history in understanding the genocide and its causes, thinking about narratives bearing witness to the 1994 Genocide against the Tutsi in Rwanda and its aftermath in terms of 'anticipatory memory' may prove fruitful for situating the genocide in its broader global historical and contemporary context. This understanding of memory allows us to read the recent testimonies by Rwandan women as future-oriented forms of writing that play a crucial role in facilitating reconciliation, fighting for justice and recognition for survivors, and in building an important cultural legacy for future generations.

---

recent Canadian political science PhD thesis examines identity formation within the Rwandan diaspora in the Greater Toronto Area (Ainsworth, 2015).

[58] See http://ryico.org.

[59] In his recent book, *Redefining Genocide*, Damien Short draws a connection between the Intergovernmental Panel on Climate Change held in April 2014 and the twentieth anniversary of the Rwandan genocide, which 'focused global attention on this gruesome act of collective violence and many politicians and activists the world over stated (yet again) their commitment to genocide prevention' (2016: 186).

## Works Cited

Ainsworth, Anna. 2015. 'Constructing Rwandan Identity in the Diaspora: Remembering the Green Hills in Cold Canada'. PhD Thesis, York University, Ontario. Available at https://yorkspace.library.yorku.ca/xmlui/handle/10315/32132 (consulted on 6 March 2018).

Banyanga, Jean d'Amour, Kaj Björkqvist and Karin Österman. 2017. 'Trauma Inflicted by Genocide: Experiences of the Rwandan Diaspora in Finland'. *Cogent Psychology* 4.1: 1–12. Available at https://www.tandfonline.com/doi/full/10.1080/23311908.2017.1333244 (consulted on 22 February 2018).

Brinker, Virginie. 2014. *La Transmission littéraire et cinématographique du génocide des Tutsi au Rwanda*. Paris: Classiques Garnier.

Clark, Phil. 2010. *The Gacaca Courts, Post-Genocide Justice and Reconciliation in Rwanda: Justice without Lawyers*. Cambridge: Cambridge University Press.

Craps, Stef. 2017. 'Climate Change and the Art of Anticipatory Memory'. *Parallax* 23.4: 479–92.

Craps, Stef, et al. 2017. 'Memory Studies and the Anthropocene: A Roundtable'. *Memory Studies* 11.4: 498–515.

Gilbert, Catherine. 2018a. *From Surviving to Living: Voice, Trauma and Witness in Rwandan Women's Writing*. Montpellier: Presses universitaires de la Méditerranée.

—. 2018b. 'Mobilising Memory: Rwandan Women Genocide Survivors in the Diaspora'. *Australian Journal of French Studies* 55.1: 54–66.

Greenspan, Henry. 2010 [1998]. *Beyond Testimony: On Listening to Holocaust Survivors*. 2nd ed., revised and expanded. St. Paul, MN: Paragon House.

Herman, Judith Lewis. 2001 [1992]. *Trauma and Recovery: From Domestic Abuse to Political Terror*. London: Pandora.

Hitchcott, Nicki. 2015. *Rwanda Genocide Stories: Fiction After 1994*. Liverpool: Liverpool University Press.

—. 2017. '"More than just a genocide country": Recuperating Rwanda in the Writings of Scholastique Mukasonga'. *Journal of Romance Studies* 17.2: 127–49.

Kayitesi-Jozan, Annick. 2017. *Même Dieu ne veut pas s'en mêler: Rwanda, une vie après*. Paris: Seuil.

Kayitesi, Annick. 2004. *Nous existons encore*. Paris: Michel Lafon.

LaCapra, Dominick. 2001. *Writing History, Writing Trauma*. Baltimore: Johns Hopkins University Press.

Mujawayo, Esther, and Souâd Belhaddad. 2004. *SurVivantes. Rwanda dix ans après le génocide*. Paris: Éditions de l'Aube.

Mukagasana, Yolande. 1997. *La Mort ne veut pas de moi*. Paris: Fixot.

—. 1999. *N'aie pas peur de savoir*. Paris: Robert Laffont.

—. 2003. *De bouche à oreille*. Paris: Éditions Menaibuc.

—. 2014. *L'Onu et le chagrin d'une négresse: Rwanda/RD-Congo, 20 ans après.* Paris: Aviso.

Mukagasana, Yolande, and Alain Kazinierakis. 2001. *Les Blessures du silence: témoignages du génocide au Rwanda.* Paris: Actes Sud.

Munyandamutsa, Naasson. 2005. 'Renouer avec les liens générationnels'. In Jean Furtos and Christian Laval (eds), *La Santé mentale en actes: de la clinique au politique.* Toulouse: Éditions Erès: 83–89.

Nsengimana, Patrick. 2014. 'Le chagrin'. *Les Temps Modernes* 680–81 (special issue: *Le Génocide des Tutsi, 1994–2014: Quelle Histoire? Quelle mémoire?*): 19–26.

Purdeková, Andrea. 2015. *Making Ubumwe: Power, State and Camps in Rwanda's Unity-Building Project.* New York and Oxford: Berghahn Books.

Roisin, Jacques. 2017. *Dans la nuit la plus noire se cache l'humanité: Récits des justes du Rwanda.* Brussels: Les Impressions Nouvelles.

Rowland, Antony. 2010. 'The Future of Testimony: Introduction'. In Richard Crownshaw, Jany Kilby and Antony Rowland (eds), *The Future of Memory.* New York and Oxford: Berghahn Books: 113–21.

rYico. 2013. *Keeping Memories: Rwandans in the UK.* Brighton: QueenSpark Books.

Short, Damien. 2016. *Redefining Genocide: Settler Colonialism, Social Death and Ecocide.* London: Zed Books.

Staub, Ervin, and Johanna Vollhardt. 2006. 'Altruism Born of Suffering: The Roots of Caring and Helping After Victimization and Other Trauma'. *American Journal of Orthopsychiatry* 78.3: 267–80.

Uwaysabye, Didacienne. 2014. 'Vivre est un combat'. *Les Temps Modernes* 680–81 (special issue: *Le Génocide des Tutsi, 1994–2014: Quelle Histoire? Quelle mémoire?*): 27–39.

# Decolonizing Trauma Therapy in Rwanda

*Caroline Williamson Sinalo*

Exposure to highly traumatic experiences such as the Genocide against the Tutsi often has distressing consequences. Although people can respond in a range of ways, negative emotions (anxiety, depression, anger, irritability, sadness, guilt, fear) and troubling, repetitive thoughts are quite common. The combination of these emotions and thoughts can lead to behavioural difficulties and even physical reactions such as fatigue, muscle tension, difficulties with breathing, feelings of jumpiness or difficulty sleeping (Calhoun and Tedeschi, 1999: 5–10). Such emotional, cognitive, behavioural and physical reactions are frequently interpreted as pathological and labelled 'post-traumatic stress disorder' (PTSD). According to leading post-traumatic growth theorists Stephen Joseph and Alex Linley, an 'illness ideology has permeated the language of clinical psychology, leading it to become the language of medicine and psychopathology' (2008: 4). In their criticism of this medicalization of trauma, Joseph and Linley (2008) argue that the pervasive illness ideology has separated the study of PTSD from that of post-traumatic growth, rather than developing an integrative perspective for understanding all responses to trauma.

Post-traumatic growth is when individuals establish new beliefs about themselves and the world, and build a new, and often enhanced, way of life following a traumatic experience (for an overview, see Calhoun and Tedeschi, 2006). Research suggests that, alongside psychological distress, many trauma survivors also experience positive changes in the wake of tragedy. A medical model nonetheless continues to dominate the study of trauma, although the concept of PTSD has come under criticism, particularly when applied in non-Western contexts. As Derek Summerfield argues, 'Western trends towards the medicalization of distress' assume that PTSD is 'a universal human response to [traumatic] events' (2004: 241). However, Western 'psychiatric universalism risks being imperialistic' in postcolonial settings by assuming that certain types of knowledge are superior to others (Summerfield, 2004: 242).

Such may be the case in Rwanda, partly because of the way in which the medical model conceives of trauma and partly because of the way therapy is conducted there. This chapter will discuss these factors and contrast them with local understandings of trauma, drawing first on an interview with traditional Rwandan trauma therapist Muganga Rutangarwamaboko, and second on an analysis of genocide survivor testimonies. In its conclusion, the chapter will advocate an alternative approach to trauma therapy in Rwanda, reconciling post-traumatic growth theory and postcolonial theory with home-grown ideas about Rwandan identity, known as *ndi umunyarwanda*, the notion of Rwandanness or 'Rwandicity'.

An official *Ndi Umunyarwanda* programme was launched by the Rwandan government in 2013 with the aim of reconciling Rwandans in advance of the twentieth anniversary of the genocide (see Benda, this volume). It consisted in a set of public meetings in which young Hutu (particularly men) were encouraged to apologize for genocide crimes. According to President Kagame, 'Le but de cette campagne est de mettre l'accent sur ce qui nous unit, la "rwandité", et de faire disparaître ce qui nous divise et qui a causé le génocide' (Soudan, 2014) [the point of this campaign is to focus on what unites us, our 'Rwandicity', and to eradicate the things that divide us and caused the genocide]. Critics of the *Ndi Umunyarwanda* programme argue that it encourages the Hutu population to apologize to the Tutsi in the name of the entire ethnic group (regardless of whether they were individually responsible for the genocide) and that this may further exacerbate ethnic divisions in Rwanda (Mbaraga, 2013). Because of the government campaign, the term *ndi umunyarwanda* (literally, 'I am Rwandan')[1] is often associated with dominant government narratives; however, the concept predates the policy.

---

[1] An alternative Kinyarwanda term sometimes used to describe this concept is *ubunyarwanda* which combines the word *umunyarwanda* [Rwandan person] with the eighth-class prefix *bu-*, indicating the abstract form of a noun. Other similar expressions include *kwitwa umunyarwanda* [to call oneself Rwandan] and *kuba umunyarwanda* [to be Rwandan]. *Ndi umunyarwanda* goes beyond all of these terms and suggests a Rwandan who embraces Rwandan culture and values.

According to Frank Rusagara, 'Rwandanness' was created in precolonial times 'through an extensive institutional infrastructure' (2009: 9). This included *amatorero*, military schools where young Rwandans were educated in Rwandan cultural values, including discipline (*imyitwarire*), courage (*ubutwali*) and patriotism (*gukunda igihugu*) (Rusagara, 2009: 48, 91). Beyond the government's use of the term, *ndi umunyarwanda* is understood as a shared set of values, being an upstanding citizen (*kuba imfura* or *inyanga-mugayo*) and having a common Rwandan identity (Williamson, 2016b). As my analysis below demonstrates, this ideology is espoused by survivors to recreate their identities, albeit in ways that often defy the government's ideology. My main argument is that by revalorizing indigenous values, culture and language, survivors demonstrate a form of positive identity change which I label 'postcolonial post-traumatic growth'. By attending to such change, the therapy approach suggested attempts to acknowledge and encourage such existing stories of positive change among survivors, providing a response to structural, chronic forms of trauma while avoiding the imposition of the Western medical model.

## A Misplaced Approach: An Event-Based Model for Long-Term Trauma

Besides importing potentially culturally alien 'practices, technologies, and narratives' (Young, 1995: 5), a significant problem with the Western medical model in a postcolonial, post-genocide context like Rwanda is its narrow understanding of what constitutes 'traumatic'. Craps argues that even the most recent American Psychiatric Association definition is still 'narrow enough to make some important sources of trauma invisible and unknowable' (2013: 25). In his view, this narrow focus on singular events tends to 'leave unquestioned the conditions that enabled the traumatic abuse such as political oppression, racism, or economic domination' (2013: 28). This means that 'problems that are essentially political, social, or economic are medicalized, and the people affected by them are pathologized as victims without agency, sufferers from an illness that can be cured through psycho-logical counselling' (Craps, 2013: 28). On first inspection, an event-based description of trauma might seem appropriate for understanding the 1994 Genocide against the Tutsi. This episode of extreme violence took place over a distinct period and went far beyond the ordinary, everyday experiences of most Rwandan people, leaving many to suffer the types of emotional, cognitive and behavioural responses associated with PTSD. A further examination of Rwandan history might cause one to reconsider this view, however, as the traumatic experiences of Rwandans date back well beyond

1994. Frantz Fanon (1961: 236) concluded that colonialism involves the 'négation systématisée de l'autre, une décision forcenée de refuser à l'autre tout attribut d'humanité', which forces the people it affects to 'se poser constamment la question: 'Qui suis-je en réalité?'[2] Colonialism had similar consequences in the Great Lakes region where, Gérard Prunier informs us, 'African social and cultural ways of doing things were neither taken into account nor questioned [by colonists]; they were simply made obsolete' (2009: xxix). This was no less the case for Rwanda and not only during the colonial period (1897–1962). The domination of Rwandan cultural identity continued well beyond independence. Writing in the 1970s, Claudine Vidal identified a 'fourth ethnic group' in Rwanda, the bourgeoisie which adopted European cultural norms but remained 'totalement dépendante du maître étranger' [totally dependent on the foreign master] (1974: 81–82).[3] According to Vidal, this bourgeoisie:

> adopte ses valeurs [européennes], copie du mieux qu'elle peut sa civilisation. Elle n'en reçoit pourtant que les miettes: quelques modes vestimentaires, des rudiments de culture, des meubles, des fêtes ... Peu de choses, juste assez pour se démarquer de la masse, mais trop peu pour égaler les Européens. (1974: 82)[4]

Unfortunately, the Rwandan experience of colonization was not simply the negation of culture but rather the re-engineering of society by the Belgians on the basis of a divisive form of scientific racism known as the 'Hamitic hypothesis'.[5] The Hamitic myth was eventually reformulated by extremist Hutu ideologues who emphasized the exploitative nature of Tutsi rule during the precolonial period and considered Tutsi to be an 'outsider' group who had invaded Rwanda. This idea eventually formed the basis of the genocidal ideology.

---

[2] 'Because it is a systematic negation of the other person and a furious determination to deny the other person all attributes of humanity, colonialism forces the people it dominates to ask themselves the question constantly: "In reality, who am I?"' (Fanon, 1963: 250).

[3] This and all subsequent quotations from this source were translated by myself.

[4] 'adopts [European] values; copies as best it can their civilization. In return, it receives nothing but a few scraps: some clothing styles, some rudimentary culture, a bit of furniture, parties ... Very few things, just enough to distinguish itself from the masses, but too little to match the Europeans'.

[5] The Tutsi were classified as a Hamitic 'race' – a subgroup of the Caucasian race – who had arrived in Rwanda from Somalia or Ethiopia and conquered the Hutu and Twa as a result of what was assumed to be their natural superiority.

The post-genocide government has attempted to respond to the identity crisis caused by colonialism, but Rwandan people continue to experience the neo-imperial demonization of their identities, particularly in popular Western representations of Rwanda. For example, in an analysis of news coverage of the Rwanda crisis in the United States, Melissa Wall concludes that when 'Rwandans were given a voice, it was only within a framework that consistently presented them as pathetic and helpless victims, as insensate, animal-like creatures or as barbaric savages' (2007: 265). Similarly, in her analysis of the perpetrator testimonies in Jean Hatzfeld's award-winning *Machete Season*, Madelaine Hron argues that the Rwandans presented in the book are generally portrayed as primitive and that the text reflects Western clichés of Africa as a dark and dangerous place (2011: 136, 141). My own research also shows a tendency to omit criticisms of the West in published translations of survivor testimonies, making them appear as passive, voiceless victims of inevitable, unstoppable violence (Williamson, 2016a; Williamson Sinalo, 2018). President Paul Kagame recognizes this reductionist tendency in international representations of Rwanda, stating that 'despite accelerating globalization, our continent is still perceived as a place apart, an alternate dimension of the human experience, at once faceless, passive, and dangerous' (Soudan, 2015: 127–28). When put in this context, it can be seen that the genocide was in fact a product of a much more complex, chronic form of trauma – caused by colonialism and the destruction of identity – that continues even today. To treat Rwandan trauma sufferers with an event-based view, such as the medical model, then, fails to capture the complex traumatic experiences of Rwandans. Such a misunderstanding, combined with the presumed superiority of the Western medical model, may thus exacerbate rather than remedy the trauma suffered in Rwanda, especially as therapies are often conducted by Western 'specialists' via a translator/interpreter.

## The Trauma of Western Therapy

As in other contexts, most studies of trauma and its consequences in Rwanda have focused on the negative consequences, drawing on an event-based medical model. Most published reports of therapy, for example, evaluate the effectiveness of an intervention on its ability to reduce levels of distress and PTSD symptoms (e.g. Chu, 2010; Gishoma et al., 2014; Godard, 2003). The paucity of resources, personnel and infrastructure to 'treat' people suffering from PTSD constitutes a significant challenge, even if we were to accept the validity of the concept. According to Isaura Zelaya Favila, all of Rwanda's psychiatrists left during the civil war (1990–1994); there was just one in 2005 and by 2008 only three psychiatrists were practising in the country (2009:

2). While the 'psychiatric infrastructure had never been good', in the years following 1994 it was 'practically nonexistent' (Favila, 2009: 3).

The restoration of mental health services in Rwanda has largely been down to the work of a single individual, the one psychiatrist left in Rwanda after 1994, Professor Naasson Munyandamutsa.[6] With support from UNICEF and the Swiss government, he established Rwanda's National Trauma Recovery Centre at Ndera Hospital in 1995 and later collaborated with the Ministry of Health to develop the Psychosocial Consultation Centre, which provides counselling for genocide survivors. In collaboration with a team of experts at the University of Rwanda, Professor Munyandamutsa developed a four-year Master of Medicine (MMED) degree in psychiatry, which is offered in the College of Medicine and Health Sciences.

Despite Munyandamutsa's efforts, however, Lauren Ng and Boniface Harerimana report that the 'availability of mental health services is still very limited due in part to a lack of trained professionals and a small budget for mental health services' (2016: 2). Most healthcare providers working at the two main mental healthcare centres (Ndera and the Psychosocial Consultation Centre) are primarily Bachelor's degree-level psychiatric nurses and psychologists. The World Health Organization's Mental Health Atlas (2017) states that there are still only 0.06 psychiatrists per 100,000 people (i.e. roughly seven for the whole country). Moreover, while the 'government has been actively decentralizing [physical] health care, [...] the great majority of mental health care is still done at the national hospital level' and 'almost all mental health services are located in Kigali' (Ng and Harerimana, 2016: 2, 7). Alongside Ndera Hospital and the Psychosocial Consultation Service, there are a number of local and international NGOs providing counselling programmes (see Favila, 2009: 12–13).[7] Levels of training in these organizations also vary considerably and many of them are based in Kigali. In addition to these infrastructural concerns, however, the main psychosocial trauma and recovery interventions are still dominated by the Western medical model, which is also espoused by the government (Ng and Harerimana, 2016: 2). The methods described in

---

[6] Professor Munyandamutsa sadly died in 2016. The Belgian Embassy in Kigali published a short obituary on its Facebook page where further bibliographical information about him can be found. See https://www.facebook.com/permalink.php?story_fbid=496125003908613&id=108988062622311 (consulted on 1 June 2018).

[7] See also http://www.sociotherapy.org/ and https://www.fracarita-international.org/mental-health-care. The focus and approach of NGOs providing psychotherapy vary considerably and many do indeed adopt more community-based, grass-roots approaches.

studies authored by Munyandamutsa and his colleagues are equally embedded within this model (e.g. Gishoma et al., 2014: 474–76).

Alongside Rwandan-authored studies on trauma interventions, a number of studies have been published by Western trauma specialists. Despite their attempts to understand Rwandan culture, many of these interventions draw unproblematically on the PTSD concept while also demonstrating other cultural insensitivities. For example, French psychologist Marie-Odile Godard (2003) offers a psychoanalytical study of the traumatic dreams of genocide survivors in Rwanda. In her book, *Rêves et traumatismes* [*Dreams and Trauma(s)*], Godard draws on Freudian psychoanalysis, particularly the ideas laid out in *Beyond the Pleasure Principle* (Freud, 2015). For her, as for Freud, the repetitive return to the scene of horror that characterizes traumatic dreams may be seen as an attempt to master or manage the state of arousal caused by the traumatic experience from which the person was unable to protect themselves.

Despite being heavily influenced by Freudian theory, Godard tries to take a culturally sensitive approach with survivors in Rwanda, making an active attempt to understand their culture. As she puts it, 'J'ai écouté, engrangé, je me suis laissé imprégner de cette culture et de ces événements' (2003: 20).[8] By listening to their interpretations of dreams, she learns that her Rwandan patients understood their nightmares and traumatic dreams as messages from the *abazimu*. According to traditional Rwandese cosmology, the *abazimu* are the spirits of dead ancestors who can either protect or bring misfortune and require regular supplication to prevent them from bringing punishments such as disease (Bagilishya, 2012; Longman, 2010: p. 36). For genocide survivors, the *abazimu* are family members who died in the genocide and who force them to relive their persecution (Godard, 2003: 52). Godard attempts to balance Freudian therapeutic methods with an understanding of the patient's desire to 'amadouer les abazimu' [appease the *abazimu*]. For Godard, therapy thus requires a certain 'va-et-vient entre le nouveau et l'ancien qui doit se faire, entre ces deux cultures dont sont pétris les Rwandais' (2003: 133).[9]

Despite her sensitivity to Rwandan culture, Godard (2003: 20) nonetheless experienced some cultural barriers. For example, she was unable to communicate with survivors in Kinyarwanda and therefore had recourse to an interpreter. She also took a somewhat limited cultural-historical view,

---

[8] 'I listened, took it all in, allowed myself to soak up this culture and these events'. This and all subsequent quotations from this source were translated by myself.

[9] 'back and forth between the new and the old, which must be done between these two cultures which have shaped Rwandans'.

seeing the source of survivors' difficulties through an event-based lens.[10] Moreover, the Rwandan interpretation does not deter Godard from returning more generally to a Freudian understanding of traumatic dreams (2003: 217). Perhaps the most unsettling aspect of Godard's work, however, is its resemblance to what Erik Linstrum refers to as the 'dream-collectors' of the early twentieth century (2016: 53). In his book, *Ruling Minds: Psychology in the British Empire*, Linstrum describes the work of 'agents', mostly anthropologists and psychoanalysts, who were sent by the imperial government to Britain's colonies in Africa and Asia to collect and interpret dreams through psychoanalysis in an attempt to better understand and ultimately control their colonial subjects. While I am not suggesting that Godard had any intention other than to help survivors, she did not problematize her methodology despite its historical use as a mechanism of control in the European colonization of Africa. Also absent from Godard's discussion is a recognition that the very same colonial anthropologists largely failed to find universal validity for Freudian psychoanalysis among African people (Linstrum, 2003: 56).

In a third type of intervention, New York-based art therapist Valerie Chu describes her work with Rwandan genocide survivors using art therapy. Recognizing that art therapy is 'a product of the West', Chu designed a creative box-making project, arguing that the box metaphor had 'functional equivalence in Rwandan culture' (2010: 4–5). Chu describes the art projects of three Rwandans, Margaret, Noah and Rosa (pseudonyms), and the impact of the therapy on them. Like others, Chu's intervention focuses on alleviating trauma 'symptoms', arguing that art therapy can help 'counter the repetitive nature of [the] trauma response' and combat 'feelings of helplessness and loss of control' (2010: 5). Moreover, like Godard, Chu relied on an interpreter to conduct her therapy sessions and, despite the supposed cultural equivalence of the box concept, she notes that the art materials used in her classes would not ordinarily be accessible to the survivors. In addition, the images provided by Chu seem inappropriate for use in a therapeutic intervention for expressing identity, as they exclusively depict white people (or at least those selected by the survivors do). The only written words appear on Rosa's box and are in English rather than in Kinyarwanda, which Chu interprets as demonstrating 'the importance of memory for Rosa' (2010: 9). However, it might also be interpreted as Rosa's attempt to create a box for her art therapist rather than for herself, given the language choice. Of course, without asking Rosa, it is not possible to know for certain.

---

[10] For example, in Godard's view, traumatic dreams are a return to 'l'événement traumatique' (2003: 26) [the traumatic event].

In sum, these examples suggest a tendency to apply a deficit-focused, medical approach in trauma therapy, rather than listening for strengths. Moreover, interventions administered by Western therapists include culturally insensitive elements. While I would not discount the contribution made by Western therapists in Rwanda, the colonial history of Rwanda, combined with global patterns of racism and inequality, are likely to create a power imbalance between therapist and survivor that may prove inappropriate or even counterproductive. I would not suggest that problems of historical inequality are insurmountable, but any Westerner conducting therapy should show sensitivity to historical and cultural factors (including choice of language) which could form part of the trauma experienced by Rwandans.

## A New Traditional Approach

Psychologist Déogratias Bagilishya agrees that 'foreign therapeutic models, organized around concepts like "post-traumatic stress disorder" must raise questions about their pertinence and their positive and negative effects' (2012: 352). 'Even if a foreign model is not necessarily harmful', he continues, 'it must be examined with extreme care to avoid destroying the fragile internal equilibrium that is trying to re-establish itself' (2012: 352). As we have seen, most therapy programmes are dominated by variations of the Western medical model despite evidence from Godard's (2003: 52) research of the continued importance of traditional Rwandan cosmology. Bagilishya calls, alternatively, for more culturally sensitive methods based on traditional cosmology which he explains in terms of its relationship to death and psychological trauma. According to him, the term *abazimu* (*umuzimu* in the singular) derives from the verb *kuzimu*, 'below, in the gloom', and signifies 'the residence of the dead' (2012: 345). The death of a loved one leads to a 'change in status and residence' of that person which results in 'a period of emotional shock that requires the work of mourning by the living' (Bagilishya, 2012: 345). The person who suffers this loss is 'given special care and attention' during the mourning period, as they must come to recognize the loved one's 'reintroduction as a new and immortal being in the family's daily life' (Bagilishya, 2012: 346). Once this period is complete, the grieving person enacts a ritual known as *ukwera*, a whitening or bleaching, an act of procreation to symbolize the 'rebirth and the return of the deceased relative among his family' (Bagilishya, 2012: 346).[11] Following the mourning process,

---

[11] This 'can be physical (e.g. sexual relations between two parents who have lost a child) or symbolic (laying on the bed when one has lost a spouse or partner)' (Bagilishya, 2012: 346).

the deceased relative, now an *umuzimu*, remains among the family 'as an ancestral protector and an intermediary between God and the members of his family' (Bagilishya, 2012: 346).

According to Bagilishya, if death occurs in circumstances in which mourning is not possible, this can be 'so crushing that any Rwandan might well suffer a traumatic reaction' (2012: 347), as evidenced by the cases described by Godard (2003). Traditionally, such cases may require the intervention of community elders, particularly from *umukecuru* [wise women/mothers], who can help the bereaved to distance themselves from their desire for revenge and prevent them from violating taboos and cultural prohibitions (Bagilishya, 2012: 350). Transgressing cultural prohibitions is seen as a 'rebellion against the ancestors and parental authority' and will subsequently be 'punished by attacks or possessions by sprits' (Bagilishya, 2012: 351). Such individuals may need to be purified by divinations performed by traditional healers.

These traditional practices have been eroded by colonialism and the introduction of Christianity, which has since become the country's main religion (Longman, 2010: 4), although Godard's work suggests that traditional cosmology also persists. Bagilishya found similarly that many Rwandans spoke of 'evil spirits and supernatural forces unleashed on the country during the genocide and massacres of 1994 and of the necessity of cleansing the country to prevent the return of these evil forces' (2012: 352). In his view, it is necessary to resituate 'ideas about grief and trauma in a framework that is coherent with Rwandan culture' (2012: 337). According to Godard, however, traditional doctors do not recognize cases of severe trauma (known in Kinyarwanda as *ihahamuka*) and instead send sufferers to churches or hospitals, where they receive treatment informed by Christianity or the medical model respectively (2003: 59). Godard suggests that this is because both trauma and genocide are seen as somehow 'extracultural' and therefore untreatable by cultural methods (2003: 59).

An exception to this is the traditional Rwandan doctor Muganga (Doctor) Rutangarwamaboko, who founded the Rwandan Cultural Health Centre LTD in an attempt to dissociate from Western models altogether.[12] Unlike the traditional practitioners discussed in Godard's book, Rutangarwamaboko does treat trauma patients and his approach is to reconnect patients with tradition. Rutangarwamaboko trained in Western clinical psychology at Rwanda's National University and began his career practicing what he grudgingly refers to as 'conventional' (i.e. Western) psychotherapy. During our meeting

---

[12] I spoke with Muganga Rutangarwamaboko during a field trip on 7 July 2016. More information can be found here: https://www.facebook.com/Rwandan-Cultural-Health-Centre-RCHCLtd-324458897613722/ (consulted on 1 June 2018).

at the Centre, he spoke of an experience which led him to move away from Western models in favour of therapies rooted in tradition. Rutangarwamaboko was working as a psychotherapist in a hospital where he met a 'patient' who was suffering with 'depression'. After much consultation, the man reluctantly spoke but all he could say was that he wanted to leave the hospital as it was 'not the place to cure him'. Rutangarwamaboko eventually discovered the cause of this man's 'depression': he had killed a wagtail. This action constituted a violation of *kirazira* [taboo] because the wagtail is the sacred bird of the Abagesera clan. This breaking of taboo was causing him acute psychological turbulence because, as Rutangarwamaboko put it, the man's spirituality had been 'poisoned'.

Taboos are a fundamental part of Rwandan culture that were gradually eroded by colonialism.[13] The genocide itself constituted the ultimate violation of taboo as the bonds of linkage between people were destroyed. To explain the importance of taboos, Rutangarwamaboko proposes a triadic model consisting in a soul, a spirit and a body. The soul is a person's reason, their thoughts and ideas. The spirit is their religiosity, their morality and, above all, their culture. According to Rutangarwamaboko, the breaking of taboos violates a person's culture, thereby poisoning their spirit and causing a troubled soul. This may eventually result in physiological problems in the body, such as psychosomatic aches and pains. To alleviate the pain of the trauma sufferer's spirit, soul and body, Rutangarwamaboko attempts to reconnect people with their culture (i.e. their spirit). He told me that the disconnection with past traditions and beliefs is such that many Rwandans who visit his centre fear that it is a satanic place when they see the traditional setting. But recognizing the limitations of event-based understandings of trauma, Rutangarwamaboko insists that the only way to address the long-term trauma of colonialism and identity destruction is to reconnect Rwandan people with their traditions. In his words, 'if you have no culture, you have nothing'. Western sceptics may argue that Rutangarwamaboko's model has no empirical basis.[14] However, it seems to me that his model offers a greater understanding of the long-term traumatic experiences of Rwandan people than the event-based, Western medical model.

---

[13] This is reflected in the Rwandan expression *Kiliziya yakuye kirazira* [the Church abolished taboos].

[14] Western psychology emphasizes the experimental model, which typically requires research with large samples to gather empirical data; this is not a method adopted by Rutangarwamaboko. Western political critics might also argue that his methods echo the government's nostalgia about Rwanda's precolonial past (e.g. Reyntjens, 2016: 63–65).

## *Ndi Umunyarwanda* and Postcolonial Post-Traumatic Growth

Rutangarwamaboko is undoubtedly influenced by the political climate in Rwanda, where the RPF government has drawn on tradition to find home-grown solutions to problems as well as emphasizing the precolonial notion of *ndi umunyarwanda*. However, the RPF and its polices have received much criticism (e.g. Longman, 2017; Purdeková, 2015; Thomson, 2013). Filip Reyntjens, a vocal RPF critic, concludes that the party's intolerance of dissent, combined with the existence of 'strong underground narratives [...] suggests that Rwanda is not heading towards long-term peace and stability' (2016: 75).

While the arguments expressed by Reyntjens and others are not altogether unfounded, there are some interesting aspects of the RPF's ideology that are keenly espoused by some Rwandans. As I have argued elsewhere, 'the concept of *ndi umuyarwanda* should not be dismissed as the ideology of a dictatorial government, as it is also being adopted and adapted from the bottom up, often in practical and constructive ways' (Williamson, 2016b: 55; see also Grayson, 2017; Blackie and Hitchcott, 2018). Taking the first-hand testimonial narratives of genocide survivors, my research has examined the ways in which men and women have reconstructed their identities since the genocide, paying particular attention to processes of post-traumatic growth (Williamson Sinalo, 2018).[15] While the testimonies in my corpus do not tend to emphasize the traditional religious beliefs observed by Godard, many draw on the concept of *ndi umunyarwanda* and other aspects of the government's ideology, combining traditional and contemporary values about Rwandan identity, including themes such as a shared identity, a focus on non-violent collaboration, the importance of dignity, self-reliance and female

---

[15] A total of 42 audiovisual testimonies were examined, recorded in Kinyarwanda and translated into English and sometimes French. All corpus testimonies come from the Genocide Archive of Rwanda which was established by the Aegis Trust in association with Rwanda's National Commission for the Fight against Genocide (CNLG). The testimonies were collected by the archive from survivors who volunteered to give their testimony. Participating men and women come from a range of geographical locations and vary in age and profession. The archive maintains that there are no criteria for selecting survivors, although survivors with dissenting views may be more reluctant to come forward. However, many survivors appear willing to criticize the government in their testimonies. All analyses were conducted on the Kinyarwanda versions of the testimonies but presented here are my English translations.

empowerment. They also reject former colonial influences and their ideas in favour of more authentic cultural expression. Overall, the testimonies demonstrate a similar pattern of 'va-et-vient entre le nouveau et l'ancien' [back and forth between new and old] as described by Godard (2003: 133). However, while for Godard 'le nouveau' refers to her 'modern' psycho-therapy methods, the approach I discuss below suggests that by drawing on past values, new identities based on indigenous culture can be created. The following analysis of testimonies provides examples of such positive identity transformation and discusses how trauma therapy could do more to recognize such stories of change.

Despite their experiences of violence, survivors tend to embrace the government's notion of a united identity and of working in peace as a nation towards their collective development, drawing on the precolonial value of *gukunda igihugu* [patriotism]. As Uwamungu puts it, 'All Rwandans need to understand that if we want to build a better future and to avoid what we went through in the past, we will have to work on it'. The importance of working for one's country may be found in several of the testimonies. Gatare, for example, states: 'Above all, we must work towards the prosperity of our families and country. We must work and live in peace with everyone'. In the original version of his testimony, Gatare repeats the word *imbere* [first or above all] three times, as if to highlight how fundamental this point is. Such emphasis on peaceful cohabitation is shared by Nshimiyimana, who suggests that 'conflicts and rivalry only make us move backwards'.

The government's emphasis on dignity (*agaciro*), autonomy and self-reliance is also reflected in the testimonies of survivors, particularly those of women. The devastation caused by the genocide made it impossible, particularly for women, to continue with traditional ways of life (Burnet, 2012: 66). With their husbands dead, in exile or in prison, women were forced to think of themselves differently and develop skills that they would not otherwise have acquired. Nakabonye, for example, was previously reliant on her husband and had to take on new roles and responsibilities after losing him in the genocide: 'Life was bad. I felt like life was over. I couldn't picture my life without Kalisa [her husband]. I felt like I'd been left, I was worthless ... a widow. I didn't know who I was any more. But today things seem to be better. It gives me hope'. Nakabonye uses the Kinyarwanda word *gusuzugurika*, meaning to be 'worthless', 'discredited' or 'dishonourable', highlighting the stigma of being a widow. However, despite feeling discredited or worthless, Nakabonye appears to have found a way to survive without her husband. She seems not only to have survived, but also to have gained hope and learned to tackle life's challenges independently: 'To see my kids growing up gives me hope. Raising my kids alone without Kalisa was inconceivable in the past. Raising them without a job … But today, I have managed. And, I have hope for the future'. Nakabonye contrasts setbacks with personal strength and agency as well as optimism for the future. This use of contrastive language, moving from setbacks to agency and hope, demonstrates Nakabonye's ability to overcome the challenges of living without a husband. Moreover, she describes her situation as 'more positive than ever'. 'I think it's better now', she states, 'because I don't consider myself the same way I did before. Life changes for the better'. Thus, out of her loss, Nakabonye appears to have gained an enhanced sense of self-reliance.

Women gained self-reliance and autonomy not only through changing gender roles but also through the services offered by the expanding women's movement in civil society. In some cases, their agency was improved through active participation in this movement. Kayiraba, for example, describes how the Association des Veuves du Génocide Agahozo (AVEGA) trained her in trauma counselling and law:

> I owe my life to AVEGA, because it trained me in trauma, it has provided me with confidence, I am now the representative of AVEGA in Rwamagana, and I enjoy helping others […] I always meet people, I am always solving other people's problems, I was trained in Law, I was trained on GBV [gender-based violence] and I often advise people, direct them to the courts.

Clearly this training has enabled Kayiraba to gain a sense of agency and purpose. One of the primary achievements of the women's movement in civil society is its role in the expansion of women's representation in politics as it gave women the skills necessary for entering politics and promoted the legitimacy and importance of women holding office. Women's inclusion in political and public life has also been a commitment of the RPF and a fundamental feature of its policy of unity and reconciliation (Powley, 2005: 159). One woman in my sample, Burizihiza, was able to benefit from this change and became the elected representative of genocide survivors in the Mukura sector. Such changes in women's identities could also be considered to reflect Rwanda's precolonial past, where women could hold powerful positions both in politics (e.g. the Queen Mother) and within the religious realm (Bagilishya, 2012; Longman, 2006: 134).

Another aspect of post-genocide identity expressed in the testimonies is the belief in the autonomy of the Rwandan nation and an outright rejection of colonial and neocolonial influence (similar to Rutangarwamaboko's ideas discussed above). Many Rwandans have become critical of the West since 1994, particularly for the role played by colonial and neocolonial powers in the genocide (Soudan, 2014). This anti-colonial sentiment is reflected in several of the testimonies. Umuhoza, for example, states unequivocally that 'The forces that caused the genocide came from outside. They came from outside this country because the people in the country have a way of living together'. Similarly, Harerimana expresses his belief that Rwandans 'share one language and it is that which unites us' and that the genocide 'ideology [was] imposed by colonizers'. Although the translation uses the term 'ideology', the word used by Harerimana, *imico*, can mean customs, virtues or norms, but is most commonly translated as 'culture'. This rejection of European ideas and culture is also expressed in his testimony: 'I think that what led people to attack their neighbours was put there by foreigners ... I used to hear my father saying that all Rwandans come from Gihanga. No one ever said if he was Tutsi, Twa or Hutu! Now we are all Rwandans'. Not only does Harerimana reiterate his belief that the ideas behind the genocide were European, he also draws on the precolonial Rwandan belief in Gihanga, the 'legendary ancestor of the dynasty and of all Rwandans' (Semujanga, 2003: 85), suggesting a revival of indigenous myths.

One might conclude from this testimonial data that survivors are simply parroting the official line, perhaps through fear of the government. Indeed, the most common criticism of the Rwandan government concerns its intolerance of dissent and the lack of free speech in Rwanda. Yet of the 42 survivor testimonies analyzed in my research (23 women, 19 men), 24 (11 women, 13 men) spoke openly and frankly about the aspects of the regime which dissatisfied them (Williamson Sinalo, 2018). Common criticisms include: anger over the government's neglect of survivors (e.g. 'they have already forgotten our people' (Rutayisire), 'survivors are not remembered, no one talks for them' (Bukumura)); the fact that there are genocide perpetrators in government (e.g. 'among our leaders there are some who committed crimes during the genocide' (Rutayisire)); the fact that (Tutsi) Rwandans returning from exile do not understand the lives of survivors (e.g. 'the way I tell it to a survivor who was here in Rwanda is not the same as the way I tell it to a person who came from exile' (Mudahogora)); and survivors' dissatisfaction with the justice system (e.g. perpetrators 'only asked for forgiveness from the government, they didn't ask for forgiveness from those they harmed' (Kavubi)). That these testimonies have been published and are accessible to local and international audiences provides evidence against the view that the RPF 'terrorizes *all* its critics or opponents into silence' (Reyntjens, 2004: 181; emphasis added). My analysis thus reveals that although survivors draw on the government's version of *ndi umunyarwanda* to reconstruct their identity in positive ways, they are not uncritically reproducing the government's ideology.

The rejection of former colonial influences and their ideas, combined with an emphasis on developing one's country through hard work, unity and a shared, indigenous language, could be conceived of as a type of postcolonial post-traumatic growth. It could also be seen as analogous to the various postcolonial theories that have developed elsewhere, such as Indigénisme in Haiti, Négritude in Africa and the Caribbean, and Antillanité and Créolité in the French Antilles. Like Rwandans before the genocide, Antilleans were, Bernabé, Chamoiseau and Confiant write, 'dans une attrape de dépendance culturelle, de dépendance politique, [et] de dépendance économique' (1993: 14).[16] For the authors of *Éloge de la Créolité* [*In Praise of Creoleness*], Créolité is about the examination of one's own culture, with 'un regard neuf qui enlèverait notre naturel du secondaire ou de la périphérie afin de le remplacer au centre de nous-mêmes. Un peu de ce regard d'enfance' (Bernabé, Chamoiseau and Confiant, 1993: 24).[17] Much as Caribbean people draw on Créolité to explore new identities, it would appear that the survivors in my corpus are engaging in a similar process of authentic identity reconstruction based on indigenous culture which is both a form of postcolonial post-traumatic growth and a reflection of broader cultural and political changes taking place in Rwanda. As President Kagame explains, 'Rwanda can't be Rwanda without its own traditions. They are the foundation we build upon' (Soudan, 2015: 98).

## Decolonizing Trauma Therapy: Facilitating Postcolonial Post-Traumatic Growth

Post-traumatic growth theory is not without limitations. As has been noted elsewhere (Williamson Sinalo, 2018; see also Grayson, 2018), scholars usually investigate the phenomenon using quantitative, self-report scales which are unable to detect the specificities of a cultural and historical context and are also blind to long-term, chronic or structural forms of trauma. However, adopting a text-based application of the theory can allow scholars to address some of these limitations by drawing on historical and cultural knowledge and listening to survivors' own understandings of the ways in which their lives have been affected by trauma. A qualitative application of post-traumatic growth theory also allows us to move beyond the medical model and its narrow understanding of what constitutes 'traumatic' and its medicalization of

---

[16] 'caught in the trick of cultural dependence, of political dependence, of economic dependence'. Translations of this source are from the bilingual version of Bernabé, Chamoiseau and Confiant (1993: 76).

[17] 'a new look capable of taking away our nature from the secondary or peripheral edge so as to place it again in the centre of ourselves, somewhat like the child's look' (Bernabé, Chamoiseau and Confiant, 1993: 85–86).

distress. One of the main advantages is that an understanding of post-traumatic growth in the Rwandan context can provide insights into how such positive change might be facilitated in a culturally and politically sensitive way.

As a result of the medicalized orientation, clinical assessments of individuals suffering the effects of trauma have tended to focus on identifying 'symptoms' by applying 'a deficit- or problem-focussed approach' (Tedeschi and Kilmer, 2005: 230). Tedeschi and Kilmer suggest that the deficit approach is insufficient and instead propose a strength-based assessment, 'attending to and assessing positive factors and pursuing means to facilitate their development or enhancement' (2005: 235). As Calhoun and Tedeschi observe, 'the exclusive focus on the need to identify and address the negative consequences of trauma may lead clinicians to overlook the possibility that some, and perhaps many, individuals can experience positive change in the wake of tragedy and loss' (1999: 54).

On the other hand, the notion of post-traumatic growth may also seem alien to some survivors, and thus, before the idea of growth is introduced, the initial focus of therapy in any context should be to help the individual to manage their psychological distress. This involves a process of desensitization by re-exposing the individual to the trauma through detailed descriptions or thinking about the experience(s) in a safe, therapeutic atmosphere. A second aim of this process is to support the individual during the rumination process so that he or she may create a narrative which will enable them to gain a model of the experience to refer to in therapy. Indeed, as Calhoun and Tedeschi suggest, therapy is 'a continual process of narrative development, where events and experiences are revisited and retold many times, with new details included in each version, and different perspectives are taken on the same events' (1999: 60). Finally, before the notion of growth is introduced, trauma treatment should also help the individual recreate a world view that encompasses what happened. According to Calhoun and Tedeschi, 'this aspect of trauma treatment is involved in the construction of the narrative that describes the trauma and provides some understanding of it' (1999: 53).

Tedeschi and Kilmer (2005) propose that a strength assessment may be made via informal qualitative methods, such as listening to the client's narrative for evidence of strengths. They advise that the clinician should make the decision as to when to introduce the notion of growth and subsequently focus questioning on positive changes. It is clear that the clinician cannot produce growth for the individual, nor should he or she try to push the individual into a conversation about growth too soon. However, labelling growth when it is apparent and discussing positive changes with an empathic understanding of the individual's world view can 'encourage further development of the cognitive processing of trauma into growth' (Tedeschi and Kilmer, 2005: 234). Overall, Tedeschi and Kilmer conclude that efforts to harness and promote post-traumatic growth may 'not only enhance the health and well-being of clients in the context of their current presenting concerns but potentially reduce their need for formal mental health services in the future' (2005: 235).

A similar approach to that just outlined could be adopted by those engaged in psychosocial work in Rwanda. When it comes to facilitating post-traumatic growth among Rwandans, historical and cultural factors must be taken into consideration, particularly the destruction of indigenous culture caused by colonialism. Given this history, the link between language and colonialism, and the challenges involved in translation (Williamson, 2016a), I would advocate that therapists and clinicians engage with survivors in Kinyarwanda. Knowledge of Rwandan language, culture and cosmology are also advocated by Bagilishya, who argues that 'traditional forms of expression (e.g. proverbs and tales) [...] offer the possibility of representing experiences and establishing a certain distance from feelings and acts of revenge' (2012: 352). Such an approach, combined with an awareness of traditional values associated with *ndi umunyarwanda*, would help therapists to recognize themes of growth among Rwandan people while also helping them to reconnect with their culture, in line with Rutangarwamaboko's approach. By listening to the testimonies of survivors, therapists can draw on post-traumatic growth theory with an awareness of the colonial and postcolonial legacy in Rwanda and the home-grown ideas about Rwandan identity that are being used to fight that legacy, to recognize and hopefully facilitate existing stories of positive change among survivors.

## Works Cited

Bagilishya, Déogratias. 2000. 'Mourning and Recovery from Trauma: In Rwanda, Tears Flow Within'. *Transcultural Psychiatry* 37.3: 337–53.

Bernabé, Jean, Patrick Chamoiseau and Raphaël Confiant. 1993. *Eloge de la Créolité* (English and French ed.). Paris: Éditions Gallimard.

Blackie, Laura E.R., and Nicki Hitchcott. 2018. '"I Am Rwandan": Unity and Reconciliation in Post-Genocide Rwanda'. *Genocide Studies and Prevention* 12.1: 24–37.

Burnet, Jennie E. 2012. *Genocide Lives in Us: Women, Memory and Silence in Rwanda*. Madison, WI: Wisconsin University Press.

Calhoun, Lawrence, and Richard Tedeschi. 1999. *Facilitating Posttraumatic Growth: A Clinician's Guide*. Mahwah, NJ: Lawrence Erlbaum.

Calhoun, Lawrence, and Richard Tedeschi (eds). 2006. *Handbook of Posttraumatic Growth: Research and Practice*. Mahwah, NJ: Lawrence Erlbaum.

Chu, Valerie. 2010. 'Within the Box: Cross-Cultural Art Therapy with Survivors of the Rwanda Genocide'. *Art Therapy: Journal of the American Art Therapy Association* 27.1: 4–10.

Craps, Stef. 2013. *Postcolonial Witnessing: Trauma out of Bounds*. London: Palgrave Macmillan.

Fanon, Frantz. 1961. *Les damnés de la terre*. Paris: François Maspero.

—. 1963. *The Wretched of the Earth*. Trans. by Constance Farrington. Paris: Présence Africaine.

Favila, Isaura Zelaya. 2009. 'Treatment of Post-Traumatic Stress Disorder in Post-Genocide Rwanda'. Global Grassroots Report. Available at http://www.globalgrassroots.org/pdf/PTSD-Rwanda.pdf (consulted on 31 January 2018).

Freud, Sigmund. 2015. *Beyond the Pleasure Principle*. Trans. by James Stachey. New York: Dover Publications.

Gishoma, Darius, Jean-Luc Brackelaire, Naason Munyandamutsa, Jane Mujawayezu, Achour Ait Mohand and Yvonne Kayiteshonga. 2014. 'Supportive-Expressive Group Therapy for People Experiencing Collective Traumatic Crisis during the Genocide Commemoration Period in Rwanda: Impact and Implications'. *Journal of Social and Political Psychology* 2.1: 469–88.

Godard, Marie-Odile. 2003. *Rêves et traumatismes: ou la longue nuit des rescapés*. Paris: Éditions Érès.

Grayson, Hannah. 2017. 'A Place for Individuals: Positive Growth in Rwanda'. *Eastern African Literary and Cultural Studies* 3.2–4: 107–30.

—. 2018. 'Articulating Growth in Rwandan Terms: Adapting the Post-Traumatic Growth Inventory'. *Studies in Testimony* 1.1: 4–30. Available at https://studiesintestimony.co.uk/issues/volume-one-issue-one/articulating-growth-in-rwandan-terms/ (consulted on 1 June 2018).

Hron, Madelaine. 2011. '*Gukora* and *Itsembatsemba*: The "Ordinary Killers" in Jean Hatzfeld's *Machete Season*'. *Research in African Literatures* 42.2: 125–46.

Joseph, Stephen, and P. Alex Linley. 2008. 'Positive Psychological Perspectives on Posttraumatic Stress: An Integrative Psychosocial Framework'. In Stephen Joseph and P. Alex Linley (eds), *Trauma, Recovery, and Growth: Positive Psychological Perspectives on Posttraumatic Stress*. Hoboken, NJ: John Wiley: 3–20.

Linstrum, Erik. 2016. *Ruling Minds: Psychology in the British Empire*. Cambridge, MA: Harvard University Press.

Longman, Timothy. 2006. 'Rwanda: Achieving Equality or Serving an Authoritarian State?' In Hannah Evelyn Britton and Gretchen Bauer (eds), *Women in African Parliaments*. Boulder, CO: Lynne Rienner: 133–50.

—. 2010. *Christianity and Genocide in Rwanda*. Cambridge: Cambridge University Press.

—. 2017. *Memory and Justice in Post-Genocide Rwanda*. Cambridge: Cambridge University Press.

Mbaraga. Robert. 2013. 'State Pushes Campaign that Critics Say it Is Ethnically Divisive'. *The East African* 16 November. Retrieved from: http://www. theeastafrican.co.ke/Rwanda/News/Mixed-reactions-to--Ndi-Umunyarwanda-initiative-/-/1433218/2075366/-/6ktcmf/-/index.html (consulted on 1 June 2018).

Ng, Lauren C., and Boniface Harerimana. 2016. 'Mental Health Care in Post-Genocide Rwanda: Evaluation of a Program Specializing in Posttraumatic Stress Disorder and Substance Abuse'. *Global Mental Health* 3.18: 1–11.

Powley, Elizabeth. 2005. 'Case Study Rwanda: Women Hold up Half the Parliament'. In Julie Ballington and Azza Karam (eds), *Women in Parliament: Beyond Numbers*, rev. ed. Stockholm: The International Institute for Democracy and Electoral Assistance: 154–63.

Prunier, Gérard. 2009. *From Genocide to Continental War: The 'Congolese' Conflict and the Crisis of Contemporary Africa*. London: Hurst.

Purdeková, Andrea. 2015. *Making Ubumwe: Power, State and Camps in Rwanda's Unity-Building Project*. New York: Berghahn Books.

Reyntjens, Filip. 2004. 'Rwanda, Ten Years On: From Genocide to Dictatorship'. *African Affairs* 103.411: 177–210.

—. 2016. '(Re-)imagining a Reluctant Post-Genocide Society: The Rwandan Patriotic Front's Ideology and Practice'. *Journal of Genocide Research* 18.1: 61–81.

Rusagara, Frank. 2009. *Resilience of a Nation: A History of the Military in Rwanda*. Kigali: Fountain Publishers.

Semujanga, Josias. 2003. *Origins of Rwandan Genocide*. New York: Humanity Books.

Soudan, François. 2014. 'Paul Kagamé: "Je ne conseille à personne de se mêler des affaires intérieures du Rwanda"'. *Jeune Afrique* 14 April. Available at http://www.j euneafrique.com/Article/JA2778p020.xml1/ (consulted on 31 January 2018).

—. 2015. *Kagame: Conversations with the President of Rwanda*. New York: Enigma Books.

Summerfield, Derek. 2004. 'Cross-Cultural Perspectives on the Medicalization of Human Suffering'. In Gerald Rosen (ed.), *Posttraumatic Stress Disorder: Issues and Controversies*. Chichester: John Wiley: 233–47.

Tedeschi, Richard, and Ryan Kilmer. 2005. 'Assessing Strengths, Resilience, and Growth to Guide Clinical Intervention'. *Professional Psychology: Research and Practice* 36.3: 230–37.

Thomson, Susan. 2013. *Whispering Truth to Power: Everyday Resistance to Reconciliation in Postgenocide Rwanda*. Madison, WI: University of Wisconsin Press.

Vidal, Claudine. 1974. 'De la religion subie au modernisme refusé. 'Théophagie', ancêtres clandestins et résistance populaire au Rwanda'. *Archives des Sciences Sociales des Religions* 38: 63–90.

Wall, Melissa. 2007. 'An Analysis of News Magazine Coverage of the Rwanda Crisis in the United States'. In Allan Thompson (ed.), *The Media and the Rwanda Genocide*. London: Pluto Press, 2007: 261–73.

Williamson, Caroline. 2016a. 'Posttraumatic Growth at the International Level: The Obstructive Role Played by Translators and Editors of Rwandan Genocide Testimonies'. *Translation Studies* 9.1: 33–50.

—. 2016b. 'Genocide, Masculinity and Posttraumatic Growth in Rwanda: Reconstructing Male Identity through *Ndi Umunyarwanda*'. *Journal of Genocide Research* 18.1: 41–59.

Williamson Sinalo, Caroline. 2018. *Rwanda after Genocide: Gender, Identity and Posttraumatic Growth*. Cambridge: Cambridge University Press.

World Health Organization (WHO). 2011. Mental Health Atlas, Department of Mental Health and Substance Abuse. Available at https://www.who.int/mental_health/publications/mental_health_atlas_2011/en/ (consulted on 4 February 2019).

Young, Allan. 1995. *The Harmony of Illusions: Inventing Post-Traumatic Stress Disorder*. Princeton: Princeton University Press.

# Promising Generations: From Intergenerational Guilt to *Ndi Umunyarwanda*

*Richard M. Benda*

Dramatic change, the kind one witnesses in post-genocide Rwanda, requires not only a synergy of well-coordinated action but, more importantly, a powerful public narrative of national reconstruction to enable this action. Politics is, after all, the synergy between mighty words and mighty actions, if Arendt (2005) is to be believed. This action and its underlying narrative have generally been attributed to the Rwandan state or more concretely to successive governments led by the Rwandan Patriotic Front (RPF). For this reason, a disproportionate bulk of literature on post-genocide recovery has focused on the agency of the RPF as the main vehicle of change (Clark, 2014; Straus and Waldorf, 2011; Reyntjens, 2013; Purdeková, 2015; Thomson, 2013). On the timeline that gradually emerged out of this literature, there seems to be a loose consensus that until 2010, the RPF's performance and underpinning narrative were viewed positively in light of evident economic growth, political stability and public order. However, since 2010, these achievements have increasingly come under scrutiny and concerns have been voiced regarding the cost of this success, especially in terms of human rights.

Phil Clark (2014) sees this emerging dichotomy as a debate between the 'developmentalists' and 'human rights activists'. The latter in particular represent post-genocide societal transformation as a top-down, Kigali elite-driven, donor-supported vision, which combines social engineering with sophisticated and transformative authoritarianism (Straus and Waldorf, 2011: 13). Social engineering, Straus and Waldorf argue, happens in four specific arenas which encompass the totality of public life in post-genocide Rwanda, namely the behavioural and social, spatial, economic and political (2011: 13–15). Authoritarianism is experienced, but not exclusively, through the monopoly of control that state elites exert over the public narrative of national reconstruction (Thomson, 2011).

Keener students of Rwanda's post-genocide recovery process have been critical of these entrenched reductionist views. The narrative models they develop fail to account for the 'complex ways in which Rwandan citizens engage with the state and participate in government-initiated community level processes' (Clark, 2014: 193). Nicola Palmer refers to dualistic diagnoses that run the risk of blurring the lines of historical contestation and subversion between the centre and the periphery (2015: 44), whilst Andrea Purdeková (2015) rejects the bipolar nature of the debate and calls for a 'complexification' of the discourse on identity politics and identity-driven change.

This essay finds common cause with this later school of thought. It is based on field research on the Youth Connekt Dialogue (YCD) initiative and offers a narrative analysis of the emergence of the *Ndi Umunyarwanda* programme out of these dialogues. Research findings in the form of hundreds of young Rwandans' life stories challenge a monistic top-bottom theory of post-genocide recovery. They point to a more complex phenomenon and a contested political space in which the national metanarrative is subtly shaped daily by a variety of agencies, factors and stakeholders. To support this argument, I will be using Edouard Bamporiki's story, which was the centrepiece of all YCD events having been adopted by the organizers as representative of the children of perpetrators' life stories.

This essay centres around three key concepts that require a note of clarification. In this contribution, 'children of perpetrators' are young Hutu of the emerging and second generation who participated in YCD and identified themselves as such. 'Emerging generation' refers to young Rwandans who were aged up to 12 years in April–July 1994. The 'second generation' are children born after the Genocide against the Tutsi (from July 1994 onward). YCD is the first phase of a series of public youth meetings which took place between 10 May and 30 June 2013 in 15 of Rwanda's 30 districts (Ngororero, Burera, Rubavu, Nyabihu, Gisagara, Nyamagabe, Nyaruguru, Kamonyi, Bugesera, Kicukiro, Gasabo, Nyarugenge, Kayonza, Gatsibo and Kirehe, as well as the Iwawa Youth Rehabilitation Centre). *Ndi umunyarwanda* literally translates as 'I am a Rwandan'. When the first phase of YCD officially closed on 30 June 2013, the political significance of the concerns raised by the dialogues and the strong reactions they generated in the Rwandan diaspora led to important decisions at the highest level of Rwandan national politics. The national leadership was sufficiently convinced that the spirit of change demonstrated by YCD should be the springboard for a national reflection on identity. In July 2013, it was decided that this programme would be called *Ndi Umunyarwanda* (National Unity and Reconciliation Commission [NURC], 2017).

It is beyond the scope of this contribution to provide an anatomy of *Ndi Umunyarwanda*, as embryonic as the concept might be (see also Williamson Sinalo, this volume). The objective is rather to narrate the birth and beginnings of *Ndi Umunyarwanda* as the next milestone and most significant change in post-genocide discourse on identity that goes beyond mere de-ethnicization (Purdeková, 2008). At its inception, this prosaic phrase expressed in the present tense of the verb *kuba* [to be] was envisioned by YCD participants as the repository of hopes for a future where the oneness – *ubumwe* [unity, oneness] – of Rwandans is no longer an ideal but an ordinary state of being and living together.[1] Secondly, this essay aims to demonstrate that, in light of the currently predominant discourse on post-genocide Rwanda, *Ndi Umunyarwanda* could be perceived as a top-down process of social engineering if only considered from the perspective of the current stage of its political dissemination. Approached from its inception stage, however, it is a bottom-up phenomenon that originates from the dialogues held between children of perpetrators, children (of) survivors and representatives of local and central governments.

In other words, the argument proposed here is that change in post-genocide Rwanda happens in different stages and at different levels. A comprehensive account of this change must take account of this multilevel and multistage dimension if we are to avoid scholarship characterized by the misleading dualistic diagnoses alluded to previously. Applied to YCD and *Ndi Umunyarwanda* as sequentially related phenomena, this approach shows that individual and group-initiated changes at grass-roots levels can and do shape the national metanarrative of post-genocide nation building. This, I argue, happens through a process of negotiation and subsequent incorporation, as points of convergence or alignment with governmental reconstruction interests are found.

In my study of YCD and *Ndi Umunyarwanda* as stages of change, I follow in the footsteps of those who study nation building in post-genocide Rwanda as an enterprise of 'labour in production of a people' (Purdeková, 2015: 11). Much like Purdeková (2015: 10), I observe actors like Edouard and Art for Peace as they nurture the idea of a generational pact and its message of a future of peace without machetes. I show how they transmit it to other children of

---

[1] *Ubumwe* is semantically encoded in the use of the singular for both the verb – *ndi* [I am] instead of *turi* [we are] – and the attribute *umunyarwanda* instead of *abanyarwanda*.

perpetrators through YCD, how the idea transforms into policy practice and action and, finally, how it is performed in the form of *Ndi Umunyarwanda*.

This study of YCD looks at children of perpetrators as agents and their stories as catalysts of change. I trace their journey from privacy and isolation, vocalized during the dialogues as a stage of transgenerational shame and guilt and rendered eloquently by Edouard Bamporiki's book *Icyaha kuri bo, Ikimwaro kuri njye* [*Their Sin, My Shame*] (2010). I suggest that YCD constituted an intermediary stage where disparate stories mutated into an in-group or generational story in the form of dialogues on shared life experiences. By bringing private stories into public space, children of perpetrators became political actors and their initiative a political enterprise. The labour of production which ultimately begat *Ndi Umunyarwanda* took place in this highly politicized arena, in the form of negotiations with state power.

## Genealogy of a Generational Story

YCD was an initiative of Art for Peace, an association of young Rwandan artists whose mission is to promote truth and reconciliation, with a particular focus on younger generations (Art for Peace, 2013). Officially, YCD fell under the tutelage of the Ministry of Youth and ICT and fit within its broader Youth Connekt programme. Rwanda's First Lady's Imbuto Foundation financed the dialogues. The slogan of the event was 'Youth Connekt Dialogue: Promise of a post-genocide generation'. The Kinyarwanda word for 'promise' in this context is *umuhigo* (plural: *imihigo*). It carries the meaning of a binding promise in which one's honour and social status are at stake.

Organizers described the dialogues as a transition from a 'rear-view mirror' to a 'windshield' perspective (Marcel, YCD Gatsibo, June 2013), which shifts the focus from exclusively survivor-centred accounts to alternative stories (Teta, YCD Kicukiro, May 2013). Such a conception of YCD might explain the notable focus on children of perpetrators. As the dialogues unfolded, it became increasingly clear that although officially all young Rwandans aged between 18 and 35 were invited,[2] it was obvious that the primary target audience were children of perpetrators and their stories. To fully appreciate the significance of YCD, it is useful to analyse the dialogues in light of the place and role assigned to children and young people in the post-genocide recovery narrative.

---

[2]  The 2006 Rwanda National Youth policy defines a 'youth' as a person aged between 14 and 35. The National Youth Council website (2018) gives an age range of 16–30. Available at https://nyc.gov.rw/index.php?id=11 (consulted on 9 March 2018).

## Childhood, Youth and Nationhood Reconstruction

There is a healthy body of work on the positioning of children and young people in post-conflict nation building (Burman, 2008; Pells, 2011; Cheney, 2007). Tradition and culture often dictate how children and young people are defined in post-conflict peace-building discourses (McEvoy-Levy, 2011). Researchers have established conceptual links between childhood and nationhood, highlighting the paradox between metaphors that romanticize children as 'pillars of the nation' and their persisting subservience to adult ideals of idyllic pasts (Cheney, 2007: 10). McEvoy-Levy (2001) suggests that this dynamic of youth-to-adult subordination reflects the reluctance to incorporate children's and young people's knowledge in post-conflict peace-building, even though there is sufficient evidence to suggest these demographic groups can and do play a variety of different, shifting roles in these contexts (UN IANYD, 2016: 13).

In light of this literature, it is fair to say that post-genocide Rwanda has taken a different route. Children and young people in general figure prominently in post-genocide narratives of recovery. Representations of children and youth as the future of the nation – *U Rwanda rw'ejo* – are a mainstay in political discourse and the popular imaginary. More pertinently, there is factual relevance for this discursive over-representation in a country where the 2012 national census estimated that the children and youth represented 78.2% of the population (Republic of Rwanda, 2015). With regard to the impact of the genocide on children and young adults, the reality is sobering. The August 2002 general census showed that 64.67% had lost both parents, 22.80% had lost their father and 4.84% their mother (Ministry of Youth, 2005: 18).

In this context, one can but agree that to neglect this demographic would be 'short-sighted and counterproductive in terms of peace building particularly in the crucial post-accord phase with its twin challenges of violence prevention [...] and societal reconciliation and reconstruction' (McEvoy, 2001: 2–3). Post-genocide governments responded to this challenging reality with an array of institutions and policies. A National Commission for Children was established by Law no. 22/2011 of 28 June 2011, as a consolidation of various outcomes of successive National Children's Summits organized since 2004 (Pells, 2011). A National Youth Council was instituted in 2003 (Law no. 24/2003 of 14 August 2003) with the stated vision of having an empowered youth at the forefront of economic development (National Youth Council, 2018). Overall, local and central governments have sought to capitalize on youth as a national asset by having youth representatives at every level of decision-making. On the other hand, pupils and students are involved in a plethora of institutions (clubs, associations, etc.) with many missions varying from peace education to unity and reconciliation.

Scholarship in this area has been steadily growing around themes such as discourses on children rights and the political instrumentalization of children's agency (Pells, 2011). Some research has focused on gaps between promised development and perceived benefits in policies that seek to make children and young people central to post-genocide reconstruction (Pells et al., 2014). Other studies have centred around themes of youth and ethnic identity (Doná, 2012; Mclean Hilker, 2012) and young people's views on narratives of the past (Mclean Hilker, 2011). In these and other studies, there is evidence that young Rwandans have creatively and subversively engaged with the official metanarrative on post-genocide recovery. Overall, through the lenses of local realities and lived experience, young people have sought to reframe the state's narrative and prove that change in post-genocide Rwanda is multilayered and multidirectional in origin.

## Children of Perpetrators: Legacy, Identity and Reconstruction

Although research into the Rwandan crisis has come a long way in the last two decades, scholarship on the legacy of the Rwandan genocide for subsequent generations has been dominated by victim-centred approaches (Sydor and Philippot, 1996; Rakita, 2003; Reider and Elbert, 2013). Despite bringing much-needed insight on important themes such as young people's physical and mental health and their post-genocide socioeconomic adjustment, these studies have failed to attend to the experiences of the children of perpetrators in post-genocide Rwanda.

It is argued above that more recent and better-informed studies of Rwanda's transitional period have called for a 'complexifying' of academic discourse (Purdeková, 2015). However, earlier studies still viewed Rwanda as a 'dualist' post-conflict society (Drumbl, 2008), one where surviving victims and perpetrators live side by side. It is estimated that after the genocide, close to 120,000 adult Hutu genocide suspects were detained. After the process of identifying all suspects, the number of *genocidaires* prosecuted by *gacaca* reached 400,000, including a small number of Tutsi (Clark, 2012). After *gacaca* and its focus on the 'sins of the parents', very little attention has been given to the plight of the children of the perpetrators, despite research demonstrating that genocide could and did generate severe psychopatho-logical reactions among all children who witnessed the massacres (Sydor and Philippot, 1996: 242–43).

For the category referred to collectively as 'children of perpetrators', post-genocide recovery comes with a loaded legacy. YCD became the forum where the psycho-political ramifications of this legacy were made public for the first time. Attentive listening, display of raw emotions and intense discussions revealed a complex and traumatic relationship between this specific group and the genocide. The dialogues also revealed a group characterized by diversity, uncovering the nomenclature of 'children of perpetrators' to be what it inevitably is, namely the kind of 'groupist' artifice which Purdeková (2008, 2015) denounces. Concepts such as 'children of Hutu' or 'children of perpetrators' are the discursive embodiment of an 'extension fallacy' (Purdeková, 2008). They bestow collective identity and (hi)story to people with disparate identities: children born of Hutu parents, Hutu children whose parents committed acts of genocide, 'Hutsi' or children of mixed parentage (Mclean Hilker, 2012), children born of the rape of Tutsi women by Hutu killers, to name but a few.

The stories told during YCD conveyed an undercurrent of frustration and exasperation that these specific identities are not well understood. However, deeper still was a feeling of inescapable guilt with which they had to live because of who had given birth to them. Gilbert (2002) and Forrest (2006) have shown that feelings of guilt are not uncommon within groups of children of perpetrators. Yet this was not the healthy innocent guilt that is a necessary element in the fundamental structure of the ethical subject, in the particular context of post-conflict work (Christensen, 2013). Nor was it the kind of transgenerational collective guilt prevalent in post-Nazi Germany that Arendt finds immoral since it confuses guilt and responsibility and thus fails to make the right distinction between politics and morality (2003: 29). It was instead a deep-seated guilt born out of a *sui generis* post-genocide context where political socialization and genealogical association are intricately connected. YCD participants felt that this situation had to change for theirs and the nation's sake.

## A Narrative Shift

As mentioned previously, Art for Peace and its sponsors wanted the dialogues to help young Rwandans face their past and move towards their future, using group discussions, personal testimonies, music and other forms of art (Art for Peace, 2013). In particular, Art for Peace envisioned the dialogues as a new paradigm for truth and reconciliation that would shift the focus from reaction to change (Teta, YCD Kicukiro, May 2013).[3]

---

[3] I discuss this temporal-directional metaphor extensively in a recent publication (Benda, 2018).

Witnessing the first dialogue as a participant observer and listener left me with a strong sense of 'surrealism', which is not uncommon among researchers in post-genocide Rwanda (Purdeková, 2015: 25–30; Lemarchand, 2018). Moving from riotous music to heartbreaking testimonies and back to more raucous entertainment, one questioned whether this was a highly charged political event or an unconventional street concert. Yet it is possible to follow Ganz's advice in viewing the dialogues as a generational celebration: a 'way that members of a community come together to honour who they are, what they have done, and where they are going' (2011: 288).

Once past the initial shock, it quickly became apparent that the format of the dialogues was designed to reaffirm the agency, actual and potential, of young people in the transformation and rebuilding of post-genocide Rwanda. The ice-breaking or warm-up entertainment started with this eloquent affirmation:

Leader: *Abajeni*! [Hey, young people!]
Audience: *Imbaraga z'igihugu kandi zubaka* [(We are) the building force of the nation]
And the songs
*Jenga jenga taifa lako, jenga taifa lako* (Swahili) [Build, build your nation] (by Masamba)
Or
*Rwanda itajengwa na sisi wenyewe, Rwanda itajengwa na sisi vijana* (Swahili) [Rwanda will be built by us, Rwanda will be built by us, the young] (Gatsibo district music group)

Purdeková has made a robust case for the significance of 'appearance' and 'characterization' in Rwanda's transitional politics. In a context of systematic 'production of gaps' between depiction of activities and their observable content, 'naming and descriptions can [...] mask and perform political work', and 'formalities and formulations are substance in their own right' (Purdeková, 2015: 6). The rousing words of self-affirmation at the beginning of the dialogues must be deciphered with this discursive political landscape in the background.

This remark and the somewhat rigid format of the dialogues, as well as the interventions by state officials, might lead to the conclusion that YCD did not differ from other state-sanctioned forums such as *ingando*, *ubudehe*, *ubusabane*,[4] and should therefore be open to the same criticism as top-down

---

4 *Ingando* means 'camp'. In post-genocide Rwanda, there are two kinds of *ingando*: *solidarity* camps, which gather elite groups including judges, politicians and university students, and *re-education* camps that host the more 'problematic'

mechanisms of social engineering (Thomson, 2011, 2013; Pells, 2011). Yet this assimilation would be inaccurate. To understand what sets YCD apart, it is more appropriate to locate it within a narrative continuity that requires analysis of its inception. Ganz suggests that it is particularly important to celebrate beginnings as a way of acknowledging the start of a new common identity (2011: 288). This return to the beginning reveals layered stories of which YCD is but a new departure, a 'resonance moment' (Gilpin-Jackson, 2014) that is neither the beginning nor the end. At the origin of the dialogues, one discovers the birth of Art for Peace, itself a result of the public emergence of Edouard Bamporiki, a young man with a big story.

## Edouard's Journey, a Personal and Paradigmatic Story of Change

Narrative, Ganz suggests, should be understood as 'the discursive means we use to access values that equip us with the courage to make choices under conditions of uncertainty, to exercise agency' (2011: 274). In this context, Edouard Bamporiki's story carries great significance for any account of Rwanda's recovery that takes the agency of the youth seriously. This story was adopted by organizers of the dialogues as the paradigm for children of perpetrators' post-genocide condition.

Edouard's story was the centrepiece of each YCD event and was recounted in all 15 districts. The excerpts used below are taken mainly, but not exclusively, from the version delivered in Kicukiro (May 2013). Typical of inspirational accounts, the story was powerful and its narration skilfully punctuated by key moments known in narrative analysis as 'critical junctures' (Palmer, 2014) or 'choice points' (Ganz, 2011). It found the right balance between entertaining anecdotes and the overall seriousness of a biographical narrative (Cohen, 2011). The result was a story which clarified, compelled attention, persuaded or reinforced beliefs, inspired and influenced the audience's view of the speaker (Lehrman, 2010: 102).

Edouard introduced his story genealogically and poetically with 'Bamporiki wa ...' going back five generations and refers to himself as 'Umusizi w'Umusinga wo kwa Nyakayaga' (Kicukiro, May 2013) [a Musinga poet from the lineage of Nyakayaga]. The emphasis on clan (*umusinga*) and lineage

---

segments of society such as confessed *génocidaires*, released prisoners and ex-soldiers. *Ubudehe* refers to a practice and culture of collective action and mutual support to solve problems within a community. *Ubusabane* are convivial gatherings in which communities come together to celebrate life through sharing food and other aspects of Rwandan culture.

(Nyakayaga) is important for students of Rwanda's post-genocide identity politics. Quesenbery and Brooks (2010) remind us that stories are created for a purpose and Edouard's sidestepping of ethnic belonging is significant. It was a purposeful distancing from the past and the marker of alignment or convergence between individual politics and the official discourse on identity in which the terms 'Hutu' and 'Tutsi' have been outlawed.

The first critical juncture in Edouard's story coincides with the start of the genocide:

> When the genocide broke out in 1994, I was nine years old and I was in the hospital of Kibogora. My mother was looking after me. There were three other people in the room [...] We heard noises of bullets outside and disturbances in the hospital. When I asked mum what was happening, she shushed me [...] when I insisted, she told me that she had heard that the Hutu were killing the Tutsi.

The story continues as Edouard invites the audience into his hospital room where a sick child – who has been reassured by his mother that he has nothing to worry about since he is *umuhutu udafunguye* or a pure *Muhutu* (Hutu) – witnesses the brutal murder of Tutsi patients by armed Hutu. In the same tableau, an adult patient is quietly tucking into his dish of macaroni whilst a little Tutsi girl sits in a pool of blood, the severed head of her father resting in her lap.

This part of the story often generated a very strong emotional response from the audience. However, the narrative intention was not to re-traumatize participants but to highlight the traumatic effect of the genocide on Hutu children and the responsibility of adult Hutu using a brief but charged passage. It also serves as a transgenerational indictment which puts the responsibility for genocide squarely on the shoulders of adult Hutu. Finally, it juxtaposes the four elements that frame the genocide against the Tutsi: Hutu killers, Hutu bystanders, Tutsi killed atrociously and child witnesses/survivors.

The next stage of the narrative reiterates adult Hutu guilt and initiates an empathetic connection between the narrator and the 'victim' group. At the same time, it keeps present the genealogical association between children and adult perpetrators.

> When the genocide was over and schools reopened, I was saddened to see that there were no Tutsi kids and teachers in the classrooms. This is when I wrote my first poem 'Iyo badatsembwa tuba dutwenga' [Had they not been exterminated, we would be laughing together], in which I question how our people – *bene wacu* – could kill teachers, children, women [...] I could never comprehend it.

From the perspective of the current literature on guilt and genocide, this segment of the story seems to render support to the presumed collective guilt of all adult Hutu and its transmission to their descendants (Eltringham, 2011; Blair and Stevenson, 2015). It also reinforces the suggestion that a perpetrator's guilt is often mediated by a sense of empathy for the victim group as opposed to shame, which is mediated by self-pity (Brown and Cehajic, 2008). However, seen from the vantage point of a ten-year-old boy, the words should be read as a lament. The poetics of lament expressed in the poem reveals a working through grief that is rarely explored in post-genocide literature, especially among young Hutu.

The second key moment in Edouard's story relates to the socio-economic condition of young Hutu in post-genocide Rwanda (Mclean Hilker, 2011; Doná, 2012). Despite his mother's efforts to ensure the continuation of his studies, life became increasingly hard and Edouard dropped out of school in the third year of his secondary studies. He struggled to find a decent job, like many young Hutu in the same situation, and ended up serving as a houseboy. This part of the story crystallizes an aspect of post-genocide reconstruction that is rarely broached in mainstream narratives, namely the feeling among young Hutu that, in comparison with young Tutsi, they are excluded from vital social policies such as access to secondary and tertiary education (Meintjes, 2013; Pells, 2011). As voiced during the dialogues, this socio-economic exclusion is accepted either as a matter of fact or with stoic resignation since it is an inevitable consequence of the crimes committed by their adult relatives in 1994. In an apt paraphrase of the prophet Ezekiel (18:3), Bamporiki notes that the children's teeth were being set on edge by the fruits of the tree planted by their parents (2010: 1). These feelings further resonate with findings by studies in social psychology on perpetrators' emotional responses to collective guilt (Branscombe and Doosje, 2004; Brown and Cehajic, 2008; Imhoff et al., 2013; Lickel et al., 2005).

The third critical juncture in Edouard's story coincides with an upturn in his fortunes, which he attributes to his talent as a poet and to the current government's willingness to give opportunities to everyone, especially young people:

> One day, I was cooking [...] when I heard an advert on the radio calling for poets and musicians to submit works on the importance of taxes! I composed a poem through the night and surprisingly I won the prize for best poem!

As a winner, Edouard had the privilege of reciting his poem as a prelude to President Kagame's speech during the tenth anniversary commemoration of the genocide. It is clear that at this juncture Edouard's story had already entered a political stage. The next and last critical juncture propelled both the narrator and his story into Rwanda's most sensitive public arena and irreversibly paved the way to YCD. In April 2006, Edouard was invited by a group of survivors in Kimironko to recite poetry as part of their mourning and commemoration wake:

> As is habitual in such occasions, survivors shared their testimonies and experiences of the genocide. I was so profoundly moved that when they asked me to perform, I felt unable to recite poetry. Instead, I asked the gathered survivors if I could give my own testimony.

Having received their permission, he proceeded to tell the story summarized above. The audience was so deeply moved by his story that most cried with him and sought to comfort him. Subsequently, they shared the experience with other groups of survivors who invited him to speak during their wakes as well.

This episode had a cathartic and catalytic effect on young Edouard. It dawned on him that his story had the potential bring a new dimension to the process of post-genocide reconciliation and reconstruction. His initial intention was to encourage adult Hutu who committed atrocities in front of their children to own up to their crimes and to seek forgiveness for the sake of the children of both groups. Unfortunately, he found most adult Hutu to be unreceptive but the Hutu youth who had relatives in prison, and young Tutsi survivors, mostly artists like him, responded positively to Edouard's message.[5] Together they founded Art for Peace as a means of creating for themselves a future of peace without machetes. It was during Youth Week in 2013 that Art for Peace approached the First Lady's Imbuto Foundation and secured support to take this message to all the districts of Rwanda.[6]

## Contours of a Generational Story of Change

Ganz suggests that for a collection of individuals to become an 'us', it requires a storyteller, an interpreter of shared experience (2011: 286). Edouard fulfilled this role in each of the 15 districts, each time he told his story, and each time he invited young Hutu in the audience who identified

---

[5] These conversations were recently published by Edouard Bamporiki under the title *My Son, it Is a Long Story* (2017).

[6] Following the success of YCD, Edouard was elected as an RPF Member of Parliament. After a four-year term, he was appointed head of *Itorero*, a traditional institution reintroduced in 2009 as a way to rebuild the nation's social fabric and mobilize Rwandans to uphold important cultural values.

with this story to come forth and share their experience. It is out of these dialogues that a generational story of guilt, shame and the pursuit of political redemption emerged. What are the most salient contours of this story? As already mentioned, it uses Edouard's personal account as the template for children of perpetrators' life stories. In it, the child of perpetrators is seen as an innocent and often traumatized witness wrestling with confusion and guilt, excluded from sociopolitical opportunities, needing the redemptive hearing of survivors' stories and the guiding hand of the state to find their place in society. The next step in our analysis is to examine the extent to which the stories of other children of perpetrators mirror this template narrative.

The general observation was that these stories did not emerge easily or fluently. Ganz (2011) has pointed to the challenging nature of participating in events like YCD where the participants' criticality and hope are in a dialectical relationship in their desire to bring about social changes. However, despite the reticence of a number of young people to speak to a big crowd, children of perpetrators told their stories in various ways. Some told their stories in the form of short autobiographical testimonies, like microscopic portals opening onto a more complex life. Others did not offer a story but asked pertinent questions, revealing in their own way where they stood with regard to Edouard's paradigmatic account. Still others spoke briefly to thank Edouard for having the courage to say what they could not say, implicitly showing that their lives mirrored Edouard's story. Others openly agreed with Edouard in blaming Hutu adults for the Genocide against the Tutsi.

To understand these short, unstructured and at times incoherent narratives, Pamphilon (1999) suggests using the meso-zoom level of life stories analysis, which makes it possible to evaluate the narrative process, themes and key phrases. This approach reveals intriguing but not unexpected differences between the main narrator's linear construction of self and the more fragmented experiences of the young people who responded to his story. In addition, a macro-zoom analysis of the cohort effects – that is to say, the immediate or remote external and historical factors that shaped their experience (Gilpin-Jackson, 2014) – provides an extra dimension for understanding the distinctiveness of narratives coming from members of the audience.

For all these incoherencies, hesitations and fragmentations, very important themes emerged out of these dialogues and were debated with a measure of openness rarely associated with Rwandan public space. The most frequently recurrent themes inevitably included the genocide and historical ambiguities, childhood, memory and trauma, intragenerational and intergenerational perception of responsibility and guilt, genealogical association and the transmission of liability in Rwandan culture, ethnic versus national identity and the sociopolitical condition of children of perpetrators. It is most revealing that these themes were discussed mostly through questioning. For instance, on the theme of genocide and its legacy on children of perpetrators, participants wondered how they could step out of the shadow cast by the genocidal criminality of their adult relatives in the context of annual commemoration (*icyunamo*) (Kicukiro, May 2013). They worried that in the absence of their imprisoned or exiled adult relatives, the justifiable anger of survivors would be transferred to them. In Gisagara district, for instance, a young woman told the story of how, when her brother was sentenced *in absentia*, she took it upon herself to do the *travaux d'intérêt général* that went with his sentence so that the family's shame might be mitigated (Gisagara, May 2013).

On the issue of social and political identity, children of perpetrators voiced the anxiety of not knowing who they were since they could no longer be referred to as Hutu, children of Hutu or children of killers. 'Are we to be called *abitwaga abahutu*, "ex-Hutu"?', one child asked in Gatsibo (June 2013). More importantly, YCD participants were unsure about the feasibility of de-ethnicization after a genocide which has been officially reframed in ethnic terms as the 'Genocide against the Tutsi'. Finally, as far as history is concerned, YCD participants questioned the many contradictory versions of history and debated whether there was a single version of historical truth. In Nyabihu district, children of perpetrators expressed their frustration that leaders and scholars were unable to agree on and teach 'real' history.

These and other themes revealed a generation of young people in transition and in search of identity and self-understanding, within a context marked by a particular legacy of genocide, a constantly revised history and complex identity politics. They also revealed a generation that is well attuned to the government's policies and underpinning narratives. At the same time, they questioned where and how they fit into these policies, not as the 'children of so and so' but as individual selves who are aware of their connection to Rwanda's tragic past yet remain committed to playing a positive role in its ongoing reconstruction. *Ndi Umunyarwanda* finds its origin in these embryonic narratives of ambiguous identities.

## From YCD to *Ndi Umunyarwanda*: Narrative Convergence and Political Incorporation

It is not easy to determine the transition moment when Edouard's story became a paradigmatic narrative for a generation of children of perpetrators. It is clear, however, that the construction of the story followed the same trajectory as the emergence of the narrator's identity. Concretely, one can surmise that both entered the public sphere between 'critical juncture 3' (winning the poetry competition) and 'critical juncture 4' (winning the hearts of survivors). At this point, the poetic of reconstruction collided with the rhetoric of memory, lament and reconciliation, creating an inspiring public narrative that political authorities could not ignore. It is here, arguably, that real political change happened.

Therefore, it is useful to examine how this narrative converged with the official narratives of national recovery in such a way that the trajectory from Edouard's story to YCD, and ultimately to *Ndi Umunyarwanda*, appears seamless. Studying this narrative convergence achieves one of the aims of this essay, namely, to interrogate the orthodoxy of current scholarship that posits the post-genocide reconstruction metanarrative as a top-down and RPF-driven discourse (Straus and Waldorf, 2011). Critical narrative analysis finds mixed validity in positing a pre-existent and monistic official narrative. Instead it suggests that individual or group lives, experiences and stories from below have the required breadth, depth and quality to begin a social momentum towards effective action on policy change or what Ganz (2011) calls the agency to turn opportunity into purpose.

Further analysis indicates that official metanarratives that usher in major changes can and do emerge as a number of these bottom-up initiatives are carefully engaged with and points of convergence or alignment with national interests are found. These initiatives are subsequently – although not always – absorbed into the government's vision through various policy innovations. It is this formative process of convergence assessment and subsequent incorporation in national policy to which current scholarship has so far failed to attend. Instead, it has tended to focus exclusively on the political end product without attempting thorough analytical distinction between the whole and the parts, the process and the outcome.

This point also highlights the importance of YCD and similar state-sponsored public forums on the formulation of official narratives and policies. In this case, the transition from Edouard's story to *Ndi Umunyarwanda* was not a simple case of public performance as some critics, particularly the opposition from the Rwandan diaspora, have suggested (BBC, July 2013). Rather, YCD was the pivotal transitional point which acted both as a testing forum and a validation process. The meticulous planning between Art for Peace, the Ministry of Youth and ICT and the Imbuto Foundation (Art for Peace, 2013) is evidence that Edouard's story, as important as it was, represented no more than the proverbial tree that does not make the forest. It had to receive public generational validation which, contrary to what critics suggest, was a contingent outcome rather than a foregone conclusion.

In this respect, YCD was the crucible in which potential turned into conviction on at least two levels. On one level, an individual story identified as a generational paradigm was tested and ultimately – but not uncritically – validated by similar or complementary stories from the targeted generation. On a second level, the government was sufficiently convinced that this bottom-up generational narrative had enough political relevance to signal a new departure in the discourse on identity politics. In Ganz's terminology, YCD was the forum in which individual stories of children of perpetrators mutated into a generational story of 'us', leading ultimately to the emergence of a national story of now in the form of *Ndi Umunyarwanda*. However, this process also confirmed what keen students of power dynamics and state agency have long observed in post-genocide Rwanda: the fact that 'though multiple initiatives are initiated outside of the state framework, the search for the "truly grassroots" obscures the way in which actors at all levels have to negotiate power and the state in their daily lives' (Purdeková, 2015: 13).

### *Ndi Umunyarwanda*: Finding Identity in the Rwandan Spirit

*Ndi Umunyarwanda*, I have pointed out, is a relatively new concept, having surfaced in the post-genocide political narrative in July 2013 (NURC, 2017). There is little doubt, however, that this concept is set to dominate Rwandan politics in the foreseeable future. One way of simplifying *Ndi Umunyarwanda* is to say that it is envisioned as the answer to almost all the historical ills that have befallen and divided Rwanda. A concept paper prepared by the NURC (2017) has attempted to provide a more refined précis of *Ndi Umunyarwanda* both as concept and policy. It is both *icyomoro* – a salve or balm for the Rwandan body politic – and *igihango*, the pact that binds Rwandans. It is a vision for the future, the embodiment of the Rwandan spirit and way of life, and a political programme (NURC, 2017: 53–57).

*Ndi Umunyarwanda* represents the absolute embodiment of *ubunyarwanda* or the Rwandan spirit, understood as the profound relational bond that unites all Rwandans. This bond is the eternal and unbreakable pact between all Rwandans, and between Rwandans and their country (NURC, 2017: 58). *Ndi Umunyarwanda* involves the embracing of *ubunyarwanda* as well as the values and taboos that underpin this spirit. These values are patriotism geared towards a positive legacy for the future, integrity, a culture of critical dialogue for conflict resolution and the promotion of national and individual progress. Genocide ideology, conspiring against Rwanda and Rwandans as a nation, and putting individual gain before national interests are proscribed by *ubunyarwanda* (NURC, 2017: 59–66). The concept paper goes on to provide specific goals, results and a code of conduct for *Ndi Umunyarwanda* dialogues.

Scoping *Ndi Umunyarwanda* is currently a difficult task since it is still going through different stages of conceptual and substantive consolidation. Once this process is deemed satisfactorily complete, *Ndi Umunyarwanda* will become the narrative and strategic framework for the majority of policies, especially in all matters related to citizenship and identity politics. One of the most promising additions to the narrative of *Ndi Umunyarwanda* is the recently created institution of *Abarinzi b'igihango* or Keepers of the Pact (NURC, 2016). This initiative aims to identify and tell the stories of special individuals who have demonstrated and upheld the highest values of *ubunyarwanda* during past instances of violence (NURC, 2016: 3). In doing so, they preserved the traditional pact between Rwandans and were the precursor of the spirit that animates *Ndi Umunyarwanda* (NURC, 2016: 4–6).

At the time of writing, two cohorts of *Abarinzi b'igihango* have been commended and rewarded ('Abarinzi', 2015; NURC, 2017). What is immediately noticeable is the fact that most of these individuals were rescuers during the Genocide against the Tutsi in 1994. Even if not all of them are Rwandans or Hutu, it is impossible not to surmise that the *Ndi Umunyarwanda* narrative is attempting to incorporate Hutu stories that are not just accounts of murder, shame and guilt. It is also true that this change should be seen as a direct consequence of YCD, the dialogues having already introduced to the public narrative the idea that the Hutu group should not be seen as a homogeneous collective with a single story. In this sense, an initiative that was started by marginalized children of perpetrators continues to exercise positive and profound influence on changes that are likely to shape discourse on identity politics in the foreseeable future.

## Conclusion

This study set out to provide a narrative analysis of YCD and to show how narratives from below shape or contribute to the official metanarrative on post-genocide societal change. The findings suggest that YCD contributed directly to the official narrative of identity by giving it grounding and validation.

YCD showcased many poignant stories retracing individual journeys of children of perpetrators as they wrestled with the intergenerational legacy of genocide, as they developed awareness of identity politics and as they engaged creatively with governmental policies. The dialogues generated fascinating narratives of transformative transition from ambiguous ethnic identities and transgenerational guilt to constructive exchanges aiming at intragenerational integration and future-oriented political responsibility. However, YCD also became a story in its own right, a narrative with at least four axes of change. It was the story of a bottom-up initiative. Secondly, it was a story of change from a 'rear-view mirror' to 'windshield' perspective in its shift of emphasis from survivors' to perpetrators' lives. It was also a narrative of political repositioning from private emotions to public visibility. Ultimately, it represented a redemptive narrative of moving from guilt to political agency.

For scholarship on post-genocide reconstruction, this analysis of YCD contributes a unique narrative insight into the condition of children of perpetrators in a *sui generis* post-conflict context. It draws the reader into the universe of political, socio-economic, psychological, moral and legal dilemmas that these young people face daily. Concretely, the study shows how children of perpetrators understand and conceptualize genocide and its legacy from a transgenerational perspective. It highlights the impact of this legacy on the formation of a complex post-genocide identity, transgenerational tensions around the issues of guilt, responsibility and accountability as well as the perceived and real handicaps of being children of perpetrators. It shows how this generation is forging credible agency to position themselves as partakers in the reconstruction of a nation whose destruction weighs heavily on their conscience through a culturally entrenched notion of genealogical transmissibility.

The stories of Edouard and other children of perpetrators should be seen as examples of a narrative journey from the 'dark side of the mind', a quest for hope during which denial and repression are worked through, so that knowledge and awareness are not shifted away from consciousness (Bar-On, 1991). When this consciousness is released from the confines of individuality and privacy, it becomes public and political, a public generational narrative. In this respect, the progression from Edouard's individual story to YCD is an intentional construction of in-group political identity. This in turn makes YCD events genuine sites of political transformative learning. The public nature of these stories should not be underestimated. They are in contra-distinction to what Schlant (1999) calls the 'language of silence', a form of political mutism that characterizes different generations of perpetrators (Oxenberg, 2003; Imhoff et al., 2012; Brown and Cehajic, 2008; Münyas, 2008). They offer a challenging and dialectic narrative in which the strong desire to reject the past is in tension with the political necessity to connect this past to the future (Berger and Berger, 2001).

Children of perpetrators used YCD to challenge narratives of ethnic identity (Eltringham, 2011; Mclean Hilker, 2011) and offered narratives that should begin to lay foundations for a genuine national Rwandan identity. Discussions around the issue of transgenerational guilt point to a desire to convert guilt as a handicap into political responsibility. *Ndi Umunyarwanda* is their stated political intentionality to rebuild a nation for all Rwandans in which *amahoro* [peace] not *imihoro* [machetes] should have the last word.

## Works Cited

'Abarinzi b'igihango 17 bagiye guhembwa ku rwego rw'igihugu'. *Muhabura Online* 5 November 2015. Available at http://muhabura.rw/amakuru/politiki/article/abarinzi-b-igihango-17-bagiye-guhembwa-ku-rwego-rw-igihugu (consulted on 9 March 2018).

Arendt, Hannah. 2003. *Responsibility and Judgement.* New York: Schocken.

—. 2005. *The Promise of Politics.* New York: Schocken.

Art for Peace. 2013. *Youth Connekt Dialogue: The Promise of a Generation. Report.* Kigali.

Bamporiki, Edouard. 2010. *Icyaha kuri bo, ikimwaro kuri jye. Igiti mwateye dushririwe n'imbuto zacyo.* Kigali: Edouard Bamporiki.

—. 2017. *My Son, it Is a Long Story. Reflections of Genocide Perpetrators.* Kigali: Edouard Bamporiki.

Bar-on, Dan. 1991. *Legacy of Silence: Encounters with Children of the Third Reich.* Cambridge, MA: Harvard University Press.

BBC Africa Gahuzamiryango. 2013. *Imvo n'imvano 1 and 2.* 22 and 29 July. London.

Benda, Richard. 2018. 'Time to Hear the Other Side. Transitional Temporality and Transgenerational Narratives in Post-Genocide Rwanda'. In Natascha Mueller-Hirth and Sandra Rios Oyola (eds), *Time and Temporality in Transitional and Post-Conflict Societies.* London: Routledge: Chapter 8.

Berger, Alan L., and Naomi Berger (eds). 2001. *Second Generation Voices. Reflections by Children of Holocaust Survivors and Perpetrators.* Syracuse, NY: Syracuse University Press.

Blair, Luke. S., and John A. Stevenson. 2015. 'What Do the Dead Say? The Architecture of Salvific Discourses in Post-Genocide Rwanda'. *Journal of Power, Politics & Governance* 3.1: 27–45.

Branscombe, Nyla R., and Bertjan Doosje. 2004. *Collective Guilt: International Perspectives.* New York: Cambridge University Press.

Brown, Rupert, and Sabina Cehajic. 2008. 'Dealing with the Past and Facing the Future: Mediators of the Effects of Collective Guilt and Shame in Bosnia and Herzegovina'. *European Journal of Social Psychology* 38: 669–84.

Burman, Erica. 2008. *Deconstructing Developmental Psychology, rev. ed.* London: Brunner-Routledge.

Cheney, Kristen. E. 2007. *Pillars of the Nation; Child Citizens and Ugandan National Development.* Chicago, IL: University of Chicago Press.

Christensen, Anne-Marie. S. 2013. 'The Role of Innocent Guilt in Post-Conflict Work'. *Journal of Applied Philosophy* 30.4: 365–78.

Clark, Philip. 2012. *How Rwanda Judged its Genocide.* London: Africa Research Institute.

—. 2014. 'Bringing the Peasants Back in, Again: State Power and Local Agency in Rwanda's Gacaca Courts'. *Journal of Eastern African Studies* 8.2: 193–213.

Cohen, S. 2011. 'The Art of Public Narrative: Teaching Students How to Construct Memorable Anecdotes'. *Communication Teacher* 25.4: 197–204.

Doná, Giorgia. 2012. 'Being Young and of Mixed Ethnicity in Rwanda'. *Forced Migration Review* 40: 16–17.

Drumbl, Mark. 2000. 'Punishment Postgenocide: From Guilt to Shame to "Civis" in Rwanda'. *New York University Law Review* 75.5: 1237–53.

Eltringham, Nigel. 2011. 'The Past Is Elsewhere: Paradoxes of Proscribing Ethnicity in Post-Genocide Rwanda'. In Scott Straus and Lars Waldorf (eds), *Remaking Rwanda: State Building and Human Rights after Mass Violence.* Madison, WI: The University of Wisconsin Press: 269–82.

Forrest, Peter. 2006. 'Collective Guilt; Individual Shame'. *Midwest Studies in Philosophy* 30.1: 145–53.

Ganz, Marshall. 2011. 'Public Narrative, Collective Action, and Power'. In Sina Odugbemi and Taeku Lee (eds), *Accountability through Public Opinion: From Inertia to Action.* Washington, DC: The World Bank: 273–89.

Gilbert, Margaret. 2002. 'Collective Guilt and Collective Guilt Feelings'. *Journal of Ethics* 6.2: 115–43.

Gilpin-Jackson, Yabome. 2014. 'Resonance as Transformative Learning Moment: The Key to Transformation in Sociocultural and Post-Trauma Contexts'. *Journal of Transformative Education* 12: 95–119.

Imhoff, Roland, Michał Bilewicz and Hans-Peter Erb. 2012. 'Collective Regret versus Collective Guilt: Different Emotional Reactions to Historical Atrocities'. *European Journal of Social Psychology* 42: 729–42.

Lehrman, Robert. 2010. *The Political Speechwriter's Companion: A Guide for Writers and Speakers.* Washington, DC: CQ Press.

Lemarchand, René. 2018. 'Rwanda: The State of Research'. *Mass Violence and Resistance – Research Network.* Available at https://www.sciencespo.fr/mass-violence-war-massacre-resistance/en/document/rwanda-state-research (consulted on 24 August 2018).

Lickel, Brian, Toni Schmader, Matthew Curtis, Marchelle Scarnier and Daniel R. Ames. 2005. 'Vicarious Guilt and Shame'. *Group Processes and Intergroup Relations* 8: 145–57.

McEvoy-Levy, Siobhan. 2001. 'Youth as Social and Political Agents: Issues in Post-Settlement Peace Building'. Kroc Institute Occasional Paper #21:OP:2. Indianapolis, IN: Kroc Institute.

—. 2011. 'Children, Youth and Peacebuilding'. In Thomas Matyók, Jesica Senehi and Sean Byrne (eds), *Critical Issues in Peace and Conflict Studies: Theory, Practice, and Pedagogy.* Plymouth: Lexington Books: 159–76.

Mclean Hilker, Lindsay. 2011. 'Young Rwandans' Narratives of the past (and present). In Scott Straus and Lars Waldorf (eds), *Remaking Rwanda: State Building and Human Rights after Mass Violence*. Madison, WI: University of Wisconsin Press: 316–30.

—. 2012. 'Rwanda's "Hutsi": Intersections of Ethnicity and Violence in the Lives of Youth of "Mixed" Heritage'. *Identities* 19.2: 229–47.

Meintjes, Cara. 2012. Keeping the Peace: Life in Rwanda Post-Genocide. Cape Town. *Mail and Guardian online* 13 December. Available at http://mg.co.za/article/2012-12-13-keeping-the-peace-life-in-rwanda-post-the-genocide (consulted on 7 March 2018).

Ministry of Youth, Culture and Sport. 2005. *The National Youth and Sports Policy Document*. Kigali.

Münyas, Burcu. 2008. 'Genocide in the Minds of Cambodian Youth: Transmitting (Hi)stories of Genocide to Second and Third Generations in Cambodia'. *Journal of Genocide Research* 10.3: 413–39.

National Unity and Reconciliation Commission (NURC). 2016. *Abarinzi b'igihango*. Kigali.

—. 2017. *Inyoborabiganiro kuri gahunda ya Ndi Umunyarwanda*. Kigali.

National Youth Council. 'Mission and Vision'. Available at https://nyc.gov.rw/index.php?id=11 (consulted on 9 March 2018).

Oxenberg, Julie. 2003. 'Mourning, Meaning, and Not Repeating: Themes of Dialogue between Descendants of Holocaust Survivors and Descendants of Nazis'. *Journal for the Psychoanalysis of Culture & Society* 8.1: 77–83.

Palmer, Nicola. 2014. 'Re-examining Resistance in Post-Genocide Rwanda'. *Journal of Eastern African Studies* 8.2: 231–45.

—. 2015. *Courts in Conflict: Interpreting Layers of Justice in Post-Genocide Rwanda*. Oxford: Oxford University Press.

Pamphilon, Barbara. 1999. 'The Zoom Model: A Dynamic Framework for the Analysis of Life Histories'. *Qualitative Inquiry* 5: 393–410.

Pells, Kirill. 2011. 'Building a Rwanda "Fit for Children"'. In Scott Straus and Lars Waldorf (eds), *Remaking Rwanda: State Building and Human Rights after Mass Violence*. Madison, WI: University of Wisconsin Press: 79–86.

Pells, Kirrily, Karen Pontalti and Timothy Williams. 2014. 'Promising Developments? Children, Youth and Post-Genocide Reconstruction under the Rwandan Patriotic Front (RPF)'. *Journal of Eastern African Studies* 8.2: 294–310.

Purdeková, Andrea. 2008. 'Building a Nation in Rwanda? De-ethnicization and its Discontents'. *Studies in Ethnicity and Nationalism* 8.3: 502–23.

—. 2015. *Making Ubumwe: Power, State and Camps in Rwanda's Unity-Building Project*. New York and Oxford: Berghahn.

Quesenbery, Whitney, and Kevin Brooks. 2010. *Storytelling for User Experience: Crafting Stories for Better Design*. Brooklyn NY: Rosenfeld Media.

Rakita, Sara. 2003. *Lasting Wounds: Consequences of Genocide and War on Rwanda's Children*. London: Human Rights Watch.

Reider, Heidi, and Thomas Elbert. 2013. 'Rwanda – Lasting Imprints of a Genocide: Trauma, Mental Health and Psychosocial Conditions in Survivors, Former Prisoners and their Children'. *Conflict and Health* 7.6. Available at https://conflictandhealth.biomedcentral.com/articles/10.1186/1752-1505-7-6 (consulted on 9 March 2018).

Republic of Rwanda. 2015. *National Youth Policy: Towards a HAPPi Generation*. Kigali.

Reyntjens, Filip. 2013. *Political Governance in Post-Genocide Rwanda*. Cambridge: Cambridge University Press.

Schlant, Ernestine. 1999. *The Language of Silence: West German Literature and the Holocaust*. New York: Routledge.

Straus, Scott, and Lars Waldorf (eds). 2011. *Remaking Rwanda: State Building and Human rights after Mass Violence*. Madison, WI: University of Wisconsin Press.

Sydor, Guy, and Pierre Philippot. 1996. 'Conséquences psychologiques des massacres de 1994 au Rwanda'. *Santé mentale au Québec* 21.1: 229–45.

Thomson, Susan. 2011. 'Reeducation for Reconciliation: Participant Observation on Ingando'. In Scott Straus and Lars Waldorf (eds), *Remaking Rwanda: State Building and Human Rights after Mass Violence*. Madison, WI: The University of Wisconsin Press: 331–42.

—. *Whispering Truth to Power: Everyday Resistance to Reconciliation in Postgenocide Rwanda*. Madison, WI: The University of Wisconsin Press.

UN IANYD. 2016. *Young People's Participation in Peacebuilding: A Practice Note*. New York: UN.

# *Imbabazi, Kwicuza* and Christian Testimonials of Forgiveness

*Madelaine Hron*

Au fond, qui parle de pardon? Les Tutsis, les Hutus, les prisonniers libérés, leurs familles ? Aucun d'eux, ce sont les organisations humanitaires. Elles importent le pardon au Rwanda, et elles l'enveloppent de beaucoup de dollars pour nous convaincre. Il y a un Plan Pardon comme il y a un Plan Sida [...] Nous, on parle du pardon pour être bien considérés et parce que les subventions peuvent être lucratives. (survivor Innocent Rwililiza in Hatzfeld, 2007: 25)[1]

I am going to die in prison. I know that but [with a big smile], I don't care any more. She came, she came to see me and she forgave me. I cannot believe how happy I am. (offender in Musanze prison, part of *Just.Equipping*'s 'Letters Project')

The two statements above reflect the contradictory perspectives on the thorny issue of forgiveness in post-genocide Rwanda. As is now well established, in 2002, the Rwandan government released some 70,000 alleged

---

[1] 'If you think about it, who is talking about forgiveness? The Tutsis? The Hutus? The freed prisoners? Their families? None of them, it's the humanitarian organizations. They are importing forgiveness to Rwanda, and they wrap it in lots of dollars to win us over. There is a Forgiveness Plan just as there is an AIDS Plan [...] As for us, we speak of forgiveness to earn their good opinion – and because the subsidies can be lucrative' (Hatzfeld, 2011: 17–18).

genocidal perpetrators languishing in overcrowded prisons back into the community and announced that the vast majority of these suspects would be tried by village justice known as *gacaca*. Over ten years, from 2002 to 2012, *gacaca* courts processed almost two million cases of people involved in the 1994 genocide, finding some 65% of the accused guilty, while the Rwandan nation engaged in the ambitious project of 'Ukuri, Ubutabera, Ubwiyunge' [Truth, Justice, Reconciliation]. At the heart of Rwanda's reconciliation project were notions of *imbabazi* [forgiveness], as well as Christian notions of *kwicuza* [remorse and repentance]. President Kagame stressed the importance of forgiveness at the official opening of the *gacaca* process when he 'invited the perpetrators to show their courage, to confess, repent and ask for forgiveness', and for 'the sins committed to be curbed and punished, but also forgiven' (Kagame, 2002). Similarly, at the closing of the *gacaca* tribunals, Kagame commended their 'truth telling', which in turn 'made it possible to ask for forgiveness in a genuine manner and to receive it' (Kagame, 2012). Kagame's lofty goals of forgiveness are echoed in various Western texts, many funded by Christian evangelical organizations.

This chapter aims to explore some of the complexities inherent in the notion of forgiveness by examining a number of Christian testimonials featuring forgiveness. There are numerous books (e.g. Irivuzumugabe, 2009; Larsen, 2009; Guillebaud, 2005) and films (e.g. Springhorn, 2005; Hinson, 2009; Freedman, 2004) about forgiveness, in addition to the three texts I will focus on in this chapter: John Rucyahana's *The Bishop of Rwanda* (2007), Frida Gashumba's *Frida: Chosen to Die, Destined to Live* (2007) and Immaculée Ilibagiza's *Left to Tell* (2006) and its various sequels. Thus far, Christian testimonials about Rwanda have received scant scholarly attention; however, their import cannot be underestimated. For instance, Ilibagiza's *Left to Tell* remained on the *New York Times* bestseller list for 20 months; similarly, Bishop Rucyahana represents a very important leader globally in the Anglican/Episcopalian schism. As such, these works written in English, and promoted by massive evangelical Christian groups abroad, have profoundly shaped the global understanding of Rwanda post-genocide, arguably more than the French literary texts which I and others have analysed elsewhere (Hron, 2009a; Hitchcott, 2015).

Before delving into this topic, however, it is salient to reveal my own evolving biases on this issue. As a Czech citizen who grew up with the legacy of the Holocaust, I was personally highly disturbed by the Rwandan government's decision to have killers live beside survivors; I could not imagine a similar situation in Central Europe wherein former Nazis would live alongside concentration camp survivors. As a scholar who had examined such topics as interviews with genocidal killers (Hron, 2011), I was very sceptical of reconciliation, which released convicted killer Fulgence Bunani defined as 'une politique très profitable. On s'en montre très satisfait' (Hatzfeld, 2007: 256).[2] Yet even Fulgence concedes that reconciliation 'est si fragile [...] Nombre restent aussi sur les quant-à-soi. Ils se montrent taiseux, ils ne sèment plus la haine, mais ils ne jettent pas les graines' (2007: 256).[3] In his trilogy, French journalist Jean Hatzfeld interviews survivors and killers from Nyamata in Rwanda, before and after the release of prisoners. I heartily agreed with survivors in Hatzfeld's last, post-release volume *La Stratégie des antilopes*, who describe reconciliation as 'la cohabitation', 'une accommodation', 'le partage équitable de la méfiance' or simply as 'une politique de l'État' (2007: 257, 263, 264).[4] Survivor Innocent, Hatzeld's translator in this trilogy, defined forgiveness even more cynically: as 'étranger', 'contraignant' or 'surnaturel' (2007: 25).[5] I wholly empathized with survivors such as Esther Mujawayo, a psychotherapist now living in Germany, who confessed that: 'Plus j'y réfléchis, plus j'ignore ce que veut dire pardonner [...] j'accepte enfin que, non je ne pardonnerai pas' (Mujawayo and Belhaddad 2006: 126).[6] Finally, as a Christian myself, I disdained many Christian texts that equated forgiveness in Rwanda with conversion to Christianity (when most Rwandans are already Christian), or that cheapened forgiveness as a facile fix, such as in the film *Living Forgiveness* directed by Ralf Springhorn, ably analysed elsewhere (Fisher and Mitchell, 2012). In this apolitical and ahistorical film, perpetrator Kamuzinzi 'confessed everything' and survivor Jean-Claude immediately forgives him, 'since it's clear that evil forces were at work within him'. The pair then tour the countryside on their motorbike preaching their message of forgiveness-as-conversion, and the film concludes with them singing and dancing before a giant inflatable screen showing the evangelical *The Jesus Film* (1979).

During research visits to Rwanda between 2009 and 2014, however, my perspective on forgiveness shifted dramatically, as I encountered various organizations working through forgiveness in admirable ways. One such

---

[2] 'a very beneficial political policy. We're quite satisfied with it' (Hatzfeld, 2011: 208).

[3] 'is so fragile [...] many folks remain aloof, closemouthed. They no longer sow hatred, but they are not throwing away the seeds' (Hatzfeld, 2011: 208).

[4] 'cohabitation', an 'accommodation', 'the equitable division of distrust' or simply as 'a state policy' (Hatzfeld, 2011: 207, 208, 212).

[5] 'having no place', being 'oppressive', if not 'outside of nature' (Hatzfeld, 2011: 18).

[6] 'The more I think about it, the less I know what it means to forgive [...] in the end I accept that, no, I will not forgive'.

grass-roots organization, the Twungubumwe Collectif, led by genocide survivor Pascal Niyomugabo, operates in the Bugesera region, the setting of Hatzfeld's trilogy. Populated in the 1960s by Tutsis exiled to this swampy region in form of reprisals, Bugesera is a particularly divided region of Rwanda, and in 1994, the killing there was exceptionally vicious and grisly; for instance, Tutsi children seeking asylum in Nyamata church were burned alive with gasoline. Despite such horror, in Twungubumwe, perpetrators and survivors now 'live together' as implied in the name *twungubumwe*. Offenders have built houses for widows and survivors, and engage in various sustainable agricultural projects such as apiculture, growing crops and raising cattle. During my first visit, a survivor proudly showed me her house and her stabled cow, and announced that all of it was provided by her neighbour living across the street – the man who had killed her family. We then chatted with this offender who poignantly explained that 'I ask [this woman] for forgiveness every day, with small acts of kindness', to which the survivor enjoined, 'And I grant him forgiveness every day'. The woman's merciful attitude contrasted starkly with the offender's own mother, who frantically rushed from the house to warn me in broken French that her son was 'a very, very bad man who has done terrible things' and that I should flee before I was harmed.

Another project that profoundly affected me was the 'Letters Project' run by a small Canadian NGO, *Just.Equipping*, which helps equip and train local prison chaplains in the Great Lakes region in restorative justice frameworks. In the Letters Project, some 400 prisoners from Rubavu prison and 30 from Gitarama and Butare prisons, wrote letters seeking forgiveness to their victims with the help of local prison chaplains. These chaplains then delivered the letters to the survivors and, if the victims wished, arranged for an encounter with the imprisoned offender. Ultimately, *Just.Equipping* facilitated a staggering 300 such encounters, and I was privileged to witness a couple of them. Though I do not speak Kinyarwanda, I could discern the dynamics of the encounter by body language. For instance, if the offender was lying, the survivor would sometimes get angry and agitated. However, in one encounter it was clear that the offender, speaking in a soft mumble with averted eyes, was profoundly remorseful, and was giving the survivor some vitally significant information. To my astonishment, that encounter culminated in the two embracing with tears flowing. This profoundly moving moment, and many others, prompted me to delve further into this complex issue of forgiveness.

## Defining Forgiveness

Forgiveness is a nebulous concept to define because, ever since the 'forgiveness movement' developed in the 1980s (Smedes, 1984), the term has been co-opted by disciplines ranging from philosophy (e.g. Derrida, 2001; Jankélévitch, 2005) to evolutionary biology (e.g. McCullough, 2008), and thus its meaning shifts in secular and religious contexts. However, most scholars generally agree on what forgiveness is not – for instance, it is not legal pardon, mercy, leniency, nor does it correlate with conciliation, excusing or forgetting and, crucially, in the Rwandan context, it does not equate with reconciliation. Forgiveness requires only one party – the offended one – to enact it, whereas reconciliation involves two parties coming together, usually for the sake of coexistence and the cessation of violence. Similarly, scholars differentiate between personal acts of forgiveness – examined here – and group forgiveness, or forgiveness in the political or legal arena, although such slippage is common in discussions about Rwanda. Likewise, both secular and religious scholars would agree that forgiveness cannot be mandated, be it by the Rwandan government or by religious institutions; rather, it is a personal choice, not a rational or calculated decision, but 'a movement of the heart, an interior free decision [...] a choice to heal that happens inside the heart of the injured person' (Nerney, 2013: 199). Finally, just as social scientists warn against superficial as opposed to genuine forgiveness (Staub, 2011: 447), theologians disparage 'cheap grace' (Bonhoeffer, 1959: 42–43) or 'false' and 'hasty forgiveness' (Schreiter, 1992: 18, 21).

For social scientists, the value of forgiveness stems from its movement from negative, retributive emotions towards more positive ones. For instance, widely cited philosopher Joanna North defines forgiveness as 'a willingness to abandon one's right to resentment, negative judgment, and indifferent behavior toward one who unjustly injured us, while fostering the undeserved qualities of compassion, generosity and even love toward him or her' (1998: 46–47). In the Rwandan context, it is unreasonable to expect forgiving survivors to foster love and munificence towards their offenders. For the purposes of this chapter, therefore, forgiveness is defined generically as a letting go of resentment, requital or vengeance, while moving towards a restorative relationship with the offender. In Christian contexts, although forgiving parties often experience inner peace or healing, it would be erroneous to consider forgiveness as simply therapeutic, a 'form of religious coping' or 'a search for significance in stressful times' (Pargament and Rye, 1998: 60).

Theologically, forgiveness is a complex concept relating to the mystery of God's merciful love, in that God so loved the world he forgave humankind's sins by letting his own son die to redeem humanity (John 3:16). Those who forgive are thus spiritually part of God's infinite love, and his creative plan of redemption: forgiveness between human beings reflects God's divine forgiveness and the 'restoration of communion – with God, with one another and with the whole of Creation' (Jones, 1995: 25). In a Christian context, then, forgiveness and reconciliation are inextricably linked; as theologian Martin Marty explains: 'in the New Testament [...] forgiveness always leads to reconciliation, and reconciliation results from mutual experiences of forgiveness. They cannot, finally be separated' (1998: 11). Crucially, in a Christian context, forgiveness does not correlate with justice, even in the Old Testament, or the Judaic tradition. As Jewish scholar Elliot Dorff clarifies when explicating Jewish approaches to forgiveness, 'you, as the victim, have to give up your claims to justice – that you have been wronged and that the offender owes you something' (1998: 33). Christian theologian Miroslav Volf (2001) echoes Dorff and elaborates that forgiveness reflects a divine, eschatological form of justice only comprehensible by enacting Christ's suffering and death on the cross.

In Rwanda, according to the 2012 census, 94.5% of the population is Christian (NISR, 2012); thus, Rwandans are somewhat familiar with these theological concepts of forgiveness. Certainly, they understand Christian obligations of forgiveness, namely to 'forgive others as God has forgiven you' (Eph. 4:32, Col. 3:13), with the caveat that 'if you do not forgive others their sins, your Father will not forgive your sins' (Matt. 6:15). In Kinyarwanda, as in English, both forgiveness, or *imbabazi*, and repentance, *kwicuza*, can be deployed in secular and religious contexts; however, as anthropologist Jennie Burnet explains, '*gusaba imbabazi* is used primarily in the legal arena, whereas *kwicuza* is used among Roman Catholics to refer to seeking pardon in the rite of confession'; post-*gacaca*, many Rwandans feel that 'certain *génocidaires* don't have the right to rejoin the community because although they have asked for mercy (*basabye imbabazi*) before the courts [...] they have not shown remorse (*batyicuza*)' (Burnet, 2011: 105–06). *Kwicuza* – linked to penitence – is not limited to Catholicism; Protestants and other Christian denominations are also supposed to confess and atone for their sins. In Christian theology, forgiveness and repentance are intimately linked: 'ultimately, there cannot be any forgiveness without repentance, and there cannot be repentance without forgiveness' (Watts, 2004: 53). In evangelical Christian denominations, seeking God's forgiveness by repenting for one's past sins often signals a hallmark in one's journey to being 'born again' as Christian. All Christians are to repent and forgive continually throughout their lives – 'forgive us, as we have been forgiven' – as mandated in the Lord's Prayer (Matt. 6:12).

To better understand the dynamics of Christian forgiveness in Rwanda, I interviewed Rev. Pierre Allard, the Canadian Baptist prison chaplain who founded *Just.Equipping* and helped organize the Letters Project.[7] In Allard's estimation, 90% of the prisoners' letters mentioned that they had heard the word of God from the chaplains in prison and that they sensed the need to repair their relationship with their victims by asking them for forgiveness. Most of these prisoners were Christian before the genocide, but had disowned or forsaken God because of their crimes; however, they felt their relationship with God restored when the chaplains shared the word of God with them in scripture and song. I myself was witness to some of these sessions, and was struck by how attentively the prisoners listened to passages about God's forgiveness, including about Dismus, the good thief (Lk 23) or the prodigal son (Lk 15). In their letters, Allard notes, the prisoners did not usually elaborate on notions of God; but nor did they mention Satan, or any demonic force (unlike the Christian texts analysed below). If they did offer excuses for their behaviour, Allard observed that they usually blamed the government for ordering them to kill. Occasionally, they compared themselves to robots on a destructive path; I also heard them comparing themselves to ignorant children. Ultimately, although many of the prisoners believed God had forgiven them, they continued to have nightmares, experience anxiety and profound unrest, as is attested in the scant psychological research about prisoners (Schaal et al., 2012). Only after receiving their victims' forgiveness did they start to sleep without nightmares and experience a new-found peace. Pierre Allard vividly remembers an older offender standing up before other prisoners and testifying that 'I am going to die in prison. I know that but [with a big smile], I don't care anymore. She came, she came to see me and she forgave me. I cannot believe how happy I am'.

Like the offenders, the forgiving survivors were also largely Christian; moreover, many affirmed that they only survived the genocide because of God's grace. According to Allard, their faith often gave these survivors the courage to meet with their offenders, and was an important factor in the encounter. The most crucial aspect in these encounters, however, was whether the offender was telling the truth. Where the offender was clearly lying, there was little possibility for forgiveness. In some cases, even when the offender told the truth and the encounter went well, forgiveness did not take place right away, but several months or years later. Allard and the *Just.Equipping* team

---

[7] Profound thanks to Pierre and Judy Allard, Adolphine Furaha, Pascal Niyomugabo and the many forgiving Rwandans who inspired me to write this chapter. The information within the next two paragraphs is gleaned from email correspondence with Rev. Pierre Allard dated 15 November 2017.

are often amazed by the generosity and mercy of the survivors; for instance, some pay school fees for offenders' children, give a field to an offender's wife or regularly leave money or food at the prison lunchroom for the offenders. Clearly, some of these survivors epitomize remarkable forgiveness, in their 'compassion, generosity and even love toward' their offender (North 1998: 47).

## John Rucyahana's *The Bishop of Rwanda*

In contrast to these remarkable stories of forgiveness, *The Bishop of Rwanda*, penned by Bishop John Rucyahana, reveals an institutional Christian perspective on the subject, albeit a fundamentalist evangelical one. Bishop Rucyahana represents a key player in global Anglicanism. At the 1998 Lambeth Conference, when the Anglican/Episcopalian Communion declared openness to the LGBTQ community, many African and Asian bishops were opposed, as were a minority of American conservatives. Some of these American conservatives created the Anglican Mission in the Americas (AMiA), a breakaway Anglican sect headquartered, surprisingly, in Rwanda, and headed by Rwandan bishops Rucyahana and Kolini. Until their retirement in December 2011, Rucyahana and Kolini therefore oversaw conservative parishes and clergy in the US, as well as their homophobic evangelization missions in North America. Problematically, until 2011, AMiA's funding was closely associated with funding targeted for post-genocide Rwanda (Cantrell, 2007: 346; Claire et al., 2012). Intriguingly, Rucyahana wholly conceals his vital role in AMiA in this book, and mentions homosexuality only once, as a result of 'spiritual failure' and 'weakness of church leaders' (2007: 44). In order not to alienate potential readers, Rucyahana describes himself as an ecumenical, non-denominational pastor who sees conversion as simply 'surrendering [one's] heart to God' (2007: 15). Yet his various references to his 'crusades' (e.g. 2007: 146, 148, 172) or anti-Catholic remarks (e.g. 2007: 12, 14, 26) betray a more fundamentalist evangelical stance. In his book, Rucyahana aligns himself with Rick Warren's evangelical Saddleback megachurch and its outreach PEACE plan, speciously described as an 'indigenous' plan '*by* the Rwandan [*sic*] and *for* Rwandans' (2007: xii; emphasis original).

Plot-wise, *The Bishop of Rwanda* is more of an historical exposé than a memoir which narrates Rwandan history from colonialism to post-genocide, as well as Rucyahana's own faith journey, from humble 'Christian rural evangelist' (2007: 38) to bishop. A born-again Christian, Rucyahana accepts Christ in a Biblical Job-like tableau – 'I fell to my knees in the mud and the dirt and cried to the Lord to accept my confused heart' (2007: 30) – and soon after his conversion, he has dream-visions of himself in clerical vestments. Throughout his faith journey, he is represented as a self-made man who achieved success with God's help because God had a divine purpose for his life (e.g. Rucyahana, 2007: 30, 43, 88); miracles and visions also guide him on his hallowed path (e.g. 2007: 112, 146–47). Although Rucyahana is not a genocide survivor, but rather an exile who lived in Uganda until 1996, the text emphasizes his persecution and heroic victimhood; for instance, in a powerful scene of personal sacrifice, he is held at gunpoint after the fall of Idi Amin in order to save fellow parishioners. Commendably, Rucyahana addresses the involvement of Christian churches in the 1994 genocide but, problematically, he explains their failings in terms of 'demonic' forces: 'They were more like members of religious clubs than real Christians [...] their beliefs were more like those of Satanists' (2007: 103).

Rucyahana's descriptions of 1994 are as shockingly gruesome as possible, so as to showcase the graphic horror of the genocide and the depravity of its killers, who are simply described as 'devils' (2007: 96–105). For instance, he sensationally alludes to killers who put 'babies into frying pans and fried them' or ground them in mortars like nuts and grains (2007: 101). In Rucyahana's world view, there is only one reason for the genocide: 'the Devil penetrated the hearts of the killers' (2007: 149). Throughout the text, there are no viable explanations offered for the killers' actions other than 'demonic possession' (2007: 97–105). Demonic possession also works to excuse what Rucyahana terms as 'victim killers', or mothers who killed 'other mothers who also had babies on their backs' or children who hacked off 'the head of a classmate to use as a soccer ball, when he was five or six years old' (2007: 98). Concomitantly, Rucyahana suggests that some of the *génocidaires* were 'Satan worshippers' (2007: 100), akin to the Nazis, who 'operated more like Satanists, and many of them had taken demonic oaths' (2007: 103). Rucyahana's descriptions of killers as demonic are problematic, in that they dehumanize these offenders as monstrous others, in a move akin to genocidal ideology itself. As psychologist and military advisor Ralph White (1984) has powerfully argued, dehumanization – which cultivates the belief that one's enemy is an inhuman monster and morally wrong – interferes with empathy, empathy being a necessary requisite in peace-building. Theologian Robert Schreiter similarly argues that theologies of otherness, that demonize, colonize or vaporize the oppressor as other, impede reconciliation (1992: 52–53). Notwithstanding, Rucyahana frames the genocide as an epic spiritual battle with demonic forces. Just as the killers' evil actions during the genocide are defined in spiritual terms, so is their post-genocide restoration within society, via forgiveness.

Rucyahana's elaborations on forgiveness and reconciliation generally reflect institutional and theological perspectives on the subject – that both can only take place within a Christian context and with divine intervention. As

Rucyahana explains, 'only God changes hearts' (2007: 200): 'to repent of such cruelty requires divine motivation and the divine presence just to attempt it. It cannot be done without God [...] and requires the cross of Jesus right in the middle of it' (2007: 96). For Rucyahana, then, forgiveness is intimately linked with conversion, both to Christianity and to a behavioural change through repentance: offenders must 'repent of their guilt' or 'heal the guilt' (2007: 181, 182). (Throughout the text, the concept of 'sin' is replaced with 'guilt' so as not to alienate readers, e.g. 2007: xvi, 98, 102). Just as Rucyahana equates genocidal killing with demonic possession, he also occasionally relates it to exorcism: as he explains, killers have been 'poisoned' by hate ideology and so need to 'vomit it out so that they may be healed [...] vomit out the memory of that experience – vomit out the problems in their heart' (2007: 169–70). Lastly, forgiveness as conversion is linked to getting a 'crown in heaven', and thus to eternal life (2007: 170). Reconciliation – the resulting consequence of forgiveness – is thus also viewed as restoring the world to a natural order, either restoring it to an Edenic Rwanda of precolonial times, where Tutsi and Hutu all lived as one people in the image of God, or to heaven, wherein 'dogs and birds, natural enemies, can play together' (2007: 200). Rucyahana also links reconciliation to the Rwandan practice of *igihong*, or a traditional blood pact (2007: 169). In the end, while Rucyahana offers an eloquent Christian apology of forgiveness, all of his discussion remains abstractly theoretical; the book lacks any personal, subjective examples of forgiveness. Moreover, because of his focus on conversion and divine reconciliation, there is little mention of forgiveness as a lengthy gradual process, or of half-hearted or failed forgiveness. There are also no viable links between forgiveness and earthly justice, namely *gacaca*. More saliently, discussions of forgiveness are limited to the offender; there is no discussion of forgiveness on the part of the survivor. In order to understand that dynamic, let us turn to testimonials by Immaculée Ilibagiza and Frida Gashumba.

## Immaculée Ilibagiza's *Left to Tell*

Immaculée Ilibagiza's *Left to Tell: Discovering God amidst the Rwandan Holocaust* features the most famous example of forgiveness by a Rwandan genocide survivor, and arguably represents the most widely read testimonial about the genocide in Rwanda. A *New York Times* bestseller two weeks after its March 2006 release, the book remained in the top 50 bestselling titles in the US for 20 months. Ilibagiza's success was furthered by an accompanying DVD, the bestselling sequel *Led by Faith: Rising from the Ashes of the Rwandan Genocide* (2008a) and a series of complementary religious books (*Our Lady of Kibeho*, 2008b; *The Boy Who Met Jesus*, 2011). In 1994, all the members of Ilibagiza's immediate family were murdered, except her brother, who was studying in Senegal. Today, Immaculée is a naturalized American citizen living in New York, a popular speaker and Catholic retreat leader.

*Left to Tell* clearly aims to appeal to the broadest readership possible. Apolitical and acultural in scope, this testimonial generalizes the 1994 genocide as 'one of history's bloodiest holocausts' (2006: xx) and makes few references to Rwandan culture. It exalts the RPF as saviour figures who made Rwanda 'free and equal' (2006: 24) and reduces the Interahamwe to 'lawless street thugs', drug-addicted homeless kids or 'devils' (2006: 34, 33, 77). Its narration draws on Holocaust conventions, as do many of these Christian testimonials. For example, the narrators in many of these texts describe idyllic childhoods until they go to school and encounter an 'ethnic roll call' akin to discriminatory Nazi identification practices or the 'selection' process in camps. To clarify for Western readers, Irivuzumbugabe dubs this practice 'segregation' (2009: 22); Rucyahana, 'partitioning education' (2007: 35); and Immaculée, her 'country's unique style of apartheid' (2008: 3). Moreover, *Left to Tell* strongly evokes Anne Frank's *The Diary of a Young Girl*: Ilibagiza survived by hiding for over 90 days in the concealed bathroom of a local cleric, Pastor Murinzi. She shared this small two-square-metre bathroom with seven other women, so they had to take turns sitting or standing, and could only rarely flush the toilet. Unlike Anne Frank, these confined women are attentive witnesses to intensifying genocidal violence: they listen to growing hate propaganda on the radio or eavesdrop on ever more murderous conversations by killers circling the pastor's compound. The carnage culminates in the women hearing the brutal murder of a woman and the slow death of her baby child. Throughout this violence, Immaculée's struggle to survive is set up as a dramatic spiritual battle: 'my battle to survive this would have to be fought inside of me [...] If I lost my faith, I knew I wouldn't be able to survive' (2006: 80).

To engage a broader evangelical audience, Ilibagiza's Catholicism is considerably downplayed in *Left to Tell*, especially when contrasted with her later works about Marian apparitions in Rwanda. In *Left to Tell*, Catholicism is reduced to paraphernalia, such as statues, scapulars and especially the rosary, to which Immaculée prays repeatedly. Furthermore, Immaculée relativizes her Catholicism: 'while my parents were Catholic, they were Christians in the broadest sense of the word' (2006: 7), 'they believed that God was found in all faiths and religions' (2008a: 2). In her description of Pastor Murinzi, who becomes increasingly unhinged and irrational, Ilibagiza also calls attention to the role of Christian churches during the 1994 genocide. *Left to Tell* also betrays the influence of her publisher, Hay House, known for its self-help New Age manuals, including the work of Wayne Dyer, who penned Ilibagiza's preface. *Left to Tell* contains numerous references to spiritual energies (e.g. 2006: 42, 80, 107), nods to visualization (2006: 118) or to positive thinking (2006: 208, 190) that are missing in her later works. Saliently, unlike other Christian texts, nowhere in any of her works does Ilibagiza urge readers to convert to Catholicism or to Christianity. Rather, she calls on people to 'heal their hearts' with love and forgiveness (2006: 209–10). In *Our Lady of Kibeho*, she even alleges that 'Our Lady has never told me that people should convert from their religions [...] she begs us to convert our hearts and love to our Father – that's what she means by "conversions"' (2008b: 66). Certainly, in her private life Ilibagiza appears less conservative than some of her Catholic followers; she is divorced and reputedly remarried to a Muslim.

At its crux, *Left to Tell* is less about Immaculée's survival in 1994 than about the survival of her faith during the genocide. Because of her Catholic upbringing, Ilibagiza does not experience any form of 'born-again' epiphany as is common in other, evangelical texts, nor is she described as 'fallen' before receiving Christ. Rather Immaculée, a model Catholic, attends church and prays regularly from a young age, and her faith is tested and rewarded with miraculous signs of God's favour. For instance, as a child, Immaculée and her brother pray their way through a mob of Interahamwe, and pass unharmed, clutching their rosaries. Immaculée's faith is similarly tested and refined in the bathroom during the genocide. Her survival is depicted as an epic spiritual battle between God and the Devil, divided into three main episodes which coincide with the three times killers search the house. At the end of each these spiritual attacks, Immaculée receives a sign of victory – a special blessing or epiphany. For instance, during the first spiritual attack, the Devil tests her faith and whispers to Immaculée to give up. She refuses, and fights the Devil by envisioning holding onto God's legs, described as pillars of light, a powerful Biblical symbol (Ex. 13:21, 22; Rev. 10:1). For not surrendering, Immaculée receives a blessing – the insight to place a wardrobe in front of the bathroom door, which protects them. Similarly, after forgiving the killers, Immaculée is divinely inspired to learn English in the bathroom; English becomes instrumental for her post-genocide life, when she applies for a job at the UN.

Immaculée's second spiritual attack revolves around forgiveness. Intriguingly, it is the Devil who challenges her to forgive the killers, and let go of her hatred and anger, mocking her as a hypocrite and a liar who prays to God but resembles the killers in her anger and hatred. Ultimately, however, Immaculée's conversion to forgiveness follows the brutal slaughter of a mother and then the slow demise of her infant, left on the road to die. As she struggles to contain her anger towards the killers, she hears God's voice stating, '*You are all my children ... and the baby is with me now*' (2006: 94; emphasis original). These words lead her to a transformative epiphany:

the killers were like children [...] cruel, vicious and dangerous, as kids sometimes can be, but nevertheless they were children [...] they were children of God, and I could forgive a child, although it would not be easy ... especially when that child was trying to kill me. In God's eyes, the killers were part of his family, deserving of love and forgiveness. (2006: 94)

Saliently, then, Immaculée is motivated to forgive the killers because she humanizes them – albeit infantilizing them – as children. Only then is she able to admit their humanity, and even their goodness and sacredness, as 'children of God,' and is able to forgive them.

At the end of *Left to Tell*, Ilibagiza actualizes the forgiveness she spiritually enacted in the bathroom when, in a highly melodramatic scene, she visits Félicien, the killer of her mother and brother, in prison. Félicien is presented as a broken, filthy, wounded wretch with 'open running sores' (2006: 203), who performs the role of remorseful penitent perfectly: a 'battered man [...] hunched and kneeling, too embarrassed to stand and face me', who could only sob from shame (2006: 204). At the sight of his wretchedness, Immaculée is so 'overwhelmed with pity for the man' that she 'wept at the sight of his suffering' (2006: 204). She excuses all his failings, drawing on demonic and pathological explanations: 'Félicien had let the devil into his heart and the evil had ruined his life as a cancer' (2006: 204). Startlingly, Immaculée even characterizes her killer as 'the victim of victims, destined to live in torment and regret' (2006: 204). When finally their eyes meet as equals she redeems him, by granting forgiveness. Immaculée's mercy is contrasted with her accompanying friend's anger; he thinks that Immaculée should spit on this murderer. Immaculée replies that her forgiveness is a freely granted gift – 'all I have to offer' (2006: 204).

Immaculée's transformative epiphany and her encounter with Félicien reflect much of the scholarship around forgiveness, which stresses the need to humanize offenders and feel empathy for them when moving towards forgiveness. Joanna North, for instance, terms this process towards humanization – of separating the wrongdoer from his/her wrongdoing – as 'reframing' (1998: 24–29). Moreover, she warns that 'forgiveness becomes a *conceptual* impossibility' when, as in Rucyahana's demonic possession, 'the wrongdoer is not "one of us," not the kind to which concepts of love, compassion and forgiveness are applicable' (1998: 28). Every model of forgiveness I have researched stresses empathy and altruism, as exemplified in Ilibagiza's text. Theologian Robert Schreiter, for example, characterizes reconciliation as an 'invitation and gift' from God (1992: 78), wherein both parties become 'a new creation', by shedding otherness, woundedness and victimhood and by cultivating empathy, care and compassion (1992: 59–62).

Similarly, psychologist Ervin Staub (2011) argues that Rwandans must learn to humanize each other, by overcoming both their fear and their distorted beliefs about the inhumanity of perpetrators, and to display empathy towards each other's suffering.

Finally, in *Led by Faith*, Ilibagiza offers further thought-provoking comments on forgiveness in relation to justice. At the end of this sequel, the reader learns that, because of her act of forgiveness in prison, Immaculée received death threats, and consequently decided to leave Rwanda with her husband for the US, where she settled permanently. She did not return for another decade, at which point the *gacaca* trials were taking place. Ilibagiza barely mentions the trials, simply stating that 'I could not bring myself to go to a *gacaca*', although others in her family found it therapeutic (2008a: 209). Immaculée never visits Félicien again, nor does she meet with other killers she knows. Sceptical critics therefore cannot help but wonder to what extent Immaculée's act of forgiveness was enabled by Félicien's perfect performance of *kwicuza* [repentance] during their encounter. Moreover, critics may question whether Immaculée's continued forgiveness is predicated on the fact that she no longer lives in Rwanda and Félicien is serving time in prison, and that, consequently, he is indeed 'destined to live in torment and regret' because secular justice has been served (2006: 204).

## *Frida: Chosen to Die, Destined to Live*

In contrast to Ilibagiza's bestsellers, Frida Gashumba's *Frida: Chosen to Die, Destined to Live* is a little-known testimonial about the author's harrowing genocide experience and her post-genocide struggle with forgiveness. Gashumba's survival story is much more disturbing than Ilibagiza's: she was buried alive in a mass killing, and then fled and hid with various Hutu rescuers. But Frida's memoir, co-authored by Sandy Waldron, lacks the vividness, melodrama and sentimentalism of Ilibagiza's texts co-written by Steve Erwin, and seems dry and disjointed in comparison. The pivotal killing and burial scene, for instance, focuses factually on external actions, such as snippets of the victims' and killers' dialogue or the sounds of butchery and burial, rather than exploring Frida's emotions in inner monologue. While this unsentimental, objective recounting may reflect the traumatized, dissociative state that may have overwhelmed Frida during this massacre – she was partially conscious throughout, buried beneath corpses of her family and bleeding from her slashed heels – it also distances readers from her ordeal, as does much of the understated narrative.

Unlike both Rucyahana's and Ilibagiza's testimonials which, like various Holocaust texts, depict childhoods before genocide as idyllic, Gashumba's is more realistic and fatalistically pessimistic. Future ethnic killings are foreshadowed in scenes of sibling rivalry, gender discrimination and the death of her infant sister; Frida's parents 'believed that the Hutu doctor administering the injection into her head had deliberately twisted it so that she would die' (2007: 46). The narrative also calls attention to massacres in the 1990s and to extermination lists. Like Immaculée's father, Frida's father is also imprisoned; unlike *Left to Tell* though, *Frida* elaborates on the torture in Rwanda's prisons, such as paraffin being poured into prisoners' ears or their fingers being cut off. As a result, Frida's life before genocide is governed by dread – 'I lived every day with the fear that cast its shadow over our lives' (2007: 35) – and when the genocide starts, she exemplifies defeatist fatalism: 'I knew that we were not going to survive' (2007: 52).

In contrast to Immaculée's sanguine childhood faith, Frida identifies as a born-again Christian post-genocide. Although she is raised Catholic, Frida relegates Catholicism to her grandfather's traditional moral order, which like him, perished during the genocide. Her grandfather's faith did not save him; rather, he died with a Bible in his hands pleading with the killers to remember their Christian faith and 'just forgive us' (2007: 71), just as a neighbouring child begged for forgiveness for being Tutsi (2007: 70). In a surprising revelation, Frida describes herself as profoundly anti-Christian: 'I hated believers. For me all Christians were hypocrites and liars […] I had no time for God' (2007: 99). Post-genocide, Frida experiences severe PTSD, ranging from 'intense pain and crippling loneliness' to 'utter despair' which leads her to attempt suicide (2007: 96–97). Eventually, she realizes that her trauma cannot be healed by psychiatric intervention, but rather by spiritual mediation (2007: 98); thereupon, she converts to become a *bona fide* believer, even marking the date as her new birthday (2007: 103–05). Frida credits her new-found faith with resolving her PTSD: 'from the time Jesus came into my life, I was a different person. I could sleep […] sing […] smile […] I was happy […] had found hope' (2007: 105). After her conversion, *Frida* follows Frida's emergent evangelism, especially her 'call to preach' and 'passion to spread the Gospel' (2007: 111–12), which is tested by her conservative Christian family who are opposed to her joining charismatic Pentecostalism, where members speak in tongues or regularly fast. Notwithstanding, Frida trains as an evangelist, marries a pastor and assumes the traditional role of wife and mother. Like Ilibagiza, she plans to create a charitable organization for orphans, and is associated with the evangelical Ellel Ministries. One of Ellel's cornerstones is deliverance ministry, which involves spiritual healing from evil spirits and demonic activity.

Unlike other aspects of her testimonial, Frida's motives for forgiveness are insightfully and thought-provokingly well-developed. In extensive interior monologue, Frida delves into her lengthy reflective process, a 'debate which raged within me for months' (2007: 116) and her reasoning for ultimately forgiving her offenders. Like Immaculée, one of Frida's initial motives to forgive stems from fear of jeopardizing her relationship with God, and 'staunch[ing] the flow of God's love in my heart' (2007: 117). While Immaculée fears God abandoning her during the atrocities, Frida fears compromising her post-genocide role as God's spokesperson. Like Immaculée, Frida also fears becoming like her offenders in her duplicitous world view, 'a hypocrite – the very thing in my mind I was often accusing Hutu Christians of being' (2007: 120). Most importantly, in order to move towards forgiveness, like Immaculée, Frida must humanize her offenders, first by finding reasons for their behaviour, such as that they were high on drugs and alcohol and, like Rucyahana, that they were possessed: 'The devil had taken over my country [...] It was the devil who had driven the Hutus to fulfill their stated aim of exterminating every single Tutsi' (2007: 119). Although Frida's book promotes Ellel's deliverance ministry, she does not propose any form of exorcism. Ultimately, Frida concludes that the killers were acting from ignorance, citing the same Biblical passage as *Left to Tell*: 'Father they do not know what they are doing' (2007: 118). Finally, in a rather remarkable insight, Frida discerns that:

> Behind the immense sense of injustice I felt was another much less noble emotion: self-pity. I wanted the world to look at me and say 'Poor Frida. Look what she has suffered.' I was cradling my loss to myself and using it as my comfort blanket [...] I began to understand that self-pity was a monster that would devour me if I continued to give in to it. (2007: 117)

In this candid statement, Frida grasps that such self-pity, suffering-as-comfort and victimhood grant her a privileged position in a power differential that I have unpacked elsewhere as 'zeroism', or suffering-as-heroism (Hron, 2009b). Writing specifically about post-conflict areas such as Rwanda, Staub likewise stresses the need to overcome one's victimhood in order to forgive, especially 'competitive victimhood', wherein one's sufferings are greater than those of offending others (2011: 470). Similarly, Schreiter argues that reconciling Christians must give up their motivations of fear, self-pity and their own woundedness, instead living as new creations in light of the resurrection (1992: 78). In order to forgive authentically, therefore, Frida must erase the differentials that separate her from her killers, including her privileged position as victim.

Finally, like Immaculée, Frida actualizes the forgiveness she has rationalized by meeting an offender in prison. Unlike *Left to Tell*, however, *Frida* describes this encounter as a lengthy, difficult process: during her first prison visits, a sobbing Frida curls into a foetal position. She is only able to return and enact forgiveness after she recognizes the suffering of killers and thus further empathizes with their plight: 'I was very aware that they were suffering [...] not at peace [...] becoming poorer and poorer [...] This understanding fueled my prayers and I was truly able to say, "Father forgive them for they did not know what they were doing"' (2007: 123). Unlike Immaculée's melodramatic meeting, Frida's encounter with her father's killer, François, is narrated drily and unsentimentally, with no mention of François's appearance, behaviour or reactions. Even Frida's reactions are muted; we only learn that forgiveness brought her 'great healing' and a 'new peace [which] increased immeasurably as I forgave the people who destroyed my life' (2007: 124). Frida never details any of these other meetings of forgiveness, described as successful. Instead, a footnote disrupts Frida's reconciliatory narrative, as the reader learns that upon being freed from prison, François denied all his actions.

Frida's subsequent meeting with François, as a free man, no longer refers to forgiveness, but to justice. This time, their conversation is recorded at length, and François's attitude is described as 'hostile and defensive' as he denies the truth; Frida is consequently no longer at peace, but rather 'extremely upset' (2007: 156, 160). She is so angry that she testifies before *gacaca*, as do witnesses of François's crimes. He is sentenced to return to prison, but disappears before the verdict. After the trial, Frida exhibits contradictory emotions. On the one hand, she insists that she 'thanks God that He has enabled her to forgive because she can live a free and happy life' (2007: 166); yet, on the other hand, she admits that it is 'very painful to live' with François at large, denying his actions (2007: 165). Similarly, though she claims to 'carry no bitterness in her heart', she insists that 'it is fundamentally right and proper to see justice carried out on those responsible for heinous acts of bloodshed' (2007: 166). In sum, Frida's act of Christian forgiveness here does not preclude a desire for secular justice and reparation, which in this case are not possible.

## Reframing Forgiveness

In conclusion, the three testimonials analysed in this chapter offer some insight into the mysterious dynamics of forgiveness enacted by offender-victim pairs in Twungubumwe and in *Just.Equipping*'s Letters Project. Rucyahana's *Bishop of Rwanda* reflects institutional Christian perspectives about forgiveness as *kwicuza*, or repentance and penitence, necessary on the part of the killers. However, he also hinders forgiveness with his problematic depiction of killers as demonically possessed, which dehumanizes these offenders as monstrous others, and so inhibits empathy towards them. Both Ilibagiza's *Left to Tell* and Gashumba's *Frida* explore the complex and lengthy dynamics of unilaterally forgiving an offender, and thus of forgiveness as *imbabazi* [pardon]. Like Rucyahana, both narrators depict their journey to forgiveness as a spiritual battle with demonic forces; however, both texts showcase the process of 'reframing' (North, 1998: 24–29) which separates the wrongdoer from his wrongdoing, as well as empathy for the offender, empathy being the necessary step in achieving forgiveness according to secular and religious scholars alike (e.g. Worthington, 1998; Staub, 2011; Schreiter, 1992). Ilibagiza humanizes her offenders by recognizing their common humanity as 'children of God', whereas Gashumba recognizes their shared suffering, in a move wherein she relinquishes her privileged position of victimhood. Finally, both Immaculée and Frida grapple with the difficulties of practically enacting forgiveness with people who had murdered their families in a secular context. Where Immaculée lives abroad and can dissociate herself from *gacaca* because her offender is duly imprisoned, Frida cannot. Frida still lives in Rwanda; she has testified before *gacaca*, but her perpetrator, convicted for his crimes, has fled justice.

Ultimately, as intimated in these Christian testimonials, religious understandings of forgiveness, albeit concerned with divine justice, do not necessarily correlate with secular justice. As theologian Miroslav Volf elucidates,

> forgiveness is more than just 'the overcoming of anger and resentment.' It always entails forgoing a rightful claim against someone who has in some way harmed or offended us. Such forgoing of a rightful claim makes forgiveness unjust and thereby precisely prevents forgiveness from falling outside the concern for justice. (2001: 38)

Altogether, these Christian testimonials about forgiveness, especially Immaculée Ilibagiza's bestsellers, work to help global audiences forgive and let go of negative emotions – but also to relinquish 'rightful claims' within secular judicial contexts – be they *gacaca* or Western court systems. In the end, I am not convinced any of these texts can fully explain the dynamics of a community such as Twungubumwe, where ex-offenders and victims live side by side, but surely fostering empathy and altruism and forgoing rightful claims play important roles there as well.

## Works Cited

Bonhoeffer, Dietrich. 1959. *The Cost of Discipleship*. New York: Simon and Schuster.

Burnet, Jennie E. 2011. '(In)justice: Truth, Reconciliation, and Revenge in Rwanda's *Gacaca*'. In Alexander Hinton (ed.), *Transitional Justice: Global Mechanisms and Local Realities after Genocide and Mass Violence.* New Brunswick, NJ: Rutgers University Press: 95–118.

Cantrell, Phillip. 2007. 'The Anglican Church of Rwanda: Domestic Agendas and International Linkages'. *Journal of Modern African Studies* 45.3: 333–54.

Claire, Dan, Chuck Colson and Tommy Hinson. 2012. 'Why Did AMiA Break Away from the Anglican Province of Rwanda?' Available at http://www.renewdc. org/wp-content/uploads/2012/01/Why-Did-AMiA-Break-with-Rwanda.pdf (consulted on 6 February 2019).

Derrida, Jacques. 2001. *On Cosmopolitanism and Forgiveness.* New York: Routledge.

Dorff, Elliott. 1998. 'The Elements of Forgiveness: A Jewish Approach'. In Everett Worthington (ed.), *Dimensions of Forgiveness: Psychological Research & Theological Perspectives.* Philadelphia, PA: Templeton Foundation Press: 29–58.

Fisher, Duncan, and Joylon Mitchell. 2012. 'Portraying Forgiveness through Documentary Film'. *Studies in World Christianity* 18.2: 154–68.

Freedman, Paul (dir.). 2005. *Rwanda: Do Scars Ever Fade?* History Channel.

Gashumba, Frida, with Sally Waldron. 2007. *Frida: Chosen to Die, Destined to Live.* Lancaster: Sovereign World.

Guillebaud, Meg. 2005. *After the Locusts: How Costly Forgiveness Is Restoring Rwanda's Stolen Years.* Grand Rapids, MI: Monarch Books.

Hatzfeld, Jean. 2007. *La stratégie des antilopes: récits.* Paris: Seuil.

—. 2009. *The Antelope's Strategy: Living in Rwanda after the Genocide.* Trans. Linda Coverdale. New York: Farrar, Straus and Giroux.

Hinson, Laura Waters (dir.). 2009. *As We Forgive.* Sound Enterprises.

Hitchcott, Nicki. 2015. *Rwanda Genocide Stories: Fiction after 1994.* Liverpool: Liverpool University Press.

Hron, Madelaine. 2009a. '"Itsembabwoko à la française"? Rwanda, Fiction and the Franco-African Imaginary'. *Forum for Modern Language Studies* 45.2: 162–75.

—. 2009b. *Translating Pain: Immigrant Suffering in Literature and Culture.* Toronto: University of Toronto Press.

—. 2011. 'Gukora and Itsembatsemba: The "Ordinary Killers" in Jean Hatzfeld's *Machete Season*'. *Research in African Literature* 42.2: 125–46.

Ilibagiza, Immaculée, with Steve Erwin. 2006. *Left to Tell: Discovering God amidst the Rwandan Holocaust.* Carlsbad, CA: Hay House.

—. 2008a. *Led by Faith: Rising from the Ashes of the Rwandan Genocide.* Carlsbad, CA: Hay House.

—. 2008b. *Our Lady of Kibeho: Mary Speaks to the World from the Heart of Africa.* Carlsbad, CA: Hay House.

—. 2011. *The Boy Who Met Jesus: Segatashya of Kibeho.* Carlsbad, CA: Hay House.

Irivuzumugabe, Eric, with Tracey D. Lawrence. 2009. *My Father, Maker of the Trees: How I Survived the Rwandan Genocide*. Grand Rapids, MI: Baker Books.

Jankélévitch, Vladimir. 2005. *Forgiveness*. Chicago, IL: University of Chicago Press.

Jones, L. Gregory. 1995. *Embodying Forgiveness: A Theological Analysis*. Grand Rapids, MI: W.B. Eerdmans.

Kagame, Paul. 2002. 'Speech at the Official Opening of *Gacaca* Courts'. 18 June. http://cnlg.gov.rw/fileadmin/templates/documents/GACACA_COURTS_OPENING.pdf (consulted on 20 April 2009).

—. 2012. 'Speech at the Official Closing of *Gacaca* Courts'. 19 June. http://paulkagame.com/?p=1355 (consulted on 6 February 2019).

Larson, Catherine Claire. 2009. *As We Forgive: Stories of Reconciliation from Rwanda*. Grand Rapids, MI: Zondervan.

McCullough, Michael E. 2008. *Beyond Revenge: The Evolution of the Forgiveness Instinct*. San Francisco, CA: Jossey-Bass.

Marty, Martin. 1998. 'The Ethos of Christian Forgiveness'. In Everett Worthington (ed.), *Dimensions of Forgiveness: Psychological Research & Theological Perspectives*. Philadelphia, PA: Templeton Foundation Press: 9–28.

Mujawayo, Esther, and Souâd Belhaddad. 2006. *La Fleur de Stéphanie: Rwanda entre réconciliation et déni*. Paris: Flammarion.

National Institute of Statistics of Rwanda (NISR). 2012. *Fourth Population and Housing Census*. Available at http://www.statistics.gov.rw/survey-period/fourth-population-and-housing-census-2012 (consulted on 30 April 2018).

Nerney, Catherine T. 2013. 'Telling the Stories of Rwanda'. In Leo Riegert, Jill Scott and Jack Shuler (eds), *Thinking and Practicing Reconciliation: Teaching and Learning through Literary Responses to Conflict*. Newcastle upon Tyne: Cambridge Scholars Press: 185–209.

North, Joanna. 1998. 'The "Ideal" of Forgiveness: A Philosopher's Exploration'. In Robert Enright and Joanna North (eds), *Exploring Forgiveness*. Madison, WI: University of Wisconsin Press: 15–34.

Pargament, Kenneth, and Mark Rye. 1998. 'Forgiveness as a Method of Religious Coping'. In Everett Worthington (ed.), *Dimensions of Forgiveness: Psychological Research & Theological Perspectives*. Philadelphia, PA: Templeton Foundation Press: 59–79.

Rucyahana, John. 2007. *The Bishop of Rwanda*. Nashville, TN: T. Nelson.

Schaal, Susanne, Roland Weierstall, Jean-Pierre Dusingizemungu and Thomas Elbert. 2001. 'Mental Health 15 Years after the Killings in Rwanda: Imprisoned Perpetrators of the Genocide against the Tutsi Versus a Community Sample of Survivors'. *Journal of Traumatic Stress* 25.4: 446–53.

Schreiter, Robert J. 1992. *Reconciliation: Mission and Ministry in a Changing Social Order*. Maryknoll, NY: Orbis Books.

Smedes, Lewis. 1984. *Forgive and Forget: Healing the Hurts We Don't Deserve.* San Francisco, CA: Harper & Row.

Springhorn, Ralf (dir.). 2005. *Living Forgiveness: Stories from Rwanda.* Vision Video.

Staub, Ervin. 2011. *Overcoming Evil: Genocide, Violent Conflict, and Terrorism.* Oxford: Oxford University Press.

Volf, Miroslav. 2001. 'Forgiveness, Religion and Justice: A Christian Contribution to a More Peaceful Social Environment'. In Raymond Hemlick and Rodney Lawrence Petersen (eds), *Forgiveness and Reconciliation: Religion, Public Policy & Conflict Transformation.* Philadelphia, PA: Templeton Foundation Press. 27–50.

Watts, Fraser. 2004. 'Christian Theology'. In Fraser Watts and Liz Gulliford (eds), *Forgiveness in Context: Theology and Psychology in Creative Dialogue.* London: T&T International: 50–68.

White, Ralph K. 1984. *Fearful Warriors: A Psychological Profile of U.S.-Soviet Relations.* New York: Free Press.

Worthington, Everett L. 1998. 'Pyramidal Model of Forgiveness: Some Interdisciplinary Speculations about Unforgiveness and the Promotion of Forgiveness'. In Everett Worthington (ed.), *Dimensions of Forgiveness: Psychological Research & Theological Perspectives.* Philadelphia, PA: Templeton Foundation Press: 29–58.

# Stories *as* Change:
# Using Writing to Facilitate Healing among
# Genocide Survivors in Rwanda

*Laura Apol*

For several years, I facilitated a collaborative project involving educators and mental health professionals in the US and Kigali, Rwanda, using narrative writing to promote healing and positive growth among university-aged survivors of the 1994 Genocide against the Tutsi in Rwanda. The rationale for using writing as a means of healing is that, by definition, traumatic memories are characterized as being disorganized and incomplete. Part of their extreme power is that they have little or no narrative content, existing primarily as fragments, feelings and physical sensations that occur without warning and at unexpected times.

Therapeutic writing – that is, narrative writing that systematically follows a deliberately therapeutic format – has been proven effective in reducing the effects of post-traumatic stress disorder (PTSD) and improving mental health because it allows an individual to organize traumatic memory by converting images and emotions into words and narrative text. Deliberately revisiting the trauma through writing allows the individual to manage the timing of the emotional response and give order and structure to what otherwise feels chaotic and disorganized. As writers learn that they can move into and back out of painful memories, they begin to experience feelings of control over previously intolerable and unmanageable emotions, eventually integrating the trauma into their ongoing life stories.

In this essay, I will present a rationale for therapeutic writing, then discuss the design for the particular writing-for-healing model that was developed and employed in this work with Tutsi survivors. I will go on to describe the participant interactions around and responses to the overall project to demonstrate the healing potential of narrative writing in response to trauma.

## Writing and Healing: The Rationale

Traumatic memories are characterized by intense emotion and corresponding alterations of the nervous system. Because these moments are marked by an increased level of adrenaline and other stress hormones, they are deeply imprinted into a part of the psyche that is pre-narrative and even pre-verbal, recorded in an area of the brain that both retains these images and gives them their emotional weight (Herman, 1997: 38–39). For this reason, individuals feel the emotion of a traumatic memory even if (and often *because*) they cannot verbalize the experience (van der Kolk, 1988: 273–80). These traumatic memories lack verbal narratives and references; therefore, they are encoded in the form of vivid sensations and images (Brett and Ostroff, 1985: 417–24), existing primarily as fragments, feelings and physical impressions – powerful 'image[s] without context' (Herman, 1997: 38) that are disorganized and incomplete.

Given that they are not connected to the normal linear flow of time-bound memory, these moments may emerge into consciousness at any point, bringing the force of the traumatic event with them (Anderson and MacCurdy, 2000: 6). And since traumatic memories are sensory, the body reacts to these unexpected intrusions with intense affects, sensations and responses, even when the conscious mind is not aware of the cause of such reactions. Because they are outside conscious awareness, these moments occur without warning when the individual smells, hears, sees or touches something that takes them back to the time the traumatic event occurred. Given that the power of these experiences is encoded non-verbally, verbalizing them is often extremely difficult. As a result, these traumatic memories are not integrated into personal awareness nor assimilated into an ongoing life story (Herman, 1997: 37).

Re-experiencing sensory details encoded during extreme life moments is at the core of trauma recovery. A difficult memory cannot be recalled without also re-experiencing the emotional charge it produces. Therefore, the images that make up the traumatic memory must be accessed and provided narrative framing if a story about the trauma is to be told. Without encountering these images and their context, the survivor will remain their prisoner (MacCurdy, 2000: 193). As Dori Laub puts it, 'There is, in each survivor, an imperative need to tell and thus to come to know one's story, unimpeded by ghosts from the past against which one has to protect oneself. One has to know one's buried truth in order to be able to live one's life' (Felman and Laub, 1992: 78). Painful moments must be processed, adapted to and ordered for the psyche, not to mention the body, to remain alive and healthy (MacCurdy, 2000: 162).

Telling and knowing one's story is central to the resolution of traumatic life events (Herman, 1997: 70).[1] Grieving and the healing that accompanies it allow the survivor to reclaim the self and its agency, to develop a representation of the self that is congruent with the experience of the survivor and to integrate both the self and its representation into a larger community of understanding (Anderson and MacCurdy, 2000: 6). Research into trauma recovery indicates that healing is more likely to occur when survivors embark on a process in which they reconstruct the story in detail – not just the events of their trauma, but also the non-narrative images their memories have encoded.

This accessing of memory can take place in speaking or in writing, and both the narrative telling of the story and the writing of the story have therapeutic value. Spoken and written testimony share healing properties, and speaking the story is often a first step towards articulating and assimilating traumatic life events. Speaking is immediate; it may require little by way of materials or planning, and the connection between speaker and listener is made in real time. However, the spoken story is also transient and fleeting; it requires a present and listening audience, and it is often in progress as it is told.

Writing is another way to construct a healing narrative. Although writing requires advanced literacy skills on the part of both writer and reader, there are many aspects of writing that are not found in speaking, among them: the ability to (independently) enter and leave the telling, control over pacing, the physical act of writing or typing, the distance involved in shaping a telling across time, an 'imagined' rather than immediate audience and the opportunity to revisit and revise the written product.

Thus, writing holds much therapeutic potential, and the process of remembering specifics and writing them down is often central to helping the individual to heal (MacCurdy, 2000: 167–68). However, remembering and recording traumatic details is rarely easy, especially when painful memories

---

[1] In Rwanda, such remembering and revisiting of the past is institutionalized in *Kwibuka* (which means 'Remember'). The national day of remembrance, with accompanying ceremonies, is followed by *Icyunamo*, the official week of mourning. During this time, local and national (and, now, international) events are held, in which survivors of the genocide gather to tell their stories, drawing on memory for the express purpose of healing and reconciliation.

are difficult to access or are unconsciously being blocked. Successful therapeutic writing, then, finds ways to access what is otherwise too difficult or too painful to engage.

## Therapeutic Writing: The Process

Therapeutic writing has been proven effective in addressing trauma. It has been documented to result in significant and substantial short-term reductions of both PTSD and depressive symptoms (van Emmerik et al., 2012; Moran, 2004), including reductions in medical visits, health concerns, depression, absentee rates, somatic symptoms and disease severity. In studies on therapeutic writing, traumatic memories become less intrusive and less distressing after writing (Pennebaker, 1997).

There are many reasons why narrative writing is therapeutic. Writing allows the individual to organize traumatic memories and to convert images and emotions into words. Through writing, the writer begins to have a sense of control over the intense, chaotic and unpredictable memories of the trauma, to mediate the timing and intensity of the emotional response, to gain some measure of feelings of safety and security, and eventually to start to integrate the trauma into a larger life story.

According to poet Gregory Orr, trauma is powerful in part because it reminds the individual of the ways in which humans are powerless and existence is chaotic. Narrative story-making becomes a major ally in preserving a person's sense of control over their destiny and circumstances. Orr writes: 'Story [...] is one of imagination's most basic ordering powers, a fundamental method of arranging the chaotic material of our experience into a form of meaning' (2002: 19), giving the self/storyteller the belief that he or she is able to order disorder and violence and make sense of it. In making a story, several things take place. Contrary to a widespread notion, it is not the catharsis of expressing pent-up emotion that is responsible for the healing. The goal is integration, not exorcism (Herman, 1997: 181); at best, venting gives only temporary relief, and at worst exacerbates the distress (Moran, 2004: 97). Rather, other factors appear to be responsible for the value of narrative writing.

Habituation, whereby in confronting a fear or a painful memory, one becomes accustomed to it and thus robs it of its power, is one source of healing (Moran, 2004: 97). By writing about traumatic experiences, writers revisit moments of intensity, transferring those moments onto the page where they can be considered, reconsidered, left and taken up again (Anderson and MacCurdy, 2000: 7), eventually losing their power over the unconscious through exposure and desensitization. Further, constructing a narrative about an event is a way of finding coherence and meaning in it (Moran, 2004: 97). Through writing, the individual shifts the crisis to a bearable distance. As Tom Glenn puts it,

> Once you write down what has happened [...] the memory exists outside of you. In the writing process, you give meaning and structure to the experience, reduce its chaos, and force yourself to face it directly, and allow yourself to see it in a new light [...] The memory doesn't become less emotional – it never weakens or goes away. But now you can face it, live with it, come to terms with it. So you're able to channel your despair into your writing, not into your living. ('Interview with Tom Glenn', 2014)

In addition, the individual is empowered through writing about trauma, actively shaping this representation of the situation rather than passively enduring it as a lived experience (Orr, 2002: 4–5). Writing through loss and trauma is a process in which writers situate themselves as agents in their own discourse rather than as objects acted upon by outside forces they cannot control (Micciche, 2001: 133).

Finally, in writing, the narrative can be revisited and revised. As Anderson and MacCurdy put it, 'Through the dual possibilities of permanence and revision, the chief healing effect of writing is thus to recover and to exert a measure of control over [...] the past. As we manipulate the words on the page, as we articulate to ourselves and to others the emotional truth of our pasts, we become agents for our own healing' (2000: 7). Revision and re-envisioning allow the writer to return to the writing, again and again; painful memories are encountered and engaged, emotions occur and then abate, resulting in their reintegration into the conscious mind.

## Therapeutic Writing: The Product

The writing process has positive therapeutic effects, but it also results in products that can be used to create a written record that is advantageous personally, culturally and historically. In her book *Writing as a Way of Healing: How Telling Our Stories Transforms Our Lives*, Louise DeSalvo outlines the characteristics of a healing narrative: it renders our experience concretely, authentically, explicitly and with a richness of details; it links feelings to events; and it reveals the insights we have achieved from our painful experiences (1999: 57–62).

Authors write about what they have lived through in order to heal themselves. However, their writing also has the potential to speak to others. There is a close relationship between therapeutic writing and what is considered to be 'writing quality'. MacCurdy observes that 'The same thing that helps us recover from traumatic experiences – describing images *in detail* to another – produces writing which is alive with sensory description' (2000: 167; emphasis added). Choosing concrete images, described in direct and specific ways, rather than opting for abstract concepts is healing in that it allows access to emotionally charged and often unconscious images and events; it also leads to more lively and immediate writing, evoking vivid and immediate experience not only in the writer, but in the reader as well. This is a reciprocal relationship; Wilma Bucci argues that writing which does not integrate concrete images (and the emotions those images convey) into the concepts that they can produce, will not provide a healing function for the individual (1995: 144; cited in MacCurdy, 2000: 169).

Written products that are made public become a source of power, given that 'writing is a form of action that has personal and social consequences: *personal* because writing enables [writers] to reflect on and revise their own narratives about loss and pain; *social* because writing about trauma involves a re-education of emotion, beginning from the personal and then moving outward to critique [larger social] systems' (Micciche, 2001: 131–32). Additionally, writing builds a sense of community, for the writer and the reader: 'If those to whom we write receive what we have to say and respond to it as we write and rewrite, we create a community that can accept, contest, gloss, inform, invent, and help us discover, deepen, and change who we have become as a consequence of the trauma we have experienced' (Anderson and MacCurdy, 2000: 7). Finally, in readers of the trauma narrative, therapeutic writing creates *witnesses* to the trauma who are vital to its recreation in narrative form. In this way, the trauma story becomes a testimony. Julie Rak writes that 'Testimonies about trauma require readers to carry on the work of agency and social responsibility to the event and its author, because the author of the testimony needs witnesses to make the story complete, and even real' (2003: 63). Such a statement reinforces the tenet in trauma studies that '[stories] of trauma [are] written from the need to tell and retell the story of the traumatic experience, to make it "real" both to the victim and to the community' (Tal, 1996: 21).

## Writing for Healing in Post-Genocide Rwanda

There is, perhaps, no greater widespread trauma than that of genocide, particularly a genocide in which neighbours, communities, families, church members and co-workers are mobilized to betray and kill those closest to them. The 1994 Genocide against the Tutsi of Rwanda, in which an estimated 800,000 to one million citizens were killed, primarily by other civilians, left an entire country deeply traumatized (Fujii, 2009). In the aftermath, genocide survivors showed high rates of mental health and psychosocial problems due to the inconceivable brutality that the majority of them had experienced or been witness to (Des Forges, 1999). Children were particularly vulnerable: Dyregrov et al. (2000) interviewed children and adolescents approximately one year after the genocide and concluded that 79% of the survivors showed moderate to severe post-traumatic stress reactions. Ongoing studies continue to report that the majority of children in Rwanda have experienced the repercussions of genocidal violence and trauma (Schaal and Elbert, 2006; Neugebauer et al., 2009; Rieder and Elbert, 2013; Rugema et al., 2013); many of these children present evidence of PTSD and related psychological trauma.

In the face of such statistics and convinced of the value of writing for healing, I went to Rwanda in 2006 with the intent of creating – with US and Rwandan colleagues – an intervention that would employ narrative therapeutic writing in the interest of diminishing the effects of PTSD and improving the mental health of genocide survivors.[2] As a writer and teacher of writing, I was certain that the path to healing through writing was to focus on written *words* – to allow survivors to work through their experiences on the page, moving towards, moving away, pacing, shaping, negotiating, owning and, in this way, to be more able to control rather than be controlled by the feelings the trauma invoked. I believed that the model we developed should assist writers in producing effective narratives that would carry with it therapeutic benefits – that we should consider both the *writing process* and the *written products* in our planning. It is important to note here that such a writing project stood in contrast to the majority of testimony projects that were taking place at the time. Many genocide survivors were providing oral testimony, sometimes in face-to-face settings, sometimes collected in audio or video format. Nearly all the written testimonies at this point consisted of stories told to writers who were not themselves survivors of the genocide.[3] Film-makers, historians, legal experts and NGOs were collecting survivor testimonies for a range of reasons.[4] Our project was unique in that our goal was to create testimonies written *by* Rwandans themselves, allowing for the therapeutic value of the writing process along with the narrative product, in

---

[2] A more detailed description of this project (including my own acknowledgement of the complexities of being a white woman working with survivors in Rwanda) may be found in Apol (2015: 71–94).

[3] See, for example, the testimonies collected by Jean Hatfield, or Wendy A. Whitworth's book *We Survived: Genocide in Rwanda* (2006).

[4] Many of these testimonies are archived in the Rwanda Genocide Memorial or are available online at the Genocide Archive of Rwanda.

this way allowing writers to create a sense of community with other writers as well as with readers. Through writing, participants would simultaneously witness and *be witnessed* through their written testimonies; they would craft their own stories for a real or imagined audience (or no audience at all) – in their own words, at their own pace, for their own unique purposes. We did not collect these testimonies as part of our work; although we did offer help with editing and suggest possible venues should the young writers decide to make their work public, we were clear from the start that the writings belonged to them, to do with as they wished.

The US team was made up of four individuals: the director of the NGO LinkingSchools, a psychiatrist, a paediatrician and myself. The Rwandan planning team consisted of a mother and daughter duo – survivors of the genocide – who ran Association Mwana Ukundwa,[5] an organization that by then had been responsible for the care of nearly 2,000 orphans of genocide. In the early stages, we had a general sense of the project that took shape as we planned: a week-long workshop made up of writing sessions, regular debriefings and a discussion at the end of the week devoted to imagining a future for the work. In response to the interests expressed by these Rwandan colleagues, we chose to work with young adults who would simultaneously participate in and learn to facilitate their own versions of the workshop in the communities in which they lived, studied and worked. These young people had experience with *telling* their stories; this would be their first opportunity to put those stories into a written form.[6]

Eventually we settled on the following model: combining a *process writing approach* (the format) with a *therapeutic writing model* (the content). In a *process approach*, writing occurs in multiple steps: brainstorming/freewriting, narrative writing and revision. The *therapeutic model* breaks the writing content into three discrete stages, life before the trauma, the trauma itself and life after the trauma (including hopes for the future), as a means to incorporate the traumatic event into the larger life story.[7] We employed

---

[5] *Mwana Ukundwa* translates as 'Beloved Children'.

[6] It was never the intention that this workshop would be a stand-alone project or that significant and lasting change would take place after only a short period of writing. Rather, the goal was to create *a model* together, testing it as we went along, then to transfer it to the young people who would use it in other areas of their lives. And although the workshop itself took place over a short period of time, the project – planning, facilitating and following up – spanned more than a decade.

[7] The therapeutic format on which our own project is based roughly adheres to the stages of recovery outlined by Judith Herman (1997: 133–236).

various psychotherapeutic techniques (including labelling of feelings, desensitization, visualizing and focusing on details) aimed at restructuring and organizing traumatic memories by converting images and emotions into words within a narrative framework, thus reducing the emotional intensity of traumatic memories.

By using a process writing approach, in which participants begin by freewriting or brainstorming, move into drafting a narrative, then work on revising the narrative, we drew on the central tenets of writing for healing: that is, we moved from essentially private writing (i.e. envisioning, detailing) into the re-forming of the images and details into a more linear, re-envisioned (and thus more controlled) telling – in short, we moved from pre-verbal and pre-narrative into narrative. From there, the revision process allowed writers to step back, imagine an audience and reshape their narrative according to purpose and intent. Thus, writers moved from private to increasingly public writing, each step of the process providing them with more distance, more control and (due to repetition and exposure) more habituation and desensitization. Throughout, we encouraged participants to use the early stages of the writing process to access details, images, moments; to identify and name emotions and the events associated with emotions; and to share and develop their writing in whatever form and to whatever extent they desired.

## The Workshop

The workshop meetings were held at the Kigali Genocide Memorial Centre, located in the heart of Kigali on a hill overlooking the city. Constructed ten years after the genocide, the Centre marks a site where more than 250,000 victims are buried in mass graves. The building is surrounded by gardens, burial vaults and walls bearing the names of victims who have been identified and are buried there. We met in a room of the on-site conference facility and took our meals together in the canteen.

Along with the US and Rwandan planning team, the group consisted of the six young people from Rwanda along with two additional Rwandans who attended as part of our agenda-setting on the first day. The young people ranged in age from 25 to 32, meaning that they had been between 12 and 19 years old at the time of genocide. All had lost extended and/or immediate family members, and several were orphans of genocide. Because their jobs and training put them in environments in which they had close contact with youth who had survived (or were the children of survivors), all had expressed a wish to use the skills learned in the workshop to work with children and young people in their various contexts. Individuals of this age, they said, often had no one to talk to about the genocide and were left to figure things out on their own, resulting in frequent misunderstanding of facts about the genocide (both the long-term history and what had taken place during the genocide); consequently, the effects and reverberations of the genocide through their lives were powerful and confusing. Some (but not all) of the participants were fluent in written and spoken English; these individuals served as translators for others in the group when needed. All the participants were skilled in reading and writing in Kinyarwanda, and all the workshop writing was done in this language; because Kinyarwanda was the participants' first language, and because it was the language of the genocide, the participants believed that it was the language that allowed them the best access to memory, and thus to trauma and therapeutic value.[8]

As we talked about possibilities for the workshop, the participants vacillated between focusing on the therapeutic value of the *writing process* and on the therapeutic value of the *written products*. The young participants were clear that although the process might have healing properties, they also wanted their written products to find a place in the world. It was clear from our conversations that they did not imagine our time together to be an end in itself; rather, this was for them a far-reaching and ongoing enterprise, creating a record of historical documents and narratives that could help inform school curriculum within Rwanda, while letting the wider world know what had taken place and what they had experienced.

We began by thinking about the *time before the genocide*, engaging in freewriting/brainstorming in which the participants listed aspects of their lives before the genocide. Together we recorded their ideas on a poster chart: people/relationships/interactions, family gatherings, school, church, neighbours and neighbourhoods, promises, home environment (rooms, foods, routines), special days, family advice and expectations, games, toys, clothes, friends, work and chores, dreams and hopes, family stories. Our goal was to use these as prompts to reconstruct detailed memories of the time before the genocide. In this way, we employed the therapeutic technique that therapists often use to encourage clients to re-experience specific moments from the past (MacCurdy, 2000: 180). We encouraged the participants to write as quickly as they could, using as much concrete detail as possible.

---

[8] One of the participants reported later that after writing his testimony in Kinyarwanda, he went back and did his own translation into English. He said, 'It took me two weeks to translate into English. It was emotional, yes, but also hard to shift language. I lost which English words to use to translate the story from Kinyarwanda. I wanted the story done in English. I didn't want the story translated by others – I wanted the story coming directly from me'.

We talked about the senses, and about description that recreates a scene or a time period. After the freewriting, we shifted into more narrative writing, encouraging the participants to choose one or a combination of the descriptions they had created and to work from there to expand their notes into a more cohesive and linear form.

When we wrote about the *time during genocide*, we began by creating a list of feelings, then writing about memories of events during genocide and describing the feelings that went along with those events. Our goal here was to transfer the moments of trauma onto the page, to create distance from the overwhelming flood of diffuse feeling and to engage the specific emotions as a way to begin to integrate them into the story. The emotions the participants listed together included: scared, fearful, hopeless, helpless, angry, terrified, rageful, revenge, empty, lonely/alone, numb, doubt, sad, betrayed and comforted. Again, the participants wrote quickly and by association, returning later to create a more coherent narrative from their notes.

Finally, when we wrote about the *time after genocide*, we separated out a list of characteristics of the present (responding to the question, 'What good things are happening in my life right now?' for which participants offered categories of marriage, career/work, achievements, education, family, friendships, politics/country), then moving into connecting the present to their hopes and dreams for the future. One again, our goal was to take what could be vague and amorphous responses and anchor them in something more concrete and explicit, in this way allowing for clearer connections and integration.

## Participant Interactions and Responses

From the start, as participants engaged in the therapeutic process of the workshop, they reported that they began to sense the potential for using writing to facilitate healing. Through their brainstorming about life before the genocide, they recognized first-hand the importance of focusing on details as a means to access larger memories and to reconstruct a narrative (see MacCurdy, 2000: 167). In this early writing, they were able to convert images into scenes and retrieve memories they had thought long forgotten. And by dividing up the stages of trauma into *before, during* and *after* the genocide, their focus on each successive stage allowed them, at the start, to revisit through memory the happier times they had experienced in the period before genocide – something most of them said they had not done in the past. One participant explained during one of our debriefing sessions that 'I was happy when I was writing [about the time before genocide] because I felt like I was back there and was with my family', while another said, 'The time for writing was too short. I want to think about this when I have enough time. I want to be as happy as I was during this writing'.

By linking feelings to events as they wrote about the time of genocide, participants were able to recognize the emotions that had overwhelmed them at the time the trauma was taking place. One participant described his state of mind during the genocide in this way: 'Two days after [the genocide began] I fell into dreaming. I was in a dream [...] I was seeing fighting, dead people, people stealing in the houses of dead people. Even when I was rescued, I was still dreaming. It's as if I was deep in the ocean. In 1999, I realized genocide took place'. One participant recalled – with surprise – the lack of feeling she experienced during the genocide, describing her repression of emotion in this way: 'Writing yesterday I remembered how I didn't feel anything when I heard someone had died during genocide. It was like I didn't care. I couldn't allow myself to express emotion'. The value of writing, one of the participants concluded, is that it encourages people to begin to come to terms with the reality of the genocide. 'Many people *still* don't want to think genocide happened', he said. 'If someone is writing, they have to acknowledge things. They *have* to recognize that things happened'. In this way, the participants were coming to terms with their trauma, facing it directly instead and learning to live with it rather than avoiding or denying it.

In discussing their writing about the present and future (the post-genocide stage), many of the participants were highly detailed in their descriptions, seeing themselves – often for the first time – as actors in their lives rather than objects acted upon by forces outside their control. Many focused on a sense of personal pride in the lives they had created and the things they had done in the years following the genocide. As one participant put it, 'Doing this, I realized I had made good things since genocide'. One talked about how her studies helped her to understand herself and her post-genocide feelings better; another talked about his recent marriage as a stage of recovery and hope. One woman felt pride in her financial independence, stating, 'Now I am able to buy groceries for myself. I have money I can lend to others'. Another woman, who had a baby at the time of the workshop, saw a positive future for herself and her new family. Part of this stage of writing allowed for a revision of the stories that they had held about their lives (see Anderson and MacCurdy, 2000: 7), reintegrating the painful memories into their life stories in ways that were empowering and healing. One young woman took a long view across the many years since the genocide; she said, 'After genocide, I thought I had no life because I had no parents. But that wasn't true. Other families have taken the place of my parents and do what parents do. I have other family members, even if they're not direct blood relatives'. As one participant summarized it, 'Before, I was fighting against death. Now

I am fighting for life'. One young man, however, questioned whether there was anything positive to write about in Rwanda, post-genocide. He said, 'It wasn't easy for me to write something after genocide. Though after genocide I have done many things – I survived as a soldier, I graduated, I helped other survivors and orphans. I participated in many things. I tried to write about good things, but bad things still came'.[9]

By the time we concluded the workshop, the participants had many tools for moving forward in their writing and many ideas for using the writing-for-healing model in their own contexts. They had a sense that writing was significantly different from telling their stories; the brainstorming process, the pacing, the level of detail, the sense of privacy, the opportunity to shape and revisit and revise – these went far beyond the spoken testimonies they had engaged with up to that point. They also had a sense that this sort of writing was of value to other survivors, creating a sense of community with readers, leaving a written record for the future, bearing witness to their own and others' lives. Through writing, then, these young people became more active agents in their own lives, shaping the representation of their experience rather than enduring it as a lived experience (see Anderson and MacCurdy, 2000: 4–5). They were gaining a sense of control over their lives. As one of the young men observed at the close of the workshops, 'To ask someone to write is to ask them to fight. To ask someone to write is to ask them to fight for life'.

## Participant Interviews

A year and a half later, in April 2009, the US group returned to Rwanda to discuss with our colleagues the results of the writing-for-healing workshop from the vantage of 18 months' distance and to learn what the participants had done with their narratives and with the writing-for-healing model.[10]

---

[9] The model we relied on assumes a 'post-genocide', post-trauma period. But, of course, the psychological and social wounds of mass violence go on, both for the individual and for the community, long after the physical violence ends. Therefore, one aspect of this sort of work is not only to nurture hope, but also to support the ongoing work of mourning – to create a context and audience for expressions of continuing anger, fear or grief.

[10] Participant interviews were held at the Hôtel des Mille Collines. The interviews – which were recorded with participant consent – were conducted in English or French, depending on the wishes of the participant. Recordings were translated in the United States by a hired translator who worked in English, French and Kinyarwanda, and who was never provided the names or any identifying information (beyond that contained in the interviews) about any of the participants.

Our interviews revealed that over the months since the workshop, several participants had continued working on their narratives and stated that it had been the workshop model that had prompted them to embark on this telling, since it was the first time they had had access to strategies and structures that allowed them to understand or to recount what they termed 'the whole story'. Continuing work on their narratives allowed them to tell and retell, through writing, the story of their trauma, and several participants said the writing allowed them to say things they had never said before (and that some had not spoken of since). Revisiting the time before genocide was a new experience for some; as one woman explained, 'No one has ever asked me to think about my family before the genocide. Everyone wants to know what happened – how my family died, how I escaped, what it was like in the camps. But no one has ever asked me about my earlier life before'.

The participants spoke with pride of the courage it required for them to initiate this sort of self-healing, trusting that on the other side of the painful negative memories would be some positive result. Several mentioned the 'release' they had found in acknowledging, through writing, the emotions they had experienced during the genocide. They saw benefits to writing that could not be found in speaking. One explained:

> In our culture, oral telling is very important. To tell or say your story is very important, because people can ask questions and you can go into other areas. But now I see writing is valuable too. There are things that I have written that I have not spoken about – not before or since. If you want to cry and you are writing, you can cry. In our culture, it's not good to show weakness [...] but in writing you can show strong emotions and weakness.

Several admitted that writing had given them an opportunity to confront parts of the story that they had protected themselves from in the past (see Felman and Laub, 1992: 78), and that through writing they were able to grieve (see Anderson and MacCurdy, 2000: 6). They affirmed the structure and content of the workshop format; as one participant explained, 'Pre-genocide, genocide, post-genocide. It's good to remember them separately. Then you can resume your own life in an understanding manner'. Their writing, then, allowed them to create a larger narrative as they ordered the disorder and violence they had experienced in an attempt to understand and make sense of it.

For several of the writers, focus on their early years brought back happy memories that continued to provide them with comfort, and looking at the progress they had made in the time since genocide was positive as well. They were able to reintegrate emotions and painful memories into their larger life story. One participant stated, 'It was very positive to recover those early experiences with my family. I want to focus on those'. And another said, 'Until the writing, I only thought of my history as sad. It was important to have a chance to write about positive experiences of my childhood and positive parts of my life post-genocide'. Another stated, 'Prior to the workshop, I didn't even like myself. Life was very dark. Now I feel much better. When I wrote about the present time, I understood that life goes on, families gather, there is hope for the future'. In this way, rather than overwhelming them entirely, the trauma of genocide could begin to be assimilated into their ongoing life story (see Herman, 1997: 37).

In 2013, six years after the workshop had taken place, on a return trip to Rwanda I met with most of the participants one more time. The reasons for my trip were many, but one goal was to talk with these young people about their experience of the writing-for-healing workshops once again – to hear about the status of their narratives, to learn whether they had conducted (and whether they still were conducting) writing workshops of their own.

The lives of these young people had changed dramatically in the years since we had first met. At the time of the original workshop, many of the participants were in school; two were married and one had a child. Six years later, three had graduated from university, two were enrolled in graduate programmes and two others were applying to doctoral programmes. There had been three more weddings and nine additional births. The interviews at this time were all conducted in English (no translation necessary), and one took place in Toronto, where one of the young men had moved.[11]

Several of the participants had continued to write; some had maintained freewriting and taking notes as memories continued to resurface, while others wrote in more formal ways. Two had completed their narratives – one in Kinyarwanda, one in English – revising and making them public to varying degrees. One participant created a blog for genocide survivors that had to do with writing and remembering, and in 2012 wrote a memory each day for the 100-day genocide remembrance period from early April to mid-July. One participant was using the writing workshop model with children, comparing their oral and written versions of family stories; one participant used the writing-for-healing format to design questionnaires for his own research interviewing survivors, and from those interviews he had created two books of survivors' testimonies.

Several themes emerged in these conversations as – from the vantage of more than half a decade – the participants talked about their writing and

---

11 I was able to speak with five of the six participants at this time. I had lost contact with one, and only later learned that she had married and had children, and that she was living in Kigali.

their lives. Most prominent was the notion that writing had allowed them to share things that until then had been private or unacknowledged. One participant said that in the workshop, 'I wrote some things I keep private [...] It was like a conversation between me and myself'; and another said, 'Prior to the workshop, I told my story only to myself; I had not shared it. After the workshop, I started talking about it'.

The workshop allowed participants to access and begin to move into their awareness some of the emotions they had repressed, and to remember events they had forgotten. One participant said of his ongoing writing, 'It is emotional to go back but I like to do it. It's good to write all these things I held inside. Through writing, I can release them, and that feels good [...] When I sit and write, something comes out of me'. Another said, 'When genocide happened, when they told me that my parents had died, I did not feel much emotion. Through writing, emotion emerged and now I can retrieve it. Now I can cry when I think about the death of my parents'. The participants found that more memories emerged through writing in the years after the workshop. As one participant put it, 'What is different about writing after the workshop: the first time I wrote there were not as many things. Over time, more things came out. There were things I'd forgotten, but as I wrote more, I was able to retrieve them. And I find more things when I go back'. Externalizing the story through writing gave participants a wider perspective on their lives and on the role of the genocide in their lives, across the years. One young woman explained, 'It's good because you can see your story from a distance and be more objective, see what you feel'. And one participant shared that writing provided her an opportunity to focus on her own story rather than the stories of others; she said, 'Even though I was training as a clinical psychologist, I did not think about *my* life, just about other people. Through writing, I could focus on my life'.

For some, the writing became an imperative. One young man said:

Now I'm done writing my story. Before I completed it, I abandoned my job duties to work on my story. I was feeling unhappy and I knew I could only have peace once I was done with my story. Everything in writing it was related to the training [the workshop]. Before, I didn't know where to start, or who would be the audience. Afterwards, I used the strategies we had practised and I felt the desire to get the story done.

Overall, the participants felt that the writing model they had worked to develop supported their trauma recovery. One participant maintained that 'The way we were asked to write our story is a therapy in itself', while another said, 'Writing your story is self-healing. You are writing yourself – self-healing the self'.

The participants not only continued with their own writing; in the hands of these young people, the writing workshop format was also being used with primary school children, with orphans, with high school students and with adults. As one of the participants explained, 'I'm still working on some of the ideas we talked about. I have a passion to do it. I feel the need. I love my country, and it's for my country, and for the people, and for myself'. Another stated, 'This method of testifying goes beyond academic; it is healing, it is deep, it gets in the quick of the life of survivors'. In this way, the stories that were written not only documented the survivors' life changes; the writings also *brought about* change. Through their writing, these young people found ways to reshape their understandings of themselves and their histories; they moved from being fearful of and trapped in their traumatic memories towards gaining a sense of control. As one participant put it, 'When you write a story, you create distance between yourself and the story [...] When someone can write his life in detail, it's already a kind of freedom. Then he can concentrate on his future rather than being a prisoner of his past'.

## Conclusion: Rwandan Stories *as* Change

In her essay, 'From trauma to writing', MacCurdy writes that:

> Narrative is the chain that links our moments together. But image is what we see in the dark of night, what we wake up with from dreams, what we remember when we recall those we love. It is image that burns itself into our minds whether we want it to or not, and it is image which can free us from a past that will always have a hold on us until we look straight at the images that live behind our eyes. (200: 190)

Given the traumatic memories that were part of the lived experiences of these young people in Rwanda, we expected that writing would be difficult because it necessitates re-experiencing the emotions associated with the traumatic events – something most survivors have carefully avoided just to cope with life. Once images start to come, so also do the feelings (MacCurdy, 2000: 172). As a result, we were intentional about scaffolding the writing we did together. We broke the writing process into clear stages and the narrative into discrete time segments. We created lists and talked throughout about the participants' experiences with the writing activities. We followed up with interviews and check-ins across time. When we asked writers to think about the time before genocide, we focused on concrete details as a way to access memory, inviting writers to recreate the past through recollections of people, places, moments and experiences. When we asked them to revisit the trauma of the genocide, we were explicit about asking them to label emotions in nuanced ways, suggesting that they return to their memories to identify both the events and the feelings associated with the events. And in the final stage, where participants were asked to think about the time following the trauma of genocide, we focused on positive aspects of the present and hopes for the future in an effort to engage writers in a feeling of community and connectedness, countering the isolation and hopelessness many survivors experience in the aftermath of trauma.

Throughout, we knew we were asking these young survivors to enter a space that they had spent years resisting – a past that time and again threatened to overwhelm them. We knew that revisiting these traumatic memories required from them both courage and trust. To be sure, the stories they wrote of their lives before, during and after the genocide *did* document change; however, writing those stories also *led to* change. By bringing together details of their lives before the genocide, emotions of the time during the genocide and descriptions of their lives – and expectations and futures – in the years that had followed, they were able to see and began to integrate traumatic memories with happier ones, creating the groundwork for a more holistic narrative of their lives and imagining ways they could help others to do the same.

Through their writing, these young people faced their personal and collective histories, revisited excruciatingly painful memories, took control of the narratives of their lives and empowered themselves and those around them to come to terms with the past. They became agents of their own healing, and in the process created stories and change – not only for themselves, but for a larger audience as well.

## Works Cited

Anderson, Charles M., and Marian M. MacCurdy. 2000. 'Introduction'. In Charles M. Anderson and Marian M. MacCurdy (eds), *Writing and Healing: Toward an Informed Practice*. Urbana, IL: National Council of Teachers of English: 1–22.

Apol, Laura. 2015. 'Epilogue: Writer as Witness'. In *Requiem, Rwanda*. East Lansing, MI: Michigan State University Press: 71–94.

Brett, Elizabeth A., and Robert Ostroff. 1985. 'Imagery in Post-Traumatic Stress Disorder: An Overview'. *American Journal of Psychiatry* 142: 417–24.

Bucci, Wilma. 1995. 'The Power of the Narrative: A Multiple Code Account'. In James W. Pennebaker (ed.), *Emotion, Disclosure, and Health*. Washington, DC: American Psychological Association, 93–122.

Des Forges, Alison. 1999. *Leave None to Tell the Story: Genocide in Rwanda*. New York: Human Rights Watch.

DeSalvo, Louise. 1999. *Writing as a Way of Healing: How Telling Our Stories Transforms Our Lives*. Boston, MA: Beacon Press.

Dyregrov, Atle, L. Gupta, R. Gjestad and E. Mukanoheli. 2000. 'Trauma Exposure and Psychological Reactions to Genocide among Rwandan Children'. *Journal of Traumatic Stress* 13.1: 3–21.

Felman, Shoshana, and Dori Laub. 1992. *Testimony: Crises of Witnessing in Literature, Psychoanalysis, and History*. New York: Routledge.

Fujii Lee Ann. 2009. *Killing Neighbors: Webs of Violence in Rwanda*. New York: Cornell University Press.

Herman, Judith. 1997. *Trauma and Recovery: The Aftermath of Violence – From Domestic Abuse to Political Terror*. New York: Basic Books.

'Interview with Tom Glenn. "Our job was to help men die." A Vietnam Vet Writes about Men Dying of AIDS'. 2014. *Washington Independent Review of Books* 6 June. Available at http://www.washingtonindependentreviewofbooks.com/index.php/features/interview-with-tom-glenn (consulted on 10 February 2018).

MacCurdy, Marian M. 2000. 'From Trauma to Writing: A Theoretical Model for Practical Use'. In Charles M. Anderson and Marian M. MacCurdy (eds), *Writing and Healing: Toward an Informed Practice*. Urbana, IL: National Council of Teachers of English: 158–200.

Micciche, Laura R. 2001. 'Writing through Trauma: The Emotional Dimensions of Writing'. *Composition Studies* 29.1: 131–41.

Moran, Molly Hurley. 2004. 'Toward a Writing and Healing Approach in the Basic Writing Classroom: One Professor's Personal Odyssey'. *Journal of Basic Writing* 23.2: 93–115.

Neugebauer, R., P.W. Fisher, J.B Turner, S. Yamabe, J.A. Sarsfield and T. Stehling-Ariza. 2009. 'Post-Traumatic Stress Reactions among Rwandan Children and Adolescents in the Early Aftermath of Genocide'. *International Journal of Epidemiology* 38.4: 1033–45.

Orr, Gregory. 2002. *Poetry as Survival*. Athens, GA: The University of Georgia Press.

Pennebaker, James W. 1997. *Opening Up: The Healing Power of Expressing Emotions*. New York: Guilford Press.

Rak, Julie. 2003. 'Do Witness: Don't: A Women's Word and Trauma as Pedagogy'. *Topia* 10: 53–71.

Rieder, Heide, and Thomas Elbert. 2013. 'Rwanda – Lasting Imprints of a Genocide: Trauma, Mental Health and Psychosocial Conditions in Survivors, Former Prisoners and their Children'. *Conflict and Health* 7.6: 1–13.

Rugema, Lawrence, Ingrid Mogren, Joseph Ntaganira and Krantz Gunilla. 2013. 'Traumatic Episodes Experienced during the Genocide Period in Rwanda Influence Life Circumstances in Young Men and Women 17 Years Later'. *BMC*

*Public Health* 13.1235. Available at https://bmcpublichealth.biomedcentral. com/articles/10.1186/1471-2458-13-1235 (consulted on 27 February 2018).

Schaal, Susanne, and Thomas Elbert. 2006. 'Ten Years after the Genocide: Trauma Confrontation and Posttraumatic Stress in Rwandan Adolescents'. *Journal of Traumatic Stress* 19.1: 95–105.

Tal, Kalí. 1996. *Worlds of Hurt: Reading the Literatures of Trauma*. New York: Cambridge University Press.

van der Kolk, Bessel. 1988. 'The Trauma Spectrum: The Interaction of Biological and Social Events in the Genesis of the Trauma Response'. *Journal of Traumatic Stress* 1: 273–90.

van Emmerik, Arnold A.P., Albert Reijntjes and Jan H. Kamphuis. 2013. 'Writing Therapy for Posttraumatic Stress: A Meta-Analysis'. *Psychotherapy and Psychosomatics* 82: 82–88.

Whitworth, Wendy A. 2006. *We Survived: Genocide in Rwanda*. Mansfield: The Quill Press.

# Notes on Contributors

**Laura Apol** is Associate Professor in the College of Education at Michigan State University. An award-winning poet, she regularly leads writing workshops in national and international contexts. Her work using writing to facilitate healing among survivors of the 1994 Genocide against the Tutsi resulted in a collection of her own poetry entitled, *Requiem, Rwanda*; the poems were translated into Kinyarwanda and published under the title *Emwe N'imvura Irabyibuka* [*Even the Rain Remembers*]. Her scholarly interests include poetic inquiry as a research methodology and the therapeutic uses of writing. She is currently completing a book about the Rwanda writing project entitled *Whose Poem is it, Anyway? The Challenge and Responsibility of Researcher as Writer and Witness* (Springer, forthcoming).

**Richard Benda** is a tutor and a research fellow at Luther King House Educational Trust/University of Manchester, where he teaches Contextual Theology and Research Methods. He holds a BA, MA and PhD in Religious Philosophy and Political Life (University of Manchester). He also holds a second cycle degree in Law from Kigali Independent University, where he taught Criminal Law and Constitutional Law in 2003–04. His research interests include genocide studies, post-conflict transitional theories, post-conflict transgenerational dynamics and contextual theology, especially African political theologies. His most recent publication is a critical analysis of transitional temporalities and transitional narratives in post-genocide Rwanda (Routledge, 2018).

**Ananda Breed** is Professor in Theatre at the University of Lincoln and AHRC Co-Investigator for the *Changing the Story* project based on building inclusive societies with, and for, young people in five post-conflict countries. She is the author of *Performing the Nation: Genocide, Justice, Reconciliation* (Seagull Books, 2014) and co-editor of *Performance and Civic Engagement* (Palgrave Macmillan, 2017) in addition to several publications that address transitional systems of governance and the arts. She has worked as a consultant for IREX and UNICEF in Central Asia on issues concerning conflict prevention and conducted applied arts workshops in the Democratic Republic of Congo, Indonesia, Japan, Kyrgyzstan, Nepal, Palestine, Rwanda and Turkey. She was founder and co-director of the Centre for Performing Arts Development (CPAD) at the University of East London and has been a research fellow at the International Research Centre Interweaving Performance Cultures at Freie University. Breed is currently Principal Investigator of AHRC GCRF Follow On Impact project '*Ubwuzu*: Shaping the Rwandan National Curriculum through Arts'.

**Eloïse Brezault** is Assistant Professor of French and African Studies at Saint Lawrence University (New York, USA) and the author of *Johnny Chien Méchant par Emmanuel Dongala* (ACEL, 2012) on the representation of child soldiers in Dongala's novel *Johnny Mad Dog*. She has published a collection of interviews with francophone African writers, *Afrique, Paroles d'écrivains* (Mémoire d'encrier, 2010). She currently serves as the associate editor of the academic journal *Nouvelles Études Francophones*, and has written numerous articles on francophone African literature and postcolonial studies. She co-edited and published a collection of articles with Erica Johnson (Pace University) on issues of memory in the postcolonial world: *Memory as Colonial Capital: Cross Cultural Encounters in French and in English* (Palgrave, 2017). Her current project deals with representations of memory in the DRC.

**Ilaria Buscaglia** holds a PhD in Cultural Anthropology from the University of Siena (Italy). She is based in Rwanda and has extensive research experience in the country, both in academia and as a consultant for local and international NGOs. Her main research interests are youth, gender, development and state/nation building.

**Bennett Collins** is a PhD candidate at the University of St Andrews and the founder of the Third Generation Project (TGP), a climate justice think tank based at the University of St Andrews, which emphasizes the rights of communities on the front lines of climate change. He has received funding for various grassroots collaborative projects documenting and examining state and global violence against marginalized communities and Indigenous peoples from the British Academy, Carnegie Trust for Scottish Universities, Aegis Trust, National Geographic Society, and the Global Research Challenges Fund. His current research centres on responses to climate-induced displacement in the US and settler colonial state violence.

**Catherine Gilbert** is a Marie Skłodowska-Curie Research Fellow in the Department of Literary Studies at Ghent University, Belgium. Her project, 'Genocide Commemoration in the Rwandan Diaspora', investigates the impact of place and displacement on commemorative practices within diasporic communities in Europe. She recently published her first monograph, *From Surviving to Living: Voice, Trauma and Witness in Rwandan Women's Writing* (Presses universitaires de la Méditerranée (Pulm), 2018). Other recent publications include an article on mobility and memory in the *Australian Journal of French Studies* (2018), and a chapter in the edited volume *Translating the Postcolonial in Multilingual Contexts* (Pulm, 2017).

**Hannah Grayson** is Lecturer in French and Francophone Studies at the University of Stirling. She was previously a postdoctoral research fellow at the University of St Andrews, where she worked on the AHRC-funded project 'Rwandan Stories of Change'. Her research on testimony in Rwanda has been published in *Eastern African Literary and Cultural Studies* and *Studies in Testimony*, and she has published more widely on postcolonial literature in French. Prior to joining St Andrews, Hannah completed a PhD in Francophone African literature at the University of Warwick and worked as a teaching fellow in French at Durham University.

**Nicki Hitchcott** is Professor of French at the University of St Andrews in Scotland. She has published widely on various aspects of African literature and her most recent books are *Rwanda Genocide Stories: Fiction after 1994* (2015) and *Francophone Afropean Literatures* (co-edited with Dominic Thomas, 2014), both published by Liverpool University Press. Nicki was Principal Investigator on the AHRC-funded research project 'Rwandan Stories of Change' (http://rwandan.wp.st-andrews.ac.uk) and in 2018 was nominated for the inaugural Wellcome Trust/AHRC Health Humanities medal in the category of Best International Research.

**Georgina Holmes** is a Leverhulme Early Career Research Fellow in the Department of Politics and International Relations at the University of Reading. She holds a PhD in International Relations and Media from the

School of Oriental and African Studies (SOAS). Her current research, funded by the Leverhulme Trust, focuses on gender and security sector reform and the integration of African and European uniformed personnel in UN and African Union peace operations. Georgina has published in several journals, including the *Journal of Intervention and State Building, International Peacekeeping, Genocide Studies and Prevention* and *The RUSI Journal*, and is the author of *Women and War in Rwanda: Gender, Media and the Representation of Genocide* (I.B. Tauris, 2013).

**Madelaine Hron** is an Associate Professor in the Department of English and Film Studies at Wilfrid Laurier University in Canada. She is the author of *Translating Pain: Immigrant Suffering in Literature and Culture* (University of Toronto Press, 2009), and of various articles related to Rwanda post-genocide, human right issues, African literature, migration, trauma and violence. In 2009, she edited a special journal issue of *Peace Review* on Rwanda 15 years post-genocide.

**Astrid Jamar** is Lecturer in Development at the Open University. She was previously a researcher in the Political Settlements Research Programme, School of Law, University of Edinburgh. For the past decade, her research has focused on transitional justice and international aid in the African Great Lakes region. From 2008 to 2011, she gained field experience working with several international and local NGOs in Rwanda and Burundi. She has worked on various dimensions of peace-building, human rights and transitional justice, and is particularly interested in the professionalization of peace-building from postcolonial perspectives and political/legal anthropology. She is currently working on a book manuscript based on her doctoral research, 'Transitional Justice Professionals in Conflict: The Truth and Reconciliation Commission in Burundi'.

**Meghan Laws** joined the School of International Relations at St Andrews in 2018 as a postdoctoral research fellow. She is also the research director of the Third Generation Project (TGP), a climate justice think tank based at the University of St Andrews, which emphasizes the rights of communities on the front lines of climate change. Meghan has collaborated extensively with fellow contributors Richard Ntakirutimana and Bennett Collins to examine the impact of government rhetoric on the Batwa of Rwanda. She volunteers for two non-governmental organizations in Rwanda: Barakabaho Foundation and African Initiative for Mankind Progress Organization (AIMPO).

**Richard Ntakirutimana** is a human rights activist and co-founder and Executive Director of the African Initiative for Mankind Progress Organization (AIMPO), an organization which focuses on improving the living standards of 'Historically Marginalized Peoples'/Twa in Rwanda. Relatedly, his research focuses on the Twa as Indigenous peoples in the Great Lakes of Africa. Richard holds an LLM degree in Human Rights and Democratization in Africa from the Centre for Human Rights, University of Pretoria, South Africa and a postgraduate diploma in Human Rights and Development from the University of Antwerp, Belgium.

**Benjamin Thorne** is an ESRC-funded doctoral candidate in Law Studies at the University of Sussex, where he researches memory and transitional justice. His doctoral thesis focuses on how processes of witness testimony at the International Criminal Tribunal for Rwanda set up conditions for the way in which individual memories of human rights violations are collectively understood. More generally, Benjamin's research interests include discourse theory and analysis, trauma narratives, the coexistence of spaces of law and faith within justice and reconciliation, human rights and subjectivity.

**Louise Umutoni-Bower** is a journalist, researcher and publisher. She is the founder of Huza Press, a Rwanda-based publishing house that runs the country's biggest prize for fiction. She has worked as a regular reporter and contributor for several newspapers and magazines, such as the *Gazette* and *Ottawa Citizen* newspapers in Canada, *New Times Rwanda*, *Rwanda Focus* and *Enterprise Magazine*. She is also a scriptwriter and radio presenter. Louise holds an MSc in African Studies from the University of Oxford, where she researched national liberation movements in Africa and women's political inclusion. Her work was selected for the Winihin-Jemide grant and an Aegis Trust research grant. She is currently a research fellow with the University of Manchester's School of Environment, Education and Development. She is part of the centre's Effective States and Inclusive Development projects, investigating the notion of pockets of effectiveness in developing countries.

**Malaika Uwamahoro** is a Rwandan actress, poet and activist, and holds a BA in Theatre Studies from Fordham University (NYC). To pursue her studies, she received a Rwandan Presidential Scholarship. Malaika has performed her own poetry around the world, most recently at the UN for the twenty-third commemoration of the Genocide against the Tutsi in Rwanda. In 2014 she made her Off-Broadway debut at the Signature Theatre in the world premiere of Katori Hall's *Our Lady of Kibeho*. Other theatre work in the USA includes *Cartography* (The John F. Kennedy Center, D.C.), *Measure Back* (The Dixon Place, NYC), *Bishop* (Fordham/Primary Stages, NYC), and *Africa's Hope* (USC Bovard Theatre, CA). Her international theatre appearances include *Les Os qui craquent* (Théatre de Poche, Belgium), and has appeared in the films *Loveless Generation* (dir. Thomas Petkovski), *Un Plan parfait* (dir. Pascal Chaumeil) and *Shake Hands with the Devil* (dir. Roger Spottiswoode).

**Julia Viebach** is a lecturer at the African Studies Centre at the University of Oxford. Previously, she was a Leverhulme Trust Early Career Fellow and a Career Development Lecturer at Oxford's Faculty of Law. Julia's research interests pertain to memory and transitional justice, in particular to witnessing, archives and societal as well as individual meaning-making processes after mass atrocity. She has specialised in post-genocide Rwanda. Julia is the curator of the 'Kwibuka Rwanda' exhibition at Oxford's Pitt Rivers Museum, which delves into the world of Rwanda's genocide memorials telling the story of survivors who clean the remains of their loved ones.

**Caroline Williamson Sinalo** is Lecturer in World Languages at University College Cork and author of *Rwanda after Genocide: Gender, Identity and Posttraumatic Growth* (Cambridge University Press, 2018). Her PhD, funded by an AHRC Collaborative Doctoral Award, was carried out in partnership with the Aegis Trust and involved spending a year working in Rwanda at the national archive. Caroline has since continued to collaborate with the Aegis Trust, twice receiving Aegis Research, Policy and Higher Education (RPHE) funding. Her research has also been supported by the Irish Research Council (IRC).

# Index